HEROINE ABUSE

HEROINE ABUSE

Dostoevsky's
Netochka Nezvanova
and the Poetics of
Codependency

THOMAS
GAITON
MARULLO

NIU PRESS DeKalb IL

Northern Illinois University Press, DeKalb 60115
© 2015 by Northern Illinois University Press
All rights reserved

24 23 22 21 20 19 18 17 16 15   1 2 3 4 5

978-0-87580-720-1 (paper)
978-1-60909-175-0 (ebook)

Book design by Yuni Dorr
Cover design by Shaun Allshouse

Library of Congress Cataloging-in-Publication Data
Marullo, Thomas Gaiton.
Heroine abuse : Dostoevsky's "Netochka Nezvanova" and the poetics of codependency / Thomas Gaiton Marullo, University of Notre Dame.
    pages   cm
Includes bibliographical references and index.
ISBN 978-0-87580-720-1 (paperback)—ISBN 978-1-60909-175-0 (ebook)
1. Dostoyevsky, Fyodor, 1821–1881. Netochka Nezvanova. 2. Dostoyevsky, Fyodor, 1821–1881—Criticism and interpretation. 3. Codependency literature. 4. Families literature. I. Title.
PG3325.N43M37 2015
891.73'3—dc23
2015016474

TABLE OF CONTENTS

PREFACE vii

1 THE BASICS
Codependency, Dostoevsky, and *Netochka Nezvanova* 1

2 ALL IN THE CODEPENDENT FAMILY (I)
Netochka and Efimov 36

3 ALL IN THE CODEPENDENT FAMILY (II)
Netochka and Katya 78

4 ALL IN THE CODEPENDENT FAMILY (III)
Netochka and Alexandra Mikhailovna 110

CONCLUSION 155

NOTES 161

BIBLIOGRAPHY 189

INDEX 197

PREFACE

Immediately prior to the publication of *Netochka Nezvanova* in 1849, an insecure Dostoevsky wrote to Alexander Kraevsky, editor of *The Fatherland Notes*, a progressive liberal journal: "I know perfectly well that . . . *Netochka Nezvanova* is a good literary work, so good that *The Fatherland Notes* can, of course, give it space *without being ashamed of it*. I also know that it is a serious piece. Indeed, I am not alone in saying this; everybody is saying it."[1]

It is well-known that with *Netochka Nezvanova*, Dostoevsky sought not only to write his first novel but also to make a literary comeback. The stunning success of *Poor Folk* (1845), a tortured correspondence between a hapless clerk and an equally ill-fated girl, had given way to several critical failures. The pundits had panned *The Double* (1846)—a short prose work depicting a deadly struggle between another clerk and his alter-ego—along with other early Petersburg tales, including "The Landlady" (1848), a Gothic *ménage à trois* involving a young scholar, an elderly sorcerer, and his young wife.

Despite Dostoevsky's hopes for *Netochka Nezvanova*, it was also judged unsuccessful, in part for the obvious reason that it remained incomplete. Dostoevsky discontinued the work in 1849 to serve a ten-year sentence in Siberia after being implicated in the Petrashevsky Affair, in which a group of intellectuals was arrested for alleged revolutionary activity. (He would not attempt a work of similar magnitude and scope until almost twenty years later, in 1866, with his great novel about an ax murderer qua "extraordinary man," *Crime and Punishment*.)

Critics of the time were confused and irritated by *Netochka Nezvanova*. Alexander Druzhinin, a conservative literary critic, saw the work as an unsuccessful adaptation of French urban realism, an unwieldy, if strained mélange of characters and scenes without purpose, measure, or idea. "For fear that . . . he and his profound ideas will not be understood," Druzhinin wrote, "Dostoevsky does not stop when he should. . . . His work smells of sweat."[2]

Dostoevsky scholars later followed suit. Soviet researchers and reviewers either ignored *Netochka Nezvanova* or noted it only fleetingly. What little attention they gave to the work often reflected the biases of Marxist ideology and official sentiment. Leonid Grossman saw *Netochka Nezvanova* as a model of critical realism in that its heroine triumphs over her oppressive, squalid beginnings and affirms the power of art by becoming a successful singer.³

Émigré and Western critics were equally remiss in their evaluations of the work. For them *Netochka Nezvanova* not only mimicked both the European fiction of such Romantic Realists as Charles Dickens, Victor Hugo, Honoré de Balzac, E. T. A. Hoffmann, and George Sand—and also Russian works by Nikolai Gogol, Vladimir Odoevsky, Alexander Herzen, and Avdotya Panaeva. It also repeated what Dostoevsky had done, more engagingly, in earlier works, including *Poor Folk* and *The Double*. More seriously, perhaps, émigré and Western critics erred in many of their assessments of the work. As will be seen, they accepted at face value the novel's claims that Efimov, the agonized musician in the first part of the piece, is gifted; that Katya, the fiendish youngster in the second part, is sweet; and that Alexandra Mikhailovna, the calculating grande dame in the third part, is innocent. As a result, critics have generally failed to appreciate the underlying images and ideas of *Netochka Nezvanova* as well as the cares and concerns of Dostoevsky at this point in his life.

Another key shortcoming of critical evaluations of *Netochka Nezvanova* recalls the fable of the blind men and the elephant: most critics focus on aspects of the novel but fail to appreciate the whole. Consider, for example, these reactions to the character Efimov: Georgy Fridlender called him one of the "outstanding artistic achievements of the young Dostoevsky."[4] Joseph Frank dubbed him Dostoevsky's "first fully developed portrait of a sadomasochistic personality";[5] and Edward Wasiolek and Victor Terras, saw in Efimov a "brilliant sketch . . . in the psychology of failure."[6]

Despite such accolades, Dostoevsky's unfinished novel remains his least studied and least understood work of long fiction. Dostoevsky's daughter, Lyubov', notes: "In *Netochka Nezvanova*, Dostoevsky wrote a genuine masterpiece of feminine psychology . . . [which] the public has not understood in a sufficient way. . . . The heroines in his early works are pale, inert, ghostlike. [Only in *Netochka Nezvanova*] did he create two remarkable feminine portraits: Netochka and Katya."[7] Frank continues: "The significance of *Netochka Nezvanova*, which has so far not been sufficiently appreciated, is that it enables us to pinpoint a pivotal moment in Dostoevsky's literary career. . . . [The work] sheds so much light on Dostoevsky's internal evolution as a writer."[8]

I could not agree more. I would also expand on Frank's assessment by arguing that, despite its sad history and prolonged neglect, *Netochka*

Nezvanova is a critical work in Dostoevsky's repertoire in that (1) it was the apex of the so-called Petersburg period, when the author made his early forays into psychological realism;[9] (2) it serves as a seedbed for many of the images and ideas that became hallmarks of his major works; and (3) it is the first piece in Dostoevsky's fictional corpus to focus on the psychology of children and to feature a woman in a leading and narrative role.[10] *Netochka Nezvanova* was also the first work in Russian literature to deal with problems of the family, and it stands out as one of the few Russian prose works by a male author from a woman's perspective.

Further, as *Netochka Nezvanova* predates Tolstoy's *Childhood* by three years, it was Dostoevsky, not his equally illustrious counterpart, who was the first to formulate a fictional conception of a Russian childhood, a searing and harsh indigenous bildungsroman that focused on the early years of the ninety-five percent who lived at the bottom of society, in contrast to the sentimental and idealized account of childhood among the five percent who lived at the top.[11] No less than Tolstoy's *Childhood*, Dostoevsky's *Netochka Nezvanova* can be seen as emblematic of an entire way of life. Moreover, in this first attempt at a novel Dostoevsky strove for a more sweeping picture of youthful formation than Tolstoy did in *Childhood*. That is, whereas Tolstoy focused on only two days in the life of his hero, Dostoevsky followed his heroine over some fifteen years. Additionally, Dostoevsky departed further from Tolstoy by setting in motion still another theme of his mature fiction. William Rowe notes in his study of children in Dostoevsky's works, that the "memories of a happy childhood are a force capable of mitigating life's vicissitudes . . . [but] an unhappy childhood pursues one long thereafter."[12] When, for example, the infamous hero of Dostoevsky's 1864 *Notes from the Underground* tells the prostitute Liza in the final chapters of the work, "If I had had a family in my childhood, I would not be the person I am now,"[13] he harkens back to Netochka's own unease over the early years of her life. It is fair to say that Dostoevsky and Tolstoy, in their early conceptions of fictional first years, initiated the two poles of written expression—models of childhood and anti-childhood,[14] so to speak—that defined Russian family chronicles in both the nineteenth and twentieth centuries.

In *Netochka Nezvanova*, Dostoevsky showed himself in a way that he had not done previously, employing favorite forms of his mature fiction—philosophical monologue and polyphonic dialogue. In *Netochka Nezvanova*, voices mix and meld in a dramatic reading of life, brimming with moral monsters, infernal women, adult-children, and children-adults. Dostoevsky's first novel features individuals who chart a tragic course through life, but without the complex intellectual or spiritual agendas of their counterparts in the writer's major novels. As such, these characters provide clear and striking examples of the workings of what psychologists today call "codependency" in that their bonding with people, things, and ideas as a way of coping with the vicissitudes of life is often deviant and destructive.

The characters of *Netochka Nezvanova* seek community to engage in security, dominance, and control, as well as to indulge in narcissism, self-defeating perversion, and other aberrant behaviors. Indeed, in no other work would Dostoevsky examine such phenomena as pedophilia and sex among children with such abandon, without the coding that marked his later investigation into such matters.[15] Men, women, and children alike in *Netochka Nezvanova* so victimize the objects of their affections that neither oppressors nor oppressed mature or grow.

This investigation thus takes *Netochka Nezvanova* as a case study in codependency and illustrates how the young Dostoevsky intuited and demonstrated the workings of the phenomenon almost a century and a half before it became the scholarly focus of doctors, psychologists, therapists, and other practitioners of mental health. I realize that this approach to Dostoevsky stands apart from traditional and/or conventional approaches to the writer. I also believe, though, that given the crisis in literary studies today, particularly the marked indifference and even outright hostility of students to fiction, it is time that scholars and critics study fiction with the methods and tools of other disciplines, and in so doing, reassert the importance of literature in both the curriculum and the academy. Additionally, I ask readers to consider the following issues.

First, I am well aware that although research into codependency is an industry unto itself, much remains to be learned about it. In no way do I assert that codependency is a sickness or a disease; that is an issue for scholars and students of human behavior to debate. But no one will disagree that aspects of codependency, together with the attendant physical and emotional human failings, are part and parcel of everyday culture and existence.[16] Indeed, I find it particularly heartening that in recent years, the phenomenon of codependency has captured the attention of scholars in the humanities, particularly gender and ethnic studies.[17]

Second, here I consider codependency exclusively as a series of outlooks and activities that investigators agree are characteristic of the phenomenon, and I use them to shed light on the relationships in *Netochka Nezvanova*, as well as on the difficulties to which they give rise. I make no statement, however, that the characters exhibiting symptoms of codependency—Efimov and Netochka's mother; Katya and her household; Katya's sister, Alexandra Mikhailovna, and her husband, Pyotr Alexandrovich; and Netochka herself—stand as real-life prototypes or fictional constructs. Like debates over codependency, this issue is beyond the scope of my investigation. I do believe, however, that my claims in *Heroine Abuse* are valid for individuals in literature or life.

Third, my study of codependency in *Netochka Nezvanova* not only extends and amplifies classical and recent studies of sexuality in Dostoevsky's works; it also answers calls for new psychological investigations into his fiction. My work extends the investigations of such scholars as Robert Louis Jackson and William Rowe on the child;[18] Louis Breger and Elizabeth Dalton on the unconscious, fantasy, and dreams;[19] Lina Steiner on bildungsroman;[20] Olga Meerson on taboo;[21] Deborah Martinsen on shame and shamelessness;[22] Iza Erlich on spontaneous regression;[23] Susanne Fusso on pedophilia, sexually abused children, and accidental and missing families;[24] Svetlana Grenier on marginal women and wards;[25] Gary Cox on bonding hierarchies;[26] Joe Andrew on mothers, fathers, and seduced daughters;[27] Vladimir Golstein on surrogate fathers;[28] Otto Rank on the psychoanalysis of doubles;[29] Nancy Ruttenburg on estrangement and psycho-social disarticulation;[30] Richard Rosenthal on projection, boundaries, space, doubles, and omnipotent rivals;[31] Bernard Paris on defense mechanisms;[32] and Steven Rosen on homoerotic language of the body.[33] To this must be added the work of Stanley Sunderwirth and Judith Spector on the codependence of Nora in Henrich Ibsen's *The Doll House*, his 1879 diatribe against conventional marriages and mores.[34] The fact that this study and the works by Erlich and Rosen were published in *The Psychoanalytic Study of the Child*, *Psychoanalytic Review*, and *Family Dynamics of Addiction Quarterly* stands as eloquent witness to what literary critics and psychologists can teach one another not only from the perspective of their disciplines, but also from their understanding and insights into one of the world's greatest artist-psychologists. The work of Lorne Tepperman et al. relates even more directly to the matter at hand. Their study on Dostoevsky's addiction to gambling is itself groundbreaking research on the writer and his work.[35]

In the words of Peter Brooks, "psychoanalysis... is a particularly insistent and demanding intertext, in that mapping across the boundaries from one territory to the other both confirms and complicates our understanding of how the mind reformulates the real, how it constructs the necessary fictions by which we dream, desire, interpret, indeed by which we constitute ourselves as human subjects. [Psychoanalysis] ... forces the critic to respond to the erotics of form, that is, to an engagement with the psychic investments of rhetoric, the dramas of desire played out in the tropes. [It] ... stands out as a constant reminder that the attention to form, properly conceived, is not a sterile formalism but rather one more attempt to draw the symbolic and fictional map of our place in existence."[36]

It is also time to reconsider the notion that nineteenth-century medical theory and practice provide the only valid perspective for studying psychology in Dostoevsky's works. Such a view places serious limits upon Dostoevsky's brilliant insights into the human mind; it fails to bring the writer into the twenty-first century and confines him to the nineteenth century (a time when what we would today consider codependency was dismissed as hysteria, a view that might strike us today as flawed, patriarchal, or wrongheaded). Indeed, what I have found to be so particularly fascinating in my study of *Netochka Nezvanova* is that, at age twenty-eight, Dostoevsky intuited—chapter and verse—the symptoms and workings of codependency more than a hundred and fifty years before it captured the attention of students and scholars.[37] With both broad and narrow outlines, he articulated the form and function of the often fatal attractions that individuals have to people, places, and ideas—along with the various mechanisms by which they sustain such ties. Just as anyone would deem it counterproductive to study Dostoevsky solely from the content and method of nineteenth-century Russian literary criticism, so would it be equally limiting and harmful to only consider the great writer's thoughts and ideas from the perspective of what passed for medicine and psychology during that same time. Further, if literary scholars and critics are to take seriously claims regarding Dostoevsky-as-psychologist, it would seem logical, even crucial, to study the writer and his works from the points of view of all the theories, hypotheses, facts, and figures that today's doctors, psychologists, therapists, and other practitioners of mental wellness and health discuss and debate about human behavior, in general, and codependency in particular. As William Mills Todd III noted apropos of investigations into *The Brothers Karamazov* in 2004: "New studies [on Dostoevsky] explore topics . . . such as sexuality that were not widely discussed in the literary criticism of the 1870s; they can draw upon fields of scholarship, such as cognitive psychology, as yet unfounded in Dostoevsky's time."[38] Increasingly, and happily, literary scholars and critics are using insights not only from psychology but also from other social sciences so that their studies realize the humanities as humane, as expressing, in a complete and awesome way, what it means to be human. Consider, for instance, how investigations into trauma now intersect with studies of literature, history, and contemporary culture. These studies explore, in the words of Cathy Caruth, how trauma becomes text, and wound becomes voice.[39]

My fourth and final claim here is that investigating codependency in *Netochka Nezvanova* explains, in a way that no other approach can, the novel's inner workings, especially the "ties" (*sviazi*) that bind the characters to one another. The physical and emotional addictions of Netochka and her fellow characters also provide a point of departure for examining other protagonists in Dostoevsky's major fiction. Indeed, it is perhaps only through the lens of codependency that one can explain adequately the tortured and enduring relationships that exist, say, among the innocent Myshkin, the demonic Rogozhin, and the crazed Nastasya Filippovna in the 1868–1869 *The Idiot*, his work of a child-like prince and the people who drive him to the brink; or among the earthy Grushenka, the aristocratic Katerina Ivanovna, and the ill-starred Dmitri in *The Brothers Karamazov*, his final 1880 piece on the interplay of faith, reason, and passion. Without understanding these hidden ties and codependencies between characters, we are at pains to explain why people in Dostoevsky's corpus cannot live with or without each other; why they move to simultaneous affirmations of love and hate; why they seek, also contemporaneously, to sacrifice and save, devour and destroy themselves and others; and ultimately, why they end up sick and shattered, insane and dead. As Frank writes, in *Netochka Nezvanova*, Dostoevsky

> brings the theme of masochistic-sadistic 'sensuality' to the foreground as the major *source* of cruelty and oppression in human relations; and the conquest of such 'sensuality' now becomes *the* overriding moral-social imperative.... Dostoevsky's focus ... is [now] on the personal qualities that the characters display in the battle against the instinctive tendency of the ego to hit back for what social-psychic lesions and traumas it has been forced to endure. The world of *Netochka Nezvanova* is thus no longer exclusively social-psychological, but already has become the moral-psychological universe of his later fiction.[40]

Heroine Abuse consists of four chapters. In the first, I will consider codependency as it is currently understood by social scientists today and use this context to discuss several complementary frameworks for analyzing *Netochka Nezvanova*. Here I will offer a brief history and summary of the work and an analysis of the personalities and outlooks of the two narrative personae, Netochka the adult and Netochka the child. In the remaining chapters, I will engage in a close reading of Dostoevsky's first novel to examine the hows, whys, and wherefores, as well as the similarities and differences, relating to Netochka Nezvanova's various codependencies: with Efimov and her mother; with Katya and Katya's household; and with Alexandra Mikhailovna and Pyotr Alexandrovich. In each case, I will show that what Netochka and her alleged loved ones experience as momentary triumph and bonding is, in reality, enduring tragedy and bondage. Racing from one person and relationship to the next, and caught in a debilitating loop that they claim to detest (but in fact sadomasochistically enjoy), Netochka and company wreak havoc on themselves and the world. They do so, moreover, with impunity, their codependency moving them to momentary exultation as self-styled extraordinary men and women. What follows is prolonged darkness and despair, and new physical and emotional addictions.

It is also my hope that scholars and students of Dostoevsky, after reading *Heroine Abuse*, will right a grievous wrong in the studies of his fiction by pursuing new and long overdue investigations into Dostoevsky's early writings and deepening our understanding of his evolution as one of the world's greatest thinkers and writers.[41] (To date, the only full-length English-language study of Dostoevsky's youthful fiction is Victor Terras's *The Young Dostoevsky (1846–1849). A Critical Study*, published more than fifty years ago.)[42] Doctors, psychologists, therapists, and other practitioners of mental wellness and health, as well as laymen and women interested in the inner workings of men, women, and children—and yes, codependents of all types—would all do well to follow in the footsteps of their predecessors who looked to Dostoevsky for insights into mind, heart, body, and soul. *Netochka Nezvanova* is instructive on the subject of the form and function of codependency, not only in the great writer's fiction, but also in real life. For this broader audience I include pertinent information on the works, characters, and real-life individuals in the text so that they may read my study with comfort and ease, look further into Dostoevsky and other Russian and European literati for archetype-exemplars of codependence, and join with scholars and students of the great writer to see literature as illuminating and explaining life.

For their assistance in this project, I wish to thank, first and foremost, Lorne Tepperman of the University of Toronto who, as I have already noted, was the first to consider the tie between Dostoevsky and addiction, and who, in a generous way, commented insightfully on my understanding of the phenomenon, as well as the second reader of my study, who gave superb recommendations to strengthen my analysis and argument. I would also like to thank Gary Saul Morson of Northwestern University, Robin Miller of Brandeis University, Kathleen Parthé of the University of Rochester, Linda Ivanits of Penn State University, and Yuri Corrigan of Boston University, all of whom read earlier versions of my study, for their generous and helpful comments and suggestions.

Here at Notre Dame, I wish to express my gratitude to Thomas Merluzzi, Director of the Institute of Scholarship for the Liberal Arts, for his continued financial support; Kenneth Kinslow, Laura Sills, Therese Bauters, and the staff of Interlibrary Loan and Document Delivery for supplying materials for research, and for their grace and tact in not asking me why I wanted books and articles on codependency and psychological breakdown; Randy Yoho, Clarence Helm, and Stephen Marks of the Computing Office of the College of Arts and Letters for keeping my computers in working order and for rescuing files from cyberspace; and Cheryl Reed, who transformed my chaotic files into a professional document. I am also indebted to Amy Farranto, Christine Worobec, and Nathan Holmes of Northern Illinois University Press for their enthusiastic reception of this new approach to Dostoevsky, as well for their professionalism and efficiency in preparing this book for publication. Finally, I wish to acknowledge the copyeditor of my study, Judith Robey, for her meticulous attention to the content and form of the narrative.

Last but not least, I thank my wife, Gloria Gibbs Marullo, for her unstinting encouragement and support; my cats, Bernadette Marie, Bridget Josephine, Benedict Joseph, and Francis Xavier (for readers of my scholarly adventures, Gonzaga and Monica Anne are in heaven) for reminding me about the importance of seeking light and warmth in life; and Sister Mary Colleen Dillon, S.N.D. and the sisters of Lourdes Hall of the Sisters of Notre Dame of Covington, Kentucky, for their unceasing prayers on my behalf.

May you all know happiness, health, and peace.

TGM

HEROINE ABUSE

CHAPTER ONE

THE BASICS
Codependency, Dostoevsky, and *Netochka Nezvanova*

CODEPENDENCY: TOWARD A DEFINITION

Social scientists and researchers understand codependency variously.[1] In the most general terms, they regard the phenomenon as embracing anything that prevents both children and adults from sustaining healthy relationships with themselves or others. More specifically, investigators see codependency in individuals who seek skewed or inordinate fulfillment in people, places, and things apart from themselves. That is, codependents choose "external referencing" or "excessive focus" in work, alcohol, romance, sex, money, power, and success; they experience "relationship addiction" in obsessive/possessive ties with people, places, and things.[2] In fact, investigators into codependency assert that it is "our most common addiction . . . underlying all other addictions."[3] Although they debate many aspects of codependency,[4] they agree about five key symptoms of the phenomenon. The first is that codependents experience a confused or lost selfhood;[5] they do not acknowledge or value their worth, they do not trust their minds and hearts; they question everything they say, think, and do. Put simply, they see themselves as errors physically, socially, and spiritually.

A second symptom is that codependents have difficulty defining or expressing their experience of the world. They have trouble distinguishing between dreams and reality or intellectual and spiritual realms. (Not surprisingly, codependents are often seen as frustrated mystics,[7] that is, beings who inhabit otherworldly realms of awareness and consciousness and who hear voices, see visions, and fall into trances but without the enlightenment therein.) The uniqueness of their own being, the functioning of their own bodies, and the origins and operation of their thoughts, feelings, and deeds are all beyond their comprehension. Additionally, perceptions of codependents are often skewed or erroneous: they may distrust or become overwhelmed by what their senses are telling them; they may filter out all but the most trifling facts and figures. Their strained emotions, feverish deliberations, and false assumptions may lead them to perceive life as war. Whether in Dostoevsky's fiction or in life, codependents are the insulted and injured of their world.

It is also axiomatic that codependent adults and children experience multiple realities and live multiple lives. From motives of fear, rejection, and the like, they mirror the lives of others as alternatives for their own. They engage in schizoid compromises;[8] they make false confessions and tell white (and black) lies; they construct, often by painful trial and error, diverse identities, roles, and modes of being. The final moments of codependents often devolve into physical and mental dissolution since they see themselves as little more than the sum of other people's hopes, dreams, and expectations.

A third symptom is that codependents react to events in exaggerated, even histrionic ways. They live life not only on the edge, but also at its extremes. They relish the addictions of codependent highs;[9] the rush of adrenaline,[10] the flood of endorphins;[11] the tensing of muscles, the beating of the heart. Because of their emotional instability, codependents are tragically bivalent. They tend to be either totally involved or fully detached. They ride a roller coaster of moods: happy and high one moment, morbid and miserable the next. It is axiomatic to say that codependents not only invite sadness into their lives, but also give it a chair to sit on. Further, codependent personalities envision few choices or solutions in life. Their outlook is complacent, conservative, and defensive of the status quo. Their approach is to split into self-canceling absolutes, in which there is only win or lose, black or white, true or false, good or bad.[12] In fact, if there is a gray area for codependents, it is found only in the deadening sameness and tedium of their lives. Days and nights they spend as dead men (and women) walking, convinced that life must be endured, not enjoyed.

A fourth attribute often found in codependents is a reluctance to acknowledge or satisfy their own needs and wants. Opting for sackcloth, they experience shame, indifference, and ignorance concerning physical necessities, emotional nurturing, and sexual exigencies. Relationship addicts believe that everything is in short supply. Localizing themselves between a hug and a hard place,[13] they scramble for people, places, and things, hoarding and clinging to them tightly, and resenting anyone or anything that threatens to come between themselves and their self-styled possessions. Additionally, such individuals do not count their blessings. They do not appreciate the proverbial glass half filled with water. Angry that they have only some water and afraid they will not get more, codependents refuse to drink it, watch the water evaporate, and then complain that now they really have nothing.[14]

A fifth symptom is that codependents ignore or repress inner inadequacy or distress by demanding perfection from themselves in everything they think, say, or do. In their disordered minds, they become geniuses, princes, princesses,[15] or even gods, with special powers and gifts. They are always strong, good, right, and perfect;[16] they are omnipotent, omniscient, and omnipresent, especially in life-threatening challenges and deeds. The result is that codependent personalities often have a distorted or nonexistent spirituality. God or other celestial powers do not bring them guidance or peace; rather, they are seen only as competitors for attention, power, and love. Further, the assumed stance of genius-god often drives codependents to distraction (and death) with worries that they (and what they do) are never good enough, and that they can be perfect if only they can figure out how. Indeed, it is in the best interest of such individuals to repress or recast their failings by blaming anyone and anything but themselves.

CODEPENDENCE: INNER AND OUTER STRUGGLES

Codependents live lives of mental anguish, of inner whirlwinds and storms. They move from bland sweetness, through emotional indifference, and to numbing delusion and denial about problems and obstacles that become even more massive and intractable with time. Such individuals wreak havoc not only for themselves, but also within their worlds. On one hand, they are experts in "impression management."[17] Master chameleons and con artists, they listen and share, charm and seduce. They say and do the right things to make people affirm their worth, do their bidding, and (most important) still the anger, restlessness, and fear from within. (Not surprisingly, such personalities relish the attention and rewards, however trivial or fleeting, that followers and friends accord them.) On the other hand, toward the outside world, relationship addicts exhibit a variety of passive-aggressive behaviors. When the perfect exteriors of their personalities show cracks, they can go on the defensive by becoming withdrawn, forgetful, and detached. They sulk and skulk until they get their way. They cast themselves as the least of God's creations, no matter how harmful, humiliating, or perverse their stance. When codependents come across as less than geniuses or gods, they can also go on the offensive and act arrogant and grandiose. They may wheedle, beg, and bribe, or they might make blind threats and withhold attention and love. In extreme situations, they can resort to "counter-dependency,"[18] rebelling against ties and bonds and becoming psychopaths and moral monsters who seek restoration in triumph over others. To their taste, they are victors over victims, possessors over the possessed.

Codependents also have a faulty awareness of boundaries, the ontological fences by which people distinguish themselves. Boundaries are internal and external. Internally, boundaries define and contain an individual's territory, their bodies, minds, and souls. Boundaries also define likes, needs, and wants, as well as the pace necessary for rest, reflection, even survival. Externally, boundaries serve as gauges, shock absorbers, and even safety valves by which children and adults can monitor the distance between themselves and the world. They also define the "subsystems" whereby individuals know the rules for the proper behavior of a group.[19]

People with functional boundaries not only safeguard their own inner sanctum, but they also respect the private terrain of others. They do not manipulate or encroach upon the personal worlds of family and friends. Further, they ask permission of presumed loved ones before they engage in tactile expressions of affection. Codependent personalities, though, abuse boundaries in several ways. They invade other people's realms, rushing in to fix other people's lives, or they allow others to rush in and fix theirs. They take on the feelings, problems, and responsibilities of others. With one and all, they identify like a sponge absorbing water. Individuals with nonexistent boundaries also have trouble protecting themselves physically, sexually, and emotionally. Gullible and easy prey, they refuse to see that they are being deceived. They lack the resources to say: "Stop, I do not want to be touched"; or "I am not responsible for your feelings, thoughts, or behavior."

Another abuse of boundaries that occurs is what investigators call "morbid codependency," or when individuals abandon or dismantle their borders to merge with others. Terrified of being alone, they fixate on someone—anyone—and become "love addicts."[20] Morbidly addictive personalities use their "love addiction like other addictive processes ... to relieve or medicate intolerable reality."[21] Because "love addicts did not bond well with their original caregivers,"[22] they seek to attract hosts in sins of omission and commission. At one end, they relish being rescued. They appear helpless, docile, and small. They yearn for a savior who will fulfill their wishes and take responsibility for their lives. Throwing responsibility to the winds, they seek highs in fantasies and fairy tales: "It's karma, destiny, fate; we are soulmates," they tell themselves.[23]

At the other end, morbidly addictive personalities relish rescuing others. They perform heroic acts of bravery, loyalty, and love (or what passes for it in their minds). For them nothing is troublesome, demanding, or time-consuming. They mother-smother, run interference, and swallow or become swallowed in sexual and other unions.[24] Their days they spend rising and falling on their partners' ups and downs, successes and failures. They spend their nights tolerating abuse, making amends, or closing their eyes to harmful situations. Morbid codependents can even bend their hosts into their own image and likeness; or, they transmute to doubles, mirroring with stunning veracity the (often bizarre and unstable) thoughts, actions, and emotions of their partners. In a restatement of a popular adage, they show their friends to the world so that they can tell it who they are. In fact, without significant others to call their own, they believe that they have no reason to exist at all.

For morbid codependents, attracting hosts is only half the battle; the other half is keeping them in tow. They cut their hosts little slack. They feel compelled "obsessively [not only] to think about, want to be with, touch, talk to and listen to their partners," but to see them as superior, even as Higher Powers."[25]

Unsurprisingly, in the course of their relationships, morbid codependents become particularly inflexible and compulsive in their attempts to keep relationships exclusive, static, and secure; they create bondage, not bonds.[26] Moreover, love addicts exhibit a peculiar sense of justice, since they hold that whatever they do from their side warrants exclusive devotion from the other. When morbidly codependent individuals sense that tit is not for tat between possessor and possessed, they move from suicidal depression to righteous indignation and from there to murderous rebellion and rage. If they regularly set their hosts on pedestals, they just as routinely knock them off as unworthy of their time and support. "Take care of me—or else" is their watchword, their stance toward people and life.[27]

Needless to say, morbid codependencies are transient affairs. Even if hosts delight in the attention of clinging fans, they soon tire of the pressures and demands of these bonds. They become inconsistent, neglectful, and abusive. Feeling manipulated and controlled, they even come to hate their partners. Morbid codependents do not surrender without a fight, though. They grit their teeth, clutch the robe, and grab more tightly. They rage, stalk, and vow revenge; they can move to homicidal jealousy and threaten suicide. Not surprisingly, one or both of the parties involved may end up battered and bloody—or worse, destroyed, physically and spiritually.

It should be noted that individuals given to codependence may only have boundary problems with certain people or under circumstances. Such souls may be able to set boundaries for spouses and children but fail to do so with colleagues and friends. They can keep the world at bay unless they encounter authority figures or are frightened, tired, or sick. Codependents also often replace boundaries with walls or barricades so that they can live in physical and mental "undergrounds." They may activate these walls in anger and aggression, in silence and daydreaming, or in indecisiveness and procrastination. In a word, they obsess over existence rather than participating in it. Soldier-like, they can also run out from behind their barricades and penetrate the boundaries of others before retreating behind their walls anew.

CODEPENDENCE AND THE FAMILY: THE SHARED PAIN OF ALCOHOLISM

Social scientists drew much of their initial understanding of codependence from studies of alcoholics and their families.[28] Their idea was that spouses, children, and other clan members were as addicted to the alcoholic as the offender was to drink. (The term used to describe this condition is "co-alcoholism.")[29] It should also be noted that in early investigations of alcoholism and codependency (if not to this day), the victims were seen as women, not children or men.[30]

Researchers studying codependence see both the oppressor and the oppressed as exhibiting similar signs of mutually skewed (and reinforcing) behavior. Families of alcoholics can become so caught up in the alcoholism of their family members that they become ill themselves. The parents, spouses, and children of alcoholics are plagued by intense feelings of anger, frustration, and shame. They seek to cope with these feelings in a variety of ways: imposing a sham order on the household; normalizing the alcoholic's abusive behavior;[31] blaming themselves for the situation;[32] or hoping for a sudden and successful resolution to the problems. They may obsess over the victim's troubles and cater to his or her whims, wants, and needs.

With increasing frequency and intensity, members of the coterie surrounding alcoholics assume diverse stances and roles. They pose as the adjuster and the rescuer; they posture as the pacifier, the protector, and the people-pleaser; they parade as the hero, the scapegoat, the doormat, and the mascot; they costume as the wallflower, the martyr, the altruist, the stoic, and the saint.[33] Both oppressors and the oppressed see all the world as a stage and self-styled heroes and heroines as drama kings and queens staging melodramas, soap operas, and tragedies to captive audiences. In their efforts to cope, members of an alcoholic and/or codependent family or group skew boundaries and subsystems in one of two ways. The first is disengagement.[34] Here the personal demarcations are so rigid that communication is difficult, restricted, and ignored. As Dostoevsky himself wrote in drafts to *A Raw Youth*, his 1875 novel of a young intellectual who is the illegitimate son of a dissolute landowner: "the idea of decomposition in everything . . . where everyone is separate . . . the Russian family with no bonds" (16:16).[35] Making oneself scarce, seeing but not telling, and walking on eggshells are the preferred modes of operation. Double binds and triangulated messages, as well as confusing and convoluted exchanges, are equally common because codependents talk to themselves, God, and everyone else but the offending party in their midst. The second path toward skewing boundaries and systems is enmeshment. Here the boundaries are unclear, blurred, and diffuse. Genders and identities become entwined in shifting coalitions and vigilance over people and events, and men and women exchange gender roles. (Feelings of castration, impotence, and the like are not uncommon.) Husbands act as brothers to their sons, and wives as sisters to their daughters. In enmeshed families, members are "trapped in glue,"[36] or they are like "pieces of string tied and retied."[37] Over-involvement is the *modus vivendi*: "vacuum cleaners gone wild."[38] Who is supposed to do what is a mystery. Everything becomes everyone's fault and responsibility. In enmeshed families, members never give in, give up, or forget. Constantly on edge, they do not trust and feel; they watch, worry, and wonder when the other shoe will drop; advancing in rage one moment, and retreating in denial the next moment, they are victims of battle fatigue.

The codependence in families living with alcoholics is often so enduring and destructive that its members actually sabotage attempts by the addict to attain sobriety. So-called facilitators or enablers do not confront the offenders with their behavior.[39] Rather, they make excuses, clean up messes, and endure abuse. However counterintuitive the idea, the addiction of one member of a codependent family makes the hearts of the others grow fonder. After all, if the alcoholic resists drink for any length of time, facilitators can lose the often considerable amount of time, energy, and emotion they have invested in the relationship and forfeit their ideas on what family and relationships should be. They will surrender their self-worth as saviors, anchors, and the like. In fact, facilitator-enablers may even develop aches and pains, and suffer from anxiety, emptiness, and depression if normalcy returns to the home.[40] It is thus to their benefit and salvation that such individuals look the other way when the alcoholic imbibes, excuse the behavior of the offender, accept the beliefs and values of the addict, resist calls for help, or even furnish the drink for the object of their codependent affection.[41]

Needless to say, the effects of facilitating are often devastating for both the alcoholic and the enabler. The alcoholic may deny—and even exacerbate—a lack of responsibility and loss of control. The victim of drink may also feel so overwhelmed by life that he or she may regress to childhood or infancy.[42] The enabler is in a similarly difficult position. The individual will vacillate between perverse satisfaction and towering rage. In fact, the strain between the two can become so intolerable that it can explode in violence, or even in death.

CODEPENDENCE AND THE FAMILY: OVERT AND COVERT ABUSE

Investigators of codependence affirm that the abuse addictive adults often mete out to their offspring can be of two types: overt and covert. The overt mistreatment of a child by a parent or an elder occurs in both physical and verbal realms. Particularly insidious are situations in which mothers, fathers, or others mistreat youngsters in a sexual way. Such misconduct is the ultimate border violation: a slaughter of innocents that brings into play the most naked, predatory, and destructive aspects of human aggression. Sexual abuse with minors includes illicit acts such as physical sex, mutual masturbation, and inappropriate kissing and fondling to the point of ecstasy. Adults who engage in exhibitionism or voyeurism with children are similarly guilty of sexual misconduct. Even though such individuals do not engage minors in a tactile way or cause them any conscious harm, exhibitionists and their ilk receive physical stimulation at the expense of the sexual and emotional well-being of their victims. Similarly seen as overt sexual misconduct are situations in which parents or authority figures engage in inappropriate talk about sex with children and adolescents. They jabber about sexual organs; they parley erotic stories or jokes; they intimate that they wish to abandon their partners for romance with their daughters, sons, or other minors in their purview.

In line with overt sexual abuse, it should be noted that even if children are not hurt by sexual misconduct, but if, for lack of other forms of physical nurturing or contact, they actually enjoy and even request fondling and other sexual favors from the seniors in their midst, they are *not* responsible for their actions. Rather, it is the abusing adult who bears the onus for the wrongdoing. This distinction, though, has an important caveat: if a youngster has been exposed to adult-like sexual behavior and has replicated it with another minor, the child is guilty of sexual abuse and must be dealt with accordingly.

The situation of children who are aware and/or experienced in sexual matters is one of the most perfidious facets of both codependence and overt abuse because such youngsters feel both empowered and disempowered by such behavior. With the former, minors draw their potency from two sources. Moved to sexual arousal and/or orgasm, they feel themselves flooded with exhilarating energy and pleasure. Also, when juveniles engage in sex with a parent or another adult, they believe that they are more credible and needed than the spurned mother, father, or significant other in the family or love triangle. (Investigators of codependence assert that, in dysfunctional homes, assuming the role of princess, daddy's girl, or doll can be among the most seductive experiences for daughters caught between dysfunctional parents.)[43] Further, children who engage in sexual activities with adults sometimes seek to sustain their privileged position by competing or declaring all-out war on a perceived rival.

Children, though, are also disempowered by sexual abuse. They are ill-equipped to satisfy the needs and wants of the offender, physically and otherwise. They are also exhausted by struggles to maintain supremacy in the household, particularly with an outcast partner or spouse. Most tragic, perhaps, is the fact that minors who are disempowered by sexual abuse come to feel shame and revulsion for who they are and what they are doing; anger and despair issue forth from relationships that defy liberation or escape.[44]

Unlike overt abuse, the covert mistreatment of minors by their elders is hidden, devious, and indirect: it embraces thoughts and actions that are unspoken, intimated, or suggested rather than said, seen, or heard. Caregivers engage in covert abuse of youngsters when they neglect or abandon their charges. These "borderline" caregivers are disengaged from the household physically, mentally, or emotionally, or they become "addicted to looking elsewhere" and seek love and esteem from outsiders in romance, sex, religion, and work.[45] They may feel so besieged by life that they lash out, retreat into inner worlds, or distract themselves with trifles. Adults are also guilty of covert abandonment and neglect of their charges when they fail to provide basic necessities and protections. Implicit desertion and neglect also include instances in which parents and children are unclear as to the roles, rules, and responsibilities of each group, or in which, either for temporary or enduring periods of time, they succumb to "parentification,"[46] exchanging positions altogether. In fact, it is another axiom of familial codependence that in functional households, adults look after children, but in dysfunctional ones, children care for adults. In the latter situation, the fear is that if youngsters do not minister to a wayward mother or father, they may lose the parent in abandonment or death. Out of necessity, therefore, they become "king babies," seizing control of the relationship by controlling the offending party in overly mature ways.[47] They mediate conflicts; they provide comfort, support, and advice; they decide a host of issues. Even worse, perhaps, they encourage sexual misconduct by becoming confidantes and pseudo-husbands and wives, and by entering into romantic or pseudo-marital relations with the failing caregiver.

It is also the case that fathers and mothers are guilty of covert abuse when they do not develop healthy boundaries in their young. Regarding internal boundaries, parents are remiss if they allow their children's inner worlds to swirl and swell; or if they leave their children to confront life's dilemmas by themselves or with solutions that are immature and incomplete. As Dostoevsky wrote in *The Diary of a Writer* in 1877:

> By its very nature, the childish imagination, particularly at a certain age, is remarkably impressionable and inclined to the fantastic. This is especially true of those families who . . . keep the children apart . . . because of the worries and perpetual lack of time of the fathers. . . . They sit with their little books in their designated corners, not even daring to swing their feet. Going off to sleep at night in a pigsty . . . or sitting at their tedious lessons, or locked up in the toilet . . . [they] might get accustomed to harboring strange fantasies, kindly, heartfelt fantasies, spiteful fantasies, or, in simple childish fashion, fabulous preposterous fantasies. (25:187)

Regarding external boundaries, parents are guilty of covert abuse when they do not protect their youngsters from mistreatment in and out of the home. It also qualifies as implicit neglect if mothers and fathers raise sons and daughters in chaotic settings, since the message they convey to their offspring is that life is without sanity or choice. In fact, the only thing young men and women in homes learn about existence is merely to expect the unpredictable and to live under the threat of crisis and mistreatment. To them relationships are not forays into love but strategies for survival.

Parents and other authority figures also transgress external boundaries covertly in their dealings with their charges when they set themselves up as gods. Such individuals are as obsessed with their own needs and wants as they are protective of their stature and authority. They do not allow higher realities or beings into their self-inscribed pantheon, nor do they admit to, excuse, or regret their wrongdoing. Maniacal about their discipleship, they also withhold love and approval from their sons and daughters until the perceived offenders submit to their control. An even worse case of covert transgression occurs when adults overwhelm minors with inappropriate advances. They may treat these children as confidants, sharing with them images and ideas that are beyond their understanding and development. A father who, consciously or unconsciously, tells a child about his difficulties or intimacies with his spouse, or who sees a tie to a son or daughter as being more important or satisfying than the one with his wife, is treading on dangerous ground with his offspring for several reasons. He is asking his charge to be a companion-caretaker who can validate his own self-worth and meet his needs for affection, excitement, or romance. Even worse, perhaps, the father is demanding that the prince or princess of his affection turn his or her back on childhood and become the adult he desires but does not have.

Confessions of marital difficulties across the generations not only mark the child as an emotional dumping ground for the distress and anger of the offending parent, they also damage the youngster's relationship with the outsider-spouse. When a parent requires adult intimacy from a child, the abandoned partner usually responds in one of three ways. The first is to feign ignorance and indifference in the face of the wrongdoing. The second is to condone the misconduct and allow the youngster to supply physical and emotional support. The third is for the forsaken husband or wife to engage the youngster in mutual revulsion and rebuke. Here the sparks can fly, since the two do everything in their power to keep the home fires burning and to destroy all opportunities for reconciliation and peace. Even more tragic, perhaps, are the instances in which both mother and father maintain an inordinately close relationship with their offspring. In the shifting "drama triangle . . . of persecutor, rescuer, and victim,"[48] they cleave the child in two. On one hand, they ensnare the son or daughter in a vicious tug-of-war between conflicting loyalties and loves. And on the other hand, they invest their charge with power and privilege as the rational actor of the family or as a double agent who can manipulate both parents at will.

Still another example of the covert violation of borders occurs when parents overprotect their children, leaving them unable to face the challenges and obstacles of life or to negotiate existence on its own terms, apart from parental guidance and controls. (Not surprisingly, a fear of failure is especially intense for codependents.) An additional issue is when parents, either directly or indirectly, interfere with their children's access to friends or peers for fear that domestic secrets will be revealed to the public.[49] In such cases, parents forbid their children to visit other homes or to have friends come to theirs. The household takes on the air of a fortress, prison, or tomb, replete with repressive rules, secret codes, and daily terror (explicit and implicit) to conceal skeletons, black sheep, and other embarrassments from outsiders. The lesson to offspring is that intimacy, loyalty, and trust, if they exist at all, are confined exclusively to individuals in home and hearth, and that, at all costs, the offending party be shielded from exposure and blame.

It should be noted here that caregivers who do not instruct their young about the boundaries of others are also guilty of implicit abandonment and neglect. If parents see their children as perfect, above others, and/or beyond the rules of social intercourse, they often do not correct their young for unwarranted incursions into alien space. Just the reverse, when parents look upon their children as mini-gods, they convey to their youngsters that the mistreatment of others can be empowering, that crime can be without punishment, and that their youngsters can assume their place in the world as offenders or victimizers (or border-jumpers) with little or no sense of ethics, compromise, or fair play. Dostoevsky would agree. Of such individuals, he noted in *The Diary of a Writer*:

> Egotists are irresponsible and cowardly when it comes to duty.... [They have] the conviction, conversely, that everyone they encounter is obligated to them in some way, is, as it were, charged with some duty to them, must pay them tribute, owes them something. However ridiculous this fantasy may seem, it finally takes root and is transformed into an irritable dissatisfaction with the entire world toward everything and everyone.... This embittered feeling often extends over to their own children.... Children are precisely the preordained victims of this capricious egotism ... [because] they are the nearest at hand. (25:85)

The children of codependent parents cope with their situation in both passive and aggressive ways. Passively, they too become borderline, withdrawing into a host of physical and mental ills. Their hope is also for fairy tales and happy endings. They seek out princes, princesses, and tall, dark, strangers; or they volunteer as beauties for beasts. Aggressively, they fix everyone's life but their own; or they move to rebels and moral monsters who seek kicks in anything from reading to sex to death-defying stunts. Either way, youngsters from codependent households are confused about sexual identity, preference, and expression. They see the institutions of marriage and the family as sources of suffering and shame. They flee surrogate parents, authority figures, and God in panic and pain. Indeed, if children tied to codependent adults express undying love or trust for anyone in the world, it is often for the very people who abuse them.

Social scientists believe that codependents suffer stress that destroys bodies and souls. The signs of such discomfort are many. Physically, they feel cold, nauseous, and dizzy. In "ceremonies of degradation,"[50] they hang their head, hunch their shoulders, cover their face, and avert their eyes. It is also common for addictive personalities to repress or reject a viable physicality in life. They often do not see their faces or torsos, but perceive themselves as bodiless heads and voices floating through space. They blush frequently and crawl under objects; they run away, hide, or disappear altogether. Mentally, codependents are prey to sudden attacks of panic, paranoia, and shame. In their disordered minds, also, they replay past scenes of hurt and abuse with sadomasochistic glee. If unchecked, addictive personalities can so internalize their distress that they endanger their health: they become relics and/or meet their end in sickness and suicide.[51] More poignantly, perhaps, they can perish from the dreadful experience of being a child forever.[52]

ON THE PATH TO RECOVERY: RETURN TO THE PAST

Codependents seemingly have insurmountable problems. They have little sense of themselves, their world, or the boundaries between the two. They confuse wants and needs. They obsess, often morbidly, over people, places, and things. They can be both oppressor and oppressed in overt and covert abuse.

Codependents can find light in the darkness, however. As a first step toward recovery, they must resurrect the inner child within and, no matter how painful the experience, unearth and relive the past.[53] They must examine their early years for moments that were abusive or less than nurturing; they must identify when and where who did what to them, and hold them accountable for their wrongdoing. It is a further step toward mental health that addictive personalities attend to their resurrected childhoods. In this mental reconstruction—the "inner child meditation"[54]—both child and adult enter into a rational, articulate, and enduring dialogue—oral and written—to correct mistakes, remedy misconceptions, resolve conflicts, expose secrets, mourn hurts, and heal wounds that have marred both their lives. The inner child must be seen and heard, and given love, attention, and guidance missed previously.[55] Simply put, the child emerging from the adult's formative years should be in the care of a senior self who, as a mentor, confessor, and guide, is everything that real-life parents and caregivers were not.

In their psychic journey to the past, recovering dependents must safeguard against defense mechanisms, the conscious and unconscious ways in which people distort their thoughts and feelings toward previous abuse in their life. As children, defense mechanisms can be helpful, even life-saving. They may insure sanity, stability, and even survival to maturity. As adults, though, defense mechanisms can counter, even nullify attempts to reconstruct childhood, adolescence, and youth in a genuine and accurate way.

Codependents, therefore, must take care not to repress or suppress the difficulties of their yesteryear. In particular, they must not fall prey to a defense mechanism known as disassociation, a process in which abused children, freezing in terror, separate mind and body. When abused children disassociate, they have out-of-body experiences in which they observe the abuse without feeling the pain of physical or psychological violence. In the most extreme forms of abuse, disassociating children may disappear deep inside themselves, finding shelter in the darkest corners of their being. No matter the direction, though, all three mental disassociations have this outcome: the pain and fear that children will be destroyed in incest, molestation, beatings, and the like attack their physical being but bypass their mental and emotional faculties, until, often years later, such abuse is brought to the fore in memories, or even chance encounters, talks, and readings about abuse.

Codependents in dialogue with their inner child must also not succumb to pitfalls of minimization, denial, projection, and delusion. When addictive personalities minimize their past lives, they recognize the harm someone has caused them, but they discount or dismiss the misconduct, as well as the havoc it has caused in their lives. Denials of an earlier existence allows these codependents to shield themselves from the pain and emotions resulting from abuse. When adults in codependence move to projection, they transfer their distress onto others. Finally, when addictive personalities suffer from delusions about their past lives, they can ignore, misconstrue, or deny the abuse that they have endured. They can perceive the pain of their youth, but they cannot accept it as valid. Rather, they enter into a fantasy bond—a "fairy-tale . . . [of a] nice-nice family," so to speak—in which their childhoods were normal and beyond reproach.[56] In fact, codependents in delusion are often so baffled by dark recollections that contradict the fantasy of their perfect past that they accept the blame for their hurt.

ON TO THE PRESENT: THE POWER OF THE WRITTEN WORD

After they have made peace with their past lives, codependents seeking recovery must live new lives in the present. First and foremost, they need to gain both self-awareness and self-respect. Searching fearlessly, they are to conduct a moral inventory, a detoxification of themselves and their "past imperfect" so that they can understand the nature of their codependence, as well as summon the time and willingness to tackle it.[57] They must avow and accept their imperfections and what Jung calls the Shadow Self, the dark aspects of the ego. Moreover, they should let the dead bury the dead.

Into the dustbin of their personal history must go their false or invented selves, as well as their learned behaviors and vulnerabilities that engendered their addictions. Codependents seeking new life in the present must also acknowledge an inner compass to guide them through life. It is crucial that they develop healthy boundaries, distinguish between internal and external worlds, modulate their stance toward self and reality, and detach from people and things that sabotage them. It is further to their benefit that they stand up for themselves when it is in their best interest to do so. They should realize that although they have no power over others, they do have power over themselves.

As investigators of codependence make clear, relationship addictive personalities can seek self-discovery and catharsis in writing. The reason for this is straightforward. On paper and probably for the first time in their lives, they can map out the confusion and captivity of their past lives and strive for independence and meaning in the present. In confession-style letters, diaries, and journals, they can take one day at a time to define and remedy what ails them. In discrete sentences and words, they can temper their whirlwind emotions and thoughts. Multiple beginnings, middles, and ends can bring codependents to understand personalities, analyze assumptions, clarify experiences, and replace tunnel vision with broad perspectives. Internal monologues and examinations of conscience can allow them to explode in fury, weep in shame, and move to closure. Self-styled plots and casts can enable them to exorcize ghosts, to seek forgiveness, and to find home physically, socially, and spiritually.[58] Using these narrative elements, codependents can move to multiple realities, to psyche, memory, intuition, and "lived time," as well as to world fiction and myth.[59] In this way they can develop a discourse of codependency in which the self is an open text or story (or rather a series of stories) in which they can conceptualize their being, account for their experiences, and make sense of their lives.[60]

As Dostoevsky again noted in *The Diary of a Writer:*

> That today's children will also have their sacred memories is, of course, beyond a doubt; otherwise there would be no more "living life." A person cannot even live without something sacred and precious from childhood to carry into life.
>
> There are some, apparently, who do not even think about it, yet they still preserve these memories unconsciously. These memories may even be painful or bitter, yet the suffering one has undergone can be later transformed into something sacred for the soul. People, in fact, are generally so created as to love the suffering they have undergone. Aside from that, people of necessity are inclined to mark off a point in their past, as it were, to orient themselves

later in life and to derive from it something whole, to provide order and edification in their lives. And here the strongest and most influential memories are almost those which remain from childhood. (25:172–173)

Sometimes codependents writing their histories construct linear narratives; at other times, their stories progress in circles and spirals.[61] These narratives can be defensive or accusatory; they may offer forgiveness or reflect upon mistakes and draw lessons from them.[62] Codependents seeking self-knowledge must finish their life stories with a certain degree of ambiguity and open-endedness. In their final chapters, they must see themselves as a work-in-progress, but with this new certainty: they have grown and attained a degree of self-mastery; they have surmounted obstacles and challenges in life—in a word, they have taken "the leaps of faith between trapezes."[63] Additionally, it is imperative that when addictive personalities record their life stories, they see patterns of two steps forward, one step back toward what will hopefully be a more balanced and productive self. Indeed, writing affirms codependents in a way that no other approach to inner knowledge can. As one researcher puts it, "The process of self-abstraction—of *having* a self—can best be understood in terms of narrative. . . . The self-abstracted person . . . is one who has acquired a biography and thereby can tell his or her life-story. A person thus defined is as a self-narrating organism."[64] Lastly, individuals seeking to understand codependence will have a uniquely personal testament of their own experience with their addiction.[65] In their hands will be a workbook-guide that they can reread and expand upon: a journey-journal of a soul that can serve as an inspiration and incentive to others.[66]

For their part, the readers of a codependent's story do not receive the tale in any passive or peaceful way. Rather, as seen by both psychologists and literary critics, the dynamics is "shared, dialogical. . . . It is prospective rather than retrospective, all the parties entering into a new search for new meanings, new possibilities which call into question the problem-saturated description or dominant story."[67] Readers of a codependent's story act as a community of peers or even as a family the codependent has never had, sharing and even reliving the trauma and pain, legitimating and supporting the writer's quest for a valid identity in life.[68] Their calming presence provides a codependent with a safe, stable, and supportive environment—a "haven in a heartless world"[69]—that serves as an anchor in what may be a swirling sea of abandoned, broken, or skewed relationships with people, communities, or institutions. For the speaker, readers of a codependent's tale mitigate embarrassment, assuage hurt, furnish courage, and applaud progress.[70] They also challenge the writer with "reality testing,"[71] and they question rationalization and falsehood, overanalysis and melodrama. They are precisely what addictive personalities need to weave the frayed stands of their childhood, adolescence, and young adulthood into a meaningful fabric of life.[72]

FINAL THOUGHTS

Codependents need ongoing energy, fortitude, and stamina to make sense of existence. In both their present and past lives, they may open and rake raw, long-festering wounds. They may experience memory gaps, repress hurtful events, employ defense mechanisms, or indulge in endless fantasies and dreams. They also may experience what psychologists call "spontaneous regression," the sudden flood of multiple and tormenting flashbacks or "screen memories" that induce physical, emotional, and spiritual suffering.[73] Physically, codependents in self-discovery may experience symptoms of abuse and feel as if they have been struck in the head or groin. They may experience rashes or even heart and *petit mal* seizures, numbness, or shock. Emotionally, addictive personalities seeking self-truth may succumb to rage, paranoia, or panic, on one hand; and on the other, they may give in to remorse, depression, or shame. Spiritually, they may turn their backs on a higher power or deny its existence altogether. The physical, emotional, and spiritual distress borne of spontaneous regression may also cause codependents to see themselves as evil, ugly, and stupid. It may also trigger in them fears and hopes of imminent demise.

Individuals seeking to deal with codependence are also likely to experience difficulty with their present. Their struggle will be to find normalcy and balance. They will wonder: Am I expecting too little or too much from people and life? Am I looking at existence with binoculars or a microscope? Am I loving the suitor or the suit? Further, whatever joy relationship addicts will have in gaining a new self, they will make up for in mourning the gaping holes in their lives. Sadness over the death of their old personae; anger and regret over years in captivity and pain; and laments of "what if" and "if only" are typical responses.

As Dostoevsky wrote in *The Diary of a Writer*:

> If the parents are kind, if their love for the children is fervent and ardent, the children can forgive them much and will later overlook many things. . . . Moreover, they will not pass final sentence on them for some of their thoroughly bad deeds; on the contrary, their hearts will undoubtedly find extenuating circumstances. . . .

> But something altogether different can happen in families where there is disharmony and harshness.... Imagine [a child] ... at the age of thirty ... and think of the disgust, the angry feeling, and the contempt with which he will recall [episodes] from his childhood.... He will take his [memories] with him to his very grave, of that there is no doubt. He will not forgive; he will develop hatred for his memories and his childhood; he will curse his former family nest and those who share that nest with him! (25:191–192)

Addictive personalities on the mend will also grieve over the loss of perceived power and control, as well as of self-consuming hopes, dreams, plans, and *idées fixes*. However perversely, they will also will feel sadness and regret over the very people whom they have hosted in codependence. Additionally, both in their private and public roles, codependents will be unsure as to where they start and others end.[74] They will find it difficult to think, act, and live alone. Without the signals, cues, and skills from partners with whom they were once joined at the hip, they will have difficulty in finding new sources of identity and commitment. The (physical and emotional) distancing from friends, families, and others will bring codependents to face opposition from exes, as well as hostility from others who will see them as failures, burdens, and even threats to their own relationships with others.

Such pressures may also move codependents to regression and relapse. Once again, they may style themselves as victims and losers for whom life is a game of chutes-and-ladders or round-the-board plays back to square one. Once again, they may drive themselves to distraction, and rush headlong from one relationship to the next, seeking to cure others or to have others cure them. Once again, they will say "yes" when they mean "no," react instead of act, laugh when they want to cry, and seek out fatal attractions in people and things. Once again, they will patch their lives with band-aids and paper clips to keep them from falling apart. Once again, they will surrender to physical and mental breakdown.

It is also possible that individuals struggling with renewed addiction may have trouble writing their personal histories. In their stories of self, they may be aghast at the wreckage of the past, the discontinuity of the present, and the uncertainty of the future. Writer's block, bouts of blackouts and "childhood amnesia,"[75] illusions and delusions of reality, and emotions of fear and shame, may cause them to spin mental wheels.[76] In similar fashion, codependents writing their life stories may dread publicizing their lives, finding meaning in loss, or recollecting abuse, abandonment, and conditional love. They will fall into ambiguity and cliché, in incessant queries and explanations. They will not say what they mean, will not mean what they say, and will not know what they mean. Rambling narratives and sheer incoherence may frame rampant contradictions, conflicting focuses, and competing directions.[77] It may also be the case that in their narratives, codependents may be unsure as to how they should portray the various "exes" in their lives, or the lingering effects of former loved ones, or their skewed ties with family and friends. They may feel dismay that, more than ever, they harbor fragments of others, body and soul. Most harmfully, perhaps, codependents in remission or relapse may direct their narratives to various plays on the truth, false confessions, or even lies.[78] They may pen narratives of victimization, taking self-indulgent and masochistic delight in rehashing and reliving the ways in which people and life have harmed them. Or, they may lapse into narcissism, grabbing the limelight to the exclusion of everyone else in their story. Or, they may come up with an *apologia pro sua vita* of self-seeking congratulation and success and announce that, *mirabile dictu*, their struggles with existence are over.

In truth, though, codependents need to know that they will never exorcize their addictions completely, but that they will live one day at a time in continuing self-soundings. There is always unfinished business to attend to; there are always myriad layers to peel back, examine, and keep or discard; there is always the inner child—frightened, vulnerable, and needy—who requires attention; there are always mountains and valleys, plains and plateaus. Most crucially, perhaps, there are always bridges to cross or jump off of, as well as decisions that are always theirs to make. Even at death, the choices are always theirs, that is, either their life flashes before their eyes—or someone else's![79]

NETOCHKA NEZVANOVA: PREFATORY REMARKS

Although codependent images and ideas occur in Dostoevsky's early fiction—the tortured relationships between Makar Devushkin and Varvara Dobroselova in *Poor Folk*, and between Golyadkin Senior and Junior in *The Double* are pertinent examples—it was only three years later, with *Netochka Nezvanova*, that Dostoevsky investigated fatal attractions over a variety of people, issues, and ideas. The plan for the writer's first novel was several years in the making. In a letter dated October 7, 1846, Dostoevsky informed his brother Mikhail of his wish to go to Italy and there, by fall 1848, to write a novel in three or four parts. "The subject, prologue and idea [for the work] is already in my head," the writer affirmed (28:128). Several weeks later, Dostoevsky told Mikhail that his novel was "already giving

[him] no peace" (28:131), and that he intended to publish it in an edition that included *Poor Folk* and *The Double*. By the end of the year, Dostoevsky was writing to Mikhail that by January 5, 1847, he was obliged to give to Kraevsky, the editor of *The Fatherland Notes*, the first part of *Netochka Nezvanova* (this was the first time he noted the title of his work),[80] and that with it he would reignite the literary excitement he had aroused with *Poor Folk*. (An announcement about the imminent publication of the work appeared in *The Fatherland Notes* on December 1, 1846.)

Indeed, with *Netochka Nezvanova*, Dostoevsky was in a fighting mood. His first novel, he told Mikhail, he was "writing day and night ... with fervor ... [as if] to start a lawsuit against all of literature ... and to establish my primacy [in fiction] ... in spite of my ill-wishers" (28:135).

Although Kraevsky announced *Netochka Nezvanova* to the public in *The Fatherland Notes* in December 1846, he soon became an unwilling player in a game of hide-and-seek with the author and his work. Indeed, to Kraevsky and others, Dostoevsky seemed to be one of his characters come to life. "Here is an anecdote for you about one fine man," an amused Vissarion Belinsky, the famed liberal critic of the era, wrote on February 19, 1847, to Ivan Turgenev, the future author of the 1861 novel *Fathers and Sons*.

> From Kraevsky this individual took more than four thousand paper rubles to deliver on December 5th the first part of his large novel, on January 5th the second, on February 5th the third, and on March 5th, the fourth. December and January go by—Dostoevsky does not appear, and where to find him, Kraevsky does not know. Finally one fine morning in February the doorbell rings in the foyer of Kraevsky's home. The servant opens the door and sees Dostoevsky. He rushes to inform Kraevsky who, it seems, is overjoyed. The servant rushes out to welcome Dostoevsky, but he sees neither galoshes, nor overcoat, nor Dostoevsky himself. He has vanished without a trace. Now truly is that not a point-by-point scene from *The Double*?[81]

By the beginning of 1847, Dostoevsky not only expressed to his brother Mikhail his hope that he would complete *Netochka Nezvanova* by fall of that year, but he also gave a tantalizing hint of his idea for the piece. "Soon you will read *Netochka Nezvanova*," Dostoevsky wrote to his brother, "it is a *confession*, like *Golyadkin*, although in a different tone and type" (25:139). It was only in mid-1848, though, that a major part of Dostoevsky's first novel came to be. Pyotr Semyonov-Tyan-Shansky, a member of the Petrashevsky circle and later a famed geographer and statistician, recalled that at a gathering at Petrashevsky's home sometime before November of that year, Dostoevsky read excerpts both from *Poor Folk* and *Netochka Nezvanova*.[82] Ippolit Debut, another *Petroshevets*, noted that what Dostoevsky read from was "much more extensive than what appeared in print."[83]

In any case, Dostoevsky published *Netochka Nezvanova* in *The Fatherland Notes* in February, March, and May 1849. The last section appeared anonymously, though, Dostoevsky having been arrested for his tie to the Petrashevsky Affair on April 23, 1849.[84] (At the time of his arrest, Dostoevsky was also working on part four of the novel and, however unrealistically, also intended to complete parts four and five as early as May. A sixth part was also planned.)

As already noted, Dostoevsky's *Netochka Nezvanova* is the first-person account of a woman who chronicles her childhood, adolescence, and youth vis-à-vis successive and/or codependent families: her mother and stepfather, Efimov; Princess Katya and her household; and Katya's sister, Alexandra Mikhailovna, and her husband, Pyotr Alexandrovich. Harriet Murav's claim that "whatever woman is in Dostoevsky—absence, image, memory trace, a blank space . . . she is not a speaking subject" is not the case in *Netochka Nezvanova*.[85] Indeed, Dostoevsky's heroine not only moves her story chronologically, but she also pursues a more intriguing dynamic. Much as the adult and child speakers will do in Andrei Belyi's 1922 *Kotik Letaev* (which relates the quasi-autobiographical experiences of an impressionistic child embracing myth, music, mathematics, history, philosophy, theology, and linguistics),[86] Netochka bifurcates her narrative in double-voicing: a polyphonic-type dialogue in which the adult persona of her present and the child self of her past try to make sense of existence, particularly the codependence that has marked their mutual life. In what is a highly singular case in Dostoevsky, the heroine's split in *Netochka Nezvanova* does not reflect physical and mental disintegration. In fact, just the opposite is true: her self-imposed duality leads her to understand the past, balance the present, and affirm the future in a way that few characters in Dostoevsky ever do.

NETOCHKA THE ADULT

In her adult mode, Netochka makes a striking impression. Her most attractive feature is that she is writing an account of her early years. The experience is for her a physical and spiritual awakening. After years of numbness and shock, she "feels as if suddenly [she] has become conscious, as if awakening from a deep sleep" (2:159).[87]

The senior Netochka puts her best foot forward, impressing her readers as intelligent and urbane. Again, in a move unusual for a Dostoevsky character, she strides boldly into her story. Her mind is clear; her eyes are penetrating; and her feet are planted firmly on the ground. The mature Netochka also exhibits a healthy self-respect. Looking back, she follows a path common to fictional accounts of childhood. She casts herself as a precocious (or even too precocious) young person who, "unusual and peculiar" (162), received life with a wisdom beyond her years.[88] Netochka is not the "very ordinary" girl that Malcolm Jones claims her to be.[89] From the moment the adult Netochka becomes aware of her existence, she boasts: "I developed remarkably quickly ... so capable of contending with many non-childlike impressions ... to think, reason, and observe ... [that] everything became clear ... swiftly and quickly" (159–160).[90] Such mental largesse only increases with time. If the adult Netochka is to be believed, her youthful persona has little trouble in monitoring all that has transpired in her life. At age eight-and-a-half, she writes, "I began to remember everything very clearly, day by day, without a break, as if it all happened only yesterday" (158).

Again, unlike many men, women, and children in Dostoevsky's writing, the adult Netochka also shows a strong moral voice. Indeed, she is quite open about her failings, particularly about what will be seen as her fatal attractions to people, places, and ideas. In further contrast to fictional colleagues in Dostoevsky, Netochka not only assumes responsibility for her addictive shortcomings, she also experiences guilt and remorse for the suffering she has caused herself and others. Ever more revealing, perhaps, Netochka comes to an understanding of her troubles without the help of others. She does not need good and bad cops (such as the saintly prostitute Lisa in *Notes from the Underground*, the avuncular police-investigator Porfiry Petrovich in *Crime and Punishment*, or the dying elder Zosima in *The Brothers Karamazov*) to be dragged kicking and screaming to the truth. Rather, in *Netochka Nezvanova*, readers encounter a speaker who works through trials on her own and with whom they can empathize and even identify in the addictive struggles of her youth.

Above all, Dostoevsky's Netochka prides herself that she is both a student and a survivor of codependency. Unlike many distressed young female characters in Dostoevsky's works—such as Nellie, the illegitimate and abused child of Prince Valkovsky (who dies from a chronic heart condition in his 1861 tale of a tortured love quadrangle, *The Insulted and the Injured*); and Matryosha (who takes her life after having been raped by Stavrogin in Dostoevsky's 1872 portrait of man-gods and the people who create and destroy them, *Devils*)—Netochka does not yield to sickness or suicide.[91]

Neither does she suffer the fate Dostoevsky foresaw for children from dysfunctional homes: "an inability to cope with life's problems . . . a blush of false shame for their past, and a dull, sullen hatred for people which perhaps, may last a lifetime" (22:8). Rather, "oriented toward life,"[92] Netochka emerges from adversity to tell her story. The observation by Frank that in *Netochka Nezvanova*, Dostoevsky's "aim, unprecedented in the Russian novel of his time, was to depict a talented and strong-willed woman who refuses to allow herself to be crushed—who becomes, in short, the main *positive* heroine of a major novel,"[93] can be understood in a new and more strategic light. That is, the adult Netochka comes to terms with "domino-like addictions"[94] to people, places, and ideas—together with those of the individuals with whom she resides—by penning a series of case studies in which she details the stimuli and responses, causes and effects of codependency, as well as offering alternatives for more life-affirming behavior. The objection raised by Charles Passage that the "interrelation of the sets of characters and of the three homes [in *Netochka Nezvanova*] is far from clear"[95] can be answered. Dostoevsky's Netochka observes emotional addiction from a variety of angles and perspectives to discover what binds people to individuals and items in an unhealthy, even destructive way.

The senior Netochka is deadly earnest in her quest. However painful her journey to the past, she leaves no trail behind, no stone upturned. Indeed, her examination of conscience often borders on the scrupulous. It is the "elementary . . . and trifling" memories that most "lacerate [Netochka's] heart . . . [and] imprint themselves on her mind" (2:160). Absent are what Wachtel calls the "epic"[96] lyricism, wonder, and delight, or the "poeticization of loss, destruction and death"[97] that inform *la recherche du temps perdu* of Tolstoy's *Childhood* (or for that matter that permeate such later idylls of Russian gentry formation as in Sergei Aksakov's 1859 *The Childhood Years of Bagrov's Grandson* or Ivan Bunin's 1927–1939 *The Life of Arseniev*). Missing also is what Wachtel terms "the open-ended nature of narrative purpose" that marks these accounts.[98] Rather, with almost clinical precision—not unlike the "analytical skill of a behavioral therapist"[99] that Martinsen identifies in Zosima in *The Brothers Karamazov*—Dostoevsky's heroine discloses wayward thoughts and emotions; works though skewed ties and relationships; categorizes responses to people and events; and questions motivations and attitudes. Most important, perhaps, in her "history of one woman" (the subtitle of her tale), the adult summarizes the mistakes and lessons of her life. Open to new consideration is the comment by Terras that the adult Netochka "is quick with her moral judgments of people, freely dispenses her worldly wisdom, and with disarming naïveté, philosophizes on subjects in which she obviously is a dilettante."[100] True, Netochka may lack the scholarly credentials to be an investigator of codependency. What she lacks in education, though, she more than makes up for in her own experience and insights into addiction. In so doing, Dostoevsky and his heroine both deserve as much respect and applause for their efforts as any researcher of human dysfunction.

The adult Netochka is also a gifted writer. Unlike other codependents, she has no problem telling the story of her life. At times, the mature Netochka acts like a reporter who, cool and calm, sifts through rumors, gossip, and anecdotes to determine the truth of personalities and events. At other times, the senior Netochka casts herself as a well-read and accomplished author with an impressive command of literary styles and trends. The hack fantasies and fairy tales that seize the imagination of other speakers in Dostoevsky's early and mature fiction do not inform her content and form. Rather, the mature Netochka is equally adept at both romantic and realist modes of writing, specifically, the content and form of gothic, sentimental, social, and empirical fiction. As has already been noted, her account resounds with strains from Romantic-Realists such as Dickens, Hugo, Balzac, Soulié, Dumas *père*, Hoffmann, Sue, Radcliffe, and Sand abroad;[101] and at home, from Gogol, Odoevsky, Herzen, Panaeva,[102] and also the writers of the Natural School, a group who espoused "type" and "daguerreotype" in Russian poetry and prose. There are also strains of bildungsroman and *Künstlerroman*, of *éducation sentimentale* and chronicle (family and otherwise); of confession and *apologia pro sua vita*; of sentimentalism and stream-of-consciousness; and of melodrama and pulp fiction. Most dramatically, perhaps, *Netochka Nezvanova* echoes other classics of unhappy and abused children of the time (e.g., Sue's *Mathilde* [1841],[103] Charlotte Brontë's *Jane Eyre* [1847],[104] and Dickens's *The Old Curiosity Shop* [1841] and *Dombey and Son* [1848]),[105] not to mention the fictional confessions of the countless girls and wards that filled French, English, and Russian journals of the late 1830s and 1840s.[106]

In *Netochka Nezvanova*, Dostoevsky's heroine points to key facets of the writer's mature fiction. She shows a marked preference for quick-paced and convoluted plots. She also likes passion and intrigue, action and sudden turns of events, and gesture and mime in which inflamed faces, averted eyes, and barely concealed grins are worth a thousand words.[107] Indeed, as Terras notes correctly, it is the silent or semi-silent scenes that are among the most magnificent parts of the work.[108] Additionally, the adult Netochka is a master of polyphony, orchestrating with skill the many voices that resound through her account. When Netochka relates the life of her stepfather, Efimov, she seeks credibility not only via her own discourse but also with appeals to the oral discourse of the musician B., a close friend of Efimov in his youth, as well as of her mother, the landowner, the Count, and the other individuals who come into her stepfather's life. Sometimes, Netochka allows characters to speak in their own right. Other times, she lays claim to anonymous rumors and stories, as well as to indirect discourse and reported speech, recasting the utterances of others as her own.

The adult Netochka is adept at adjusting both the length and breadth of her literary focus. In some scenes, she displays omniscience, furnishing information about people and events with confidence and aplomb. In others, the senior Netochka imparts details to her readers sparingly. About an individual's thoughts and actions, she can be absolutely clear one moment and maddeningly vague the next. Images and ideas have contradictory meanings and signs. Dostoevsky's heroine even promises to speak of characters and events "later ... at greater length and detail" (71).

Whatever the source or style of her account, the adult Netochka is highly solicitous of her readers. Unlike the often rambling and duplicitous speakers in both Dostoevsky's early and mature fiction, she seeks to tell her story in a way that "[will] be understood" (7) in a space that is logical, a time that is precise, and a style that, as Albert Guerard notes, expresses "rich conscious and unconscious psychological insights . . . in an extremely economical way."[109] Netochka's paragraphs are short. Her sentences are rudimentary, almost stenographic. It is her manner to have beginnings precede middles and ends. Before the woman tells anything about her present, she feels compelled to "explain the sort of childhood she has had" (158). The mature Netochka stops herself if she believes that she is getting too far ahead with people and events. She closes gaps in her narrative first by telling her readers what she "forgot to mention" (44), and then by supplying details she deems worthy of note. Further striking in *Netochka Nezvanova* is the periodic willingness of the grown self to step back from the story to review events and to explain the motivations of herself and others. Akin to the adult personae in Tolstoy's and Aksakov's fictional childhoods, she makes cosmic generalizations, renders avuncular advice, and engages in psychological analyses.[110] Additionally, it is part of the adult Netochka's strategy to be omnipresent. Even when she narrates scenes and stories that do not involve her personally, the mature Netochka is always either in the middle of events or just off to the side, where like a stage manager, she directs action and dialogue. No detail escapes her notice.

In further contrast to many speakers in Dostoevsky, the adult heroine of *Netochka Nezvanova* seeks to be on equal terms with her readers. In no way does she seek to overwhelm her readers with weighty articles, manuscripts, legends, and discourses on good, evil, truth, beauty, God, Christ, Christianity, or humankind. She stands apart from Underground Man, with his *apologia pro sua vita* in *Notes from the Underground*; and Raskolnikov, with his article on "extraordinary men" in *Crime and Punishment*; and Ivan Karamazov, with his "Legend of the Grand Inquisitor"; and also Zosima, with his life and teachings in *The Brothers Karamazov*. Moreover, the senior Netochka does not resort to pettiness to arouse pity or scorn. In fact, throughout her story, she appears painfully human and as normal and flawed as her listeners.

For all her strengths, the adult Netochka also shows key weaknesses. There is another side to what Terras claims is the "kindly, mature, and cultured lady of great standing for the foibles of the people around her ... [an individual] whose virtue and honor are never in doubt."[111] As she is the first to admit, the adult Netochka never feels whole or complete; rather, she sees herself as a work-in-progress, with considerable growing and living to do. With apologies to the already noted Liza in *Notes from the Underground*, as well as Sonya, the virtuous prostitute-heroine in *Crime and Punishment*, she is no saint or model of "terrible perfection."[112] Indeed, just the opposite is the case. Personal issues hound and confound; identity and esteem cede to darkness and doubt; feelings of guilt and forgiveness—"the most difficult Dostoevskian dilemma"[113]—fester and burn.[114] The senior Netochka never uses her formal—if mellifluous and romantic-sounding—name of "Annetta." Rather, she prefers to underscore the *"nyet"* of her personality and life with the pejorative Netochka. The adult Netochka is without a patronymic or family name. Instead, she calls herself "Nezvanova" or "No-name" or "Appearing Uninvited," emphasizing not only her loneliness and lack of kin,[115] but also her stance as Everywoman or, for that matter, Everyman.

The senior Netochka shows little awareness of herself physically. Not once in her narrative does she tell her readers if she is tall or short, fat or thin, pretty or plain. In fact, throughout *Netochka Nezvanova*, the adult persona appears as a disembodied voice, as a mélange of mind, heart, and soul that are often disconnected and at war with each other. What the adult Netochka does not talk about externally, though, she makes up for internally. She is deeply conflicted about her past and present. A smile never crosses her face; she never laughs even when she hurts.[116] With apologies to Dickens, it was and is for her the worst of times. Regarding her past, the senior Netochka laments wrong paths, actions, and choices. She mourns lost lives and loves that, in truth, were never hers to call her own. In fact, their absence has made her heart grow fonder.[117] Further, unlike, say, Gorky's 1913 *Childhood*, in which later light and understanding emerge from earlier tunnels of poverty, brutality, and despair,[118] Netochka's account of her early life is so filled with pain and regret that she sometimes loses control over herself and her narrative. Narcissism, victimization, and sadomasochism come to the fore. In true Dostoevskian fashion, temporizing, justification, and gaps in memory (purposeful and planned) keep pace with indictments of everyone but herself.

The senior Netochka is similarly displaced in the present. Unknown are her current location and calling, as well as her life after the events of her youth. Even the adult persona's age at the time of her account is undisclosed; the remark by Terras that she is middle-aged notwithstanding.[119] Indeed, the only thing that is certain about the adult Netochka's present is that she is quite alone. Even God—never a great concern in nineteenth-century fictional childhoods[120]—does not measure up to the designation of referee or surrogate father that Terras and Fusso assign to the Almighty in the existential conflicts that consume the senior Netochka's life.[121]

Most seriously, in her account, the adult Netochka often succumbs to what is seen as one of the most nefarious features of Dostoevsky's mature characters. Presaging Marmeladov (who flaunts the ruin of his daughter Sonya before Raskolnikov in *Crime and Punishment*) and Stavrogin (who in *Devils* boasts to Bishop Tikhon that he raped Matryosha), she is guilty of "false confession." It is, perhaps, the most telling mark of her duality that she is conflicted about her wrongdoing. Even as she laments her shortcomings in saint-like fashion, she also vaunts them with a sinner's satisfaction.

When the senior heroine of *Netochka Nezvanova* tells her story, she often pursues several questionable options. First, she often discloses her addictive faults and failings not with contrition and sorrow, with bowed head and beaten breast, but with boasting and glee, with sneers and stubborn smirks, even with renewed pleasure at committing forbidden acts.[122] Indeed, the senior Netochka so delights in shocking bourgeois sensibilities with her uninhibited, self-abasing (and also self-aggrandizing) confessions of codependency that she invests her tale with a sadist-masochistic allure. Second, fearing that she has advanced too much to both her readers and herself regarding her emotive afflictions, Netochka often retreats into modes of self-preservation and survival. Suspecting that she has incriminated herself, or that she appears to be weak, talentless, confused—in a word, "ordinary"— or that she finds herself in an interrogation room that is airless, isolated, and closed, or that she is tied, fatally, to people, places, ideas, and events, she clouds transparency. Periodically, in deception and self-deception, she hides the truth about her addictions behind lies, excuses, rationalizations, and games. She even appeals to her own amnesia, which she uses to stifle memories and "[erase] internal dimensions . . . to become a purely outward, relational phenomenon."[123]

In this way the adult Netochka leads herself down a dead-end path of self-contradiction. As much as she closes cans of codependent worms, she opens them. As much as she exposes herself to readers, she shields herself from them. As much as she rescues her mind, heart, and soul, she also sabotages them. As much as she lives life, she succumbs to hyperconsciousness, an "endless awareness of awareness."[124] As much as she hides in the shadows, she seeks the spotlight. As much as she seeks dialogue, she pursues monologue. As much as she wants an audience, she ignores it altogether. As much as she says *mea culpa*, she also boasts her sins.

Finally, and most seriously, whatever contrition or remorse the adult Netochka shows for her codependency is often short-lived. She tells her sins with "official resignation, a sort of philosophical calm" (4:13), recalling the prisoner-criminals in Dostoevsky's 1861 *The House of the Dead*, his quasi-autobiographical memoir of imprisonment in Siberia. As a result, the adult Netochka never knows spiritual growth, relief, or peace. For her failings, also, she never experiences pardon, reconciliation, or absolution—"the indispensable goad of all confession, sacramental and secular," and with it "the end of the episode, the closing of the chapter, the liberation from the oppression of memory."[125] The senior Netochka also forgoes a rehabilitation of self, a reintegration into community, a return to righteousness, and a right to divine pardon of body and soul.

She belongs to those of Dostoevsky's characters who mistake crisis for conversion.[126] When she reaches a physical and mental breaking point, she often imagines, wrongly, that she has crossed a "threshold" to a realm beyond that offers mystical knowledge.[127] Invariably, though, false moments of illumination cede to genuine periods of darkness. After imagined flights into heaven, the senior Netochka presages the painful crash landings into mental and spiritual hell that beleaguer the Underground Man in *Notes from the Underground*, Raskolnikov in *Crime and Punishment*, Stavrogin in *Devils*, and Ivan and Dmitri Karamazov in *The Brothers Karamazov*. She, too, becomes obdurate. She, too, returns to despondent melancholy, endless soul-searching, panic attacks, benumbed indifference to life and human values—and of course, new (and old) codependencies. In a word, she begins the addictive cycle again. Like almost all characters in Dostoevsky, she is often her own worst enemy.

NETOCHKA THE CHILD

When the adult Netochka appeals to the child within, she resurrects a double, fledgling self. Like her adult self, her child self prefers the name Netochka to Annetta, perhaps because the former name emphasizes her physical absence. The youthful Netochka eschews her own physicality: although she begins her story as an eight-year-old and ends it as a seventeen-year-old with an adult body,[128] she never refers directly to her torso or face. References to physical details (e.g., dark eyes, crimson lips, flaming cheeks, and tousled hair), which mark the descriptions of children in Dostoevsky's later writing (e.g., Nellie in *The Insulted and the Injured*), are absent here. Nowhere also are there signs of beauty, nobility, and peace just under the physical suffering.[129] The child Netochka is never depicted looking into a mirror; she denies herself the satisfaction of fulfilling what psychiatrist Jacques Lacan sees as the desire to unite the inner and outer selves.[130] In fact, if the fledgling Netochka is aware of her physicality at all, it is usually as diminished or dissociated entities.[131] Like her adult self, she, too, is a disembodied voice. As Pyotr Pol'zinsky notes astutely, Netochka is portrayed more psychically than physiologically.[132]

The child Netochka mirrors her adult persona in that even among people, she is alone for long periods of time,[133] "forgotten in a corner" and enveloped in a silence that is "increasingly oppressive" (164, 165). While the youthful protagonists of Tolstoy and Aksakov see their childhood estates as a golden age or paradise lost, Netochka has no such experience.[134] She also does not have the parents, parents, siblings, nannies, serfs, or animals that attend fictional gentry children. Her life is also quite different from that of the children leading hardscrabble lives in most literature of the time. In contrast to the childhoods in, say, Charlotte Brontë's *Jane Eyre* and Dickens's *Oliver Twist* (1838, in which he depicts the sordid lives of criminals), no Dodgers, Fagins, Nancies, Helens, or Rochesters assist her along the way. Indeed, no matter what her situation—living with her mother and stepfather, Efimov; with Katya and her household; or with Alexandra Mikhailovna and Pyotr Alexandrovich—the youthful Netochka is the quintessential outcast, neglected physically and emotionally and left to her own devices to make her way through the world.[135]

There are, however, substantial differences between Netochka the adult and Netochka the child. The issue of identity is for the child more contentious and painful than it is for the adult. The youthful Netochka has no idea who she is other than the butt of life's jokes, reversals, and injustices.[136]

As the adult Netochka readily admits, though, much of the child's grief is her own doing. In no way does she conform to Rowe's (or Ivan Karamazov's) idea of the Dostoevskian child-victim: "a passive sacrifice to the adult world's cruelty and injustice."[137] If the senior Netochka is determined to rise in life, the fledgling Netochka is equally intent upon falling.[138] The idea of Jean Jacques Rousseau, the eighteenth-century philosopher and writer, that the child's soul is purer than that of the adult—a key component of the myth of happy childhood as expressed in, again, Tolstoy's and Aksakov's accounts of childhood[139]—is debunked cruelly in Dostoevsky's *Netochka Nezvanova*. No matter what her situation, the child Netochka eschews virtue. She is not the angel that Dostoevsky ascribes to, say, Aley, the prayerful youth in *The House of the Dead*, or the monk-like Alyosha in *The Brothers Karamazov*.[140] She also behaves badly. She never counts her blessings, she rejects the kindness of strangers, and she even bites the hand that feeds her. Indeed, she sees herself as "crushed and rather silly" (72).

The child Netochka also has skewed notions about her place in life. Days and nights are bland, without meaning. The young Netochka also passes over the vivid details of home life that engage the children in Dickens, Hugo, Balzac, and the mature Dostoevsky. Unlike Tolstoy's and Aksakov's child protagonists, the fledgling Netochka never comes to know the country. She never encounters the natural world (real or imagined), which for Varvara Dobroselova in Dostoevsky's *Poor Folk*, Nikolai Irtenev in Tolstoy's *Childhood*, and young Arseniev in Bunin's *The Life of Arseniev* serves as "a sphere of goodness standing against both social evils and personal problems."[141] Her childhood is spent in a series of sparse domiciles. In the first part of her tale, she, her mother, and her stepfather, Efimov, live in an attic with walls that are grey, a paper screen that is torn, and a sofa that is dusty and dilapidated. No matter what the child Netochka's abode, closets and corners, airless and dark, are often her preferred refuge. Even the grand homes of the second and third parts of her account are like prisons and tombs (key motifs in the fiction of the mature Dostoevsky), indistinguishable metaphysically from the garret in which she begins her story. Beyond her four walls, the youngster Netochka is similarly blasé. Crowded apartments, swirling canals, swarming streets, and littered staircases, all mainstays of both the Natural School and Dostoevsky's later urban novels, do not enter her purview. Rather, in the rare moments when she leaves home, the fledgling Netochka only notes her presence on various stairs or streets without further identifying details.

Unlike her adult persona, Netochka has some awareness of God, but only as a dark, shadowy figure—a keeper of societal admonitions and rules. But whatever religion or faith the youthful Netochka encounters in her early years is punitive, ritualistic, and ineffective; it does not promise happiness in this world or the next and even appears to favor evil over good. Noting only "a little lamp burning before an old-fashioned icon in the dark corner of a room" (158), the child Netochka has little confidence in higher powers. Even when her back is against the wall, she never begs God for deliverance.

The youthful Netochka also has difficulties with people. She is as quick to revere individuals as angels as she is to damn them as devils: small wonder that she loves with boundless love or hates with equally unrestrained hate. Borders, her own and that of others, are equally problematic. The girl transgresses other people's domains (physical and psychic) as readily as she allows others to invade hers. On one level, the child Netochka assumes the world's problems as her own, seeking to fix all the unhappiness and misery she encounters. On another level, the youthful Netochka is akin to an emotional highway, open to having both high and low drive through and leave treads in their path.

Of necessity, the child Netochka moves to an "interior life," a protracted wandering between "thinking and dreaming" (165) between and among intersecting selves and self-consciousness. For once she is like the young Irtenev in Tolstoy's *Childhood*: she, too, is the center of the universe.[142] If Tolstoy's hero looks to the natural world for his bearings, though, Dostoevsky's heroine fashions her existence from fairy tales and dreams. If he is rooted firmly in reality, she flies with the greatest of ease. "I was always silent, brooding, and fretting, trying to reach somewhere else in my dreams" (164), Netochka recalls. "I found myself living in a world of my own," she adds, "and everything around me started turning into a fairy tale . . . which I interpreted as reality" (160). Necessarily, and not unlike Raskolnikov in *Crime and Punishment* twenty years later, the youthful Netochka relishes a fate that "moves in mysterious ways" and makes life "melodramatic . . . unaccountable, even fantastic" (72). Wherever she is in this world, out of it or somewhere in between, the child Netochka is never at peace. Rather, she is a tangle of thoughts and feelings, impressions and ideas, sensations and impulses, ramblings and ruminations—all of which are so "unintelligible and obscure" that she seems to have regressed to the state of a "wild forest animal" (165).

A key problem for the youthful Netochka is that what she sees as her inner development has been "rapid . . . exhaustive . . . [and] incomprehensible" (160). Because "her faculties have come into being at such an unnaturally early age," the fledgling Netochka also admits that she "cannot interpret things properly" (160). Specifically, she cannot prioritize incoming data or assign appropriate values. "Facts" are indistinguishable from "fiction" (165); chance remarks, from dreams and theories. Feelings, "miserable and vivid," grow "stronger . . . and leave indelible impressions" (159). Images, "shrouded in a strange gloomy color," progress in "dreamlike fashion" (159). Ideas become "twisted and refashioned in imagination" (160). Nowhere is there reason or restraint. Rather, the child Netochka's head so "brims with incredible daydreams . . . utter chaos . . . and the wildest and most impossible phantoms . . . [that she] loses all faculties of judgment . . . all sense of time and reality" (165). In a word, she has "no idea where she is" (165).

The pronounced instability of her physical and psychic worlds makes the child Netochka a prime candidate for codependence, particularly in its morbid variant. Believing love to be in short supply, she rushes headlong into obsessive relationships, clinging to people, ideas, and things as if her life depends on them. Sometimes the process by which the youthful Netochka co-opts others is internal. Willingly, she forgoes, even sacrifices, her shaky sense of self and the world to mirror and even assume the personalities, roles, and behaviors of her hosts. A master of external referencing and of impression management, the fledgling Netochka adopts their likes and dislikes, sorrows and joys, no matter how ludicrous or harmful their opinions and ideas. She even models their addictions, tailoring them to her needs. She lies to and cheats her partners; she makes false confessions (and indulges in the self-exposing logic of exhibitionism and the complications to which they give rise).[143] She tolerates, even invites and relishes abuse. The youthful Netochka is the archetypal facilitator-enabler. She fulfills others' desires, performs heroic acts of sacrifice, and arouses them sexually. It is also in her ken to shield hosts from reality and truth and even to worship them as gods.

Initially, in morbid codependency with others, the child Netochka enjoys untold happiness. To her the advantages are obvious. She can take from others what she believes she lacks. Tied to a significant other, the youthful persona believes that she has not only a physical and spiritual roof over her head, but also an enduring Eden- or fairy-tale-like state of security, peace, and love that casts her as a mythical Eve or a beauty-cum-beast in the world. To engage her host in mental and physical games, to explore sexual avenues and largesse, to cry out in triumph or defeat (in truth, she does not care which); and, to focus on a one-and-only—is for her the essence of life. In morbid codependency, masochism and melodrama are for the child Netochka the order of the day. What Julia Kristeva said about Dostoevsky can also be applied to his early heroine: "suffering seems to be an 'in excess,' a force, a sensual pleasure. . . . It gives way to a passionate torrent, to a hysterical effect . . . [to a] fluid overflowing . . . which carries away the placid signs and quiescent compositions of 'monological' literature."[144]

It is routine for Netochka to show her skewed "inner architecture"[145] with ear-splitting laughter one moment and in the next to convulse in hysterical shudders and wails. Rarely does a moment go by when the child Netochka's heart does not "ache from pity and pain," and her soul "weigh heavily with fear, confusion, and doubt" (163). Such histrionics become increasingly frequent and addictive: they are the only highs she experiences in life.

Whatever benefit the young Netochka believes she derives from these morbid relationships is outweighed by the burden of maintaining them. Like a worker at a machine, she checks constantly for light, air, water, and fuel; she gauges temperature and pressure; she greases or replaces parts that show wear and tear. The child Netochka experiences panic and outrage at the slightest disjunction or failure in a relationship. She blames and berates herself and others for problems that develop. Fearing abandonment, she latches onto her host with gritted teeth and white-knuckled hands. Even when the tie is (momentarily) stable, the child Netochka is not content to be second in command. No sooner does she enter into morbid codependency with another than she seeks to reverse the flow of authority and power so as to possess the object of her affection.

In this bid for control, the young Netochka is at her most riveting. Her stance is classically passive-aggressive. At times, the youthful Netochka sighs and sulks, moans and groans to get her way. Other times, she drives people to the brink with roles, masks, and games. One way or another, the child Netochka will have her psychic utopia. Herself a master of abuse, she is neither innocent nor naïve. Particularly when she feels threatened by a rival for another's attention and love, she can be as great a moral monster as the other villains in her tale. Finally, to her repeated dismay, the child Netochka finds that her morbid attractions are often fatal. With people, the bond between host and hostess is often so tight that neither can move, think, or breathe. If the two are not parted by others, they separate themselves. In anger, panic, and/or disgust, they flee, die, or destroy each other.

The saddest aspect of the child Netochka's morbid codependency is this: like a true daughter of Dostoevsky, she never learns from her mistakes. No sooner does the girl uncouple from one host than she latches onto another. She continues to judge people poorly; she remains frustrated and alone; she ties and reties mind, heart, and soul in feelings and emotions; she erects and dethrones idols and gods. In fact, it is only at the end of her narrative that Netochka the child has learned enough from herself and others to understand codependency.

Given her distress, it is not surprising that unlike her senior self, the youthful Netochka speaks in a voice that is fitful, random, and chaotic. Although she claims to "analyze every word spoken by anyone" (160), she cares little for empiricism or objectivity. She is prone to (if not adept at) minimalization, denial, delusion, and projection. In classic accounts of addiction, also, the many stories and scenes of the child Netochka's narrative not only lack beginnings, middles, and ends—they are also notoriously devoid of logic, information, and connection.[146] Events big and small "take sudden and different unexpected turns" (145). She complicates her story with digressions, omissions, and lapses in memory; with non sequiturs, half-truths, even lies; with appeals to "suddenly" and "moment"; and with flashbacks and spontaneous regressions which for her are more real than her present. The child Netochka rarely gives a complete account of a person or event; rather, she throws only a few tantalizing details to her readers, thereby forcing them either to piece the story together themselves or to cling to her more closely in the hope that they will learn more later. Awkward diction, run-on sentences, and unclear references further complicate the narrative voice.[147]

ADULT AND CHILD TOGETHER

If, as Wachtel notes apropos of Tolstoy's *Childhood*, the relationship between the adult and child Irtenev is "fluid and purposely ill-defined,"[148] the tie between the senior and fledgling Netochka is markedly delineated, stable, and concrete. Further, in marked contrast to other split selves in Dostoevsky, one is almost always on good terms with the other. There is no struggle of the child's id with the adult's superego. Rather, the dialogue between the two is fruitful and direct, a concerted effort to understand and reconcile both sides of the self and their penchant for codependency. At times, the adult Netochka looks upon the child Netochka as a dutiful parent would. Literally on a daily basis,[149] with unwavering attention and unconditional love, the senior persona fulfills wants and needs, prescribes warnings and restraints, and exhorts correction and repentance. At other times, adult and child are sisters, even soul mates who enjoy mutual love and respect. In fact, there are times in *Netochka Nezvanova* when the two Netochkas are so close—intellectually and spiritually—that it is difficult to tell precisely who is thinking, speaking, and advancing through life.

As parent or pal, the adult Netochka allows her younger self considerable freedom to test hypotheses, make mistakes, and, most importantly, to develop a viable psyche with which to negotiate life. Sometimes this freedom is physical. Although the senior Netochka routinely ensconces the child in surroundings that are constrained and closed, she also often leaves her younger self with ample avenues for discovery and exploration. The dark and dingy attic abode that is the youngster Netochka's first home has this redeeming quality: it is situated atop a six-story house with windows that look out onto the street and the roofs of other domiciles. Taking in the town from her windows, Netochka can imagine herself mistress of the universe. More important, perhaps, the youngster Netochka learns that she must work for her self-styled grandeur. The panes of the windows in the child's attic home are latticed and jail-like: "short and broad like chinks" (159). They are also so high above the floor that she must climb both a table and a chair to see out from them. Such difficulties, though, do not disturb her. Revealing a resiliency and independence that will prove to be her salvation, the youthful Netochka takes every opportunity to mount the table and chair to survey life from the heights of her home.

Sometimes the freedom that the adult Netochka grants the child anima is metaphysical. Seminal in *Netochka Nezvanova* are the moments when the senior persona brings her child self to trust her intuition and inner voice.[150] Readers can almost see the senior Netochka nod in satisfaction when like almost all fictional children,[151] the child Netochka lays claim to the "power and force" of her understanding of existence; or when she announces: "In my own way, I did understand something" about the people and events about her; or when she asserts: "Again I do not know how I came to understand, but I did understand" (160). Even more satisfying to the adult Netochka are those instances when the child attests to a genuine life as an antidote to her addictive fantasies, dreams, and ideas. Forays into pure consciousness, together with bouts of near mystical experiences, allow her to penetrate into the very workings of life. "There are moments," the adult Netochka recalls of her early years, "when you go through more in your inner consciousness than [you do] in a lifetime" (179).[152]

In part because of the dialogue between adult and child, Dostoevsky's heroine lives to tell not only her own story, but also those of others. Via both selves, she synthesizes her own insights into codependency and, in typical Dostoevskian fashion, from multiple angles and points of view concerning her mother and Efimov, Katya and her household, and Alexandra Mikhailovna and Pyotr Alexandrovich. It is human, Netochka believes, to have addictive relationships. It is also only from the detailed observation of one, then another, and then still another that she can come to a sympathetic awareness of the phenomenon for herself and her readers. By detailing her life with her mother and Efimov, with Katya and her household, and with Alexandra Mikhailovna and Pyotr Alexandrovich, Dostoevsky's heroine presents codependency as a kaleidoscope with different patterns and designs.

CHAPTER TWO

ALL IN THE CODEPENDENT FAMILY (I)
Netochka and Efimov

BAD BEGINNINGS

From the first sentence of her story, Netochka notes that her family situation has been less than ideal. Her biological father died when she was two years old, and her mother's second marriage to an individual named Efimov began with love "[but ended in] great suffering" (142). She hints at an important root cause of her codependencies when she discloses a major source of sorrow and conflict in her life: the wedge between her mother and herself. She links her initial distress at the world to the very person who brought her into it. The myth of the "perfect mother," so prevalent in Tolstoy's *Childhood* and other fictional "happy childhoods" of Russian gentry writers, is not hers to enjoy.[1] Huddling under her bedclothes, Netochka recalls her mother as her "greatest terror" (159) and relives the impressions of her mother that "have wounded [her] heart" (160). Netochka's recollections include being trampled by a horse; suffering from a three-month illness; and suffering through frightening and morbid nights followed by days that are quiet and still, save for scurrying and scratching mice.

From the ages of four to nine, her relationship with Efimov fills the perceived void of her life. But before she details her own time with her stepfather, she talks about his difficulties in life, particularly his addictive relationships.

From the beginning, Netochka's story of Efimov is problematic. Much of the information she discloses about him comes not from her stepfather himself but, as has been noted, from an allegedly famous musician B., who was a close friend and companion in Efimov's youth. Before Netochka meets her stepfather, then, she considers him through the eyes (and discourse) of another. Efimov is thus the handiwork of two voices, not one. But whatever credibility Netochka gains for herself and her initial portrait of her stepfather vis-à-vis B. is undermined by this fact: the musician is as ill-defined and unstable as she herself is. Netochka never tells her readers precisely who this second speaker is. She also keeps them in the dark as to B.'s personal and professional credentials, the reasons for his fame, or even what instrument he plays. Like Netochka herself, the musician B. enters the tale as a disembodied voice. As will be seen, the story Netochka-cum-B. tells about Efimov abounds with gaps, illogicalities, and non sequiturs; but, as also will be evident, it is difficult to tell precisely where the breakdown is. Is the dislocation the fault of Netochka, the musician B., or (what is most likely) the two together? Is it accidental or (what is most probable) purposeful? Another problem with the mechanics of Efimov's biography is that almost all of the information the musician B. imparts to Netochka about her stepfather is rendered as indirect discourse. Rarely does B. speak in his own right; rather, he talks only under the watchful and selective aegis of Dostoevsky's heroine. The joint discussion that Netochka and B. have about Efimov suffers from a problem of spatial and emotional distance.

One thing is certain: Netochka controls the story. Before she lets the musician B. discuss Efimov, she sets up the parameters for understanding her stepfather. Her approach is simple and direct: Efimov was and continues to be for her an extraordinary man. If the father figures in Russian gentry fiction are recalled by their offspring as distant, as either overbearing managers of estates or devil-may-care devotees of hunting and cards,[2] Efimov is rendered by Netochka not only as immediate and intimate, but, more importantly, also with superlatives that magnify and even immortalize his being. Her stepfather, she writes, "was destined to lead a most remarkable life"; he was "the strangest and most extraordinary person whom [she] has ever known"; he exerted "too powerful an influence over her early childhood . . . and entire life" (142).

From the beginning, though—and as will be the case with all alleged supermen in Dostoevsky—Netochka has difficulties in sustaining the aura about Efimov. She provides no information about her stepfather's beginnings, appearance, and path to becoming a musician. Even his name is only given late in the story. Dostoevsky's heroine also shows Efimov as living a carefree, if privileged life. Efimov is no oppressed and humiliated artist. Rather, he is a clarinetist in the employ of a sensitive, cultured, and kind landowner (who goes unnamed). In fact, the master loves music so passionately that he "gives way to displays of emotion" (147) whenever he hears a well-played piece. To Efimov's further comfort and ease, the landowner puts his money where his soul is. He not only spends almost his entire income on a "fairly respectable orchestra" (142), he is also lauded throughout the region for treating his musicians with dignity and respect.

Netochka's case for Efimov as an extraordinary man is flawed. For the picture of her stepfather, she throws together the conventional, if time-worn tropes of Gothic romantic fiction. The details are almost embarrassing in their triteness. Efimov comes into possession of a violin, courtesy of a conductor: an anonymous and evil Italian—a "very bad . . . and strange man" (142)—who has been dismissed for (again) unspecified misconduct by his employer, a rich and (again) unidentified count. The man sinks into "complete degradation" (142) and spends his days wandering, begging, and drinking. He dies of apoplexy and is found in a ditch, but not before he furnishes Efimov with a violin. There is more. As the musician B. tells it to Netochka, the tie between the conductor and Efimov is "inexplicable and strange"[3]—so much so that when Efimov "imitates his friend" (143), the landowner forbids contact between the two men (but later turns a blind eye to the relationship). Questions abound. Who is this conductor, why is he in Russia, and what is the nature of his wrongdoing? Netochka does not say.[4] Moreover, she is mum about the harm the conductor has caused Efimov, the nature of the imitation between the two men, the reasons for the landowner's half-hearted edict, and the motivation behind the gift of the violin.

Without pausing for a breath, Netochka moves to even greater complications. Although the violin is quite ordinary, it becomes the object of a tug-of-war between Efimov on one side and the landowner and the Count on the other. For reasons also unknown, the Count seeks, long after the conductor's death and at all costs, to purchase the violin. For equally undisclosed reasons, Efimov ignores the Count's request not once, but twice. In the scuffle, the Count acts like a gentlemen, but Efimov does not. As told by Netochka via B., the Count does not exploit Efimov's "simplicity and ignorance" (143); he also does not take the violin by force. Rather, in exchange for the instrument, the Count offers the "honest sum" (143) of three thousand rubles, and appeals to the landowner only with Efimov's recalcitrance. Efimov is surly and rude to both the Count and the landowner. He tells them—"first seriously . . . and then with a chuckle"—that he will not sell the violin, but also that it is the "master's affair" (143) if he is forced to relinquish the instrument.

Again, in her story, Netochka raises more issues than answers. She does not explain why long after the conductor's demise, the Count wants the violin so earnestly. Additionally, she does not elaborate as to why Efimov clings to the instrument, since, it will be recalled, he is a clarinetist. This time, though, clarity pierces through the narrative haze. When Efimov looks upon the landowner as a master (and by implication, himself as a man), he brings to the relationship a patriarchal aura that Netochka and B. have not noted previously. It will be recalled that when the two began Efimov's story, just the opposite was the case: the landowner had treated his musicians with a light hand, almost as his superiors, and artists in their own right. A more genuine, if sinister dynamic seems to have been afoot, though—one that not only redefines the tie between Efimov and the landowner but also casts all involved as untrustworthy in anything they say, think, or do.

With new prodding by Efimov, Netochka and the musician B. disclose details they have omitted earlier. Efimov's challenge over the violin, both now admit, touches upon a "sensitive spot" (143) of his employer: the landowner and the members of his orchestra are bound in an unhealthy way. Close inspection reveals that the landowner in *Netochka Nezvanova* is not the "humane and benevolent man ... genuinely devoted to music ... [and a model] of rectitude and true humanity" that Terras, Frank, Grossman, and others claim he is.[5] The dysfunction is twofold. The landowner is often neither cultured nor kind. Rather, he "dreads his temper so greatly" (144) that he banishes offenders from his sight for fear that he will harm them bodily. The landowner also prides himself on accommodating his musicians not from love of music but to ensure that his orchestra is "not only superior to the Count's," but "as good as any in Moscow or Petersburg" (143). With such admissions by Netochka and the musician B., it is fair to say that Efimov's landowner sees his musicians not as people but as objects and status symbols. An additional claim by the two speakers casts further doubt on the man. The landowner does not direct or inspire his musicians. Rather, he indulges and spoils them, since "not for anything in the world does he wish to be stern with his 'artists'" (144). The relationship between the landowner and his players, then, is similar to one between a remiss parent and his delinquent children. Given such a dynamic, readers of *Netochka Nezvanova* can only wonder at the performances of the landowner's orchestra—another issue Netochka chooses to ignore.

In what comes to be seen as an emerging codependent schema—master and man bound tightly, to the detriment of both—it comes as little surprise that the landowner is both surprised and angered by Efimov's revolt. Even more understandable is the fact that when, again for unspecified reasons, the landowner himself offers to his charge the similar sum of three thousand rubles for the violin, he becomes "quite beside himself" (144) when Efimov rejects his bid also. The landowner has additional reasons for anger at his employee. For one thing, he fears that the obstinate Efimov will disrupt the dependent equilibrium—a codependent ecosystem, so to speak—between his musicians and himself. With the members of his orchestra, the landowner values "good behavior... as much as, if not more, than their musical ability" (145). The landowner also panics that, with his obstreperous hireling, "unfavorable conclusions regarding the position of musicians in his orchestra" (144) may reach the Count or others in the area.

Still more salient grounds for the landowner's ire at Efimov speak to the heart of the codependency between the two men. The sudden revelation by the landowner (and, by implication, Netochka and the musician B.) that Efimov is a "poor clarinetist" (143) suggests that the employer had kept his employee out of pity, not pride. In the harangue over the violin, the landowner sees Efimov as an "ungrateful creature... [whom he] has fed, clothed, and compensated... and [even elevated] to a gentleman... [and] an artist" (144). In outraged righteousness, the man banishes Efimov from his sight.

Further evidence of the relationship addiction between master and man occurs when Efimov is charged with criminal conduct and the landowner comes to his rescue. A month after the confrontation over the violin, the first violinist in the Count's orchestra instigates a "terrible affair" (144). He insists that Efimov has caused the Italian conductor's death through excessive drink but not before forcing the man to bequeath the violin to him. The charge, though, is dismissed because of a lack of evidence. The violinist cannot produce witnesses; medical examiners find nothing amiss in the autopsy of the conductor's body. In an odd development, *both* the landowner and the Count forget their acrimony and rush to Efimov's defense with the argument that the violinist is angry at not having acquired the violin for himself. Matters do not end there. Undeterred, the Count's violinist now demands a second inquest and accuses Efimov of having poisoned the Italian conductor; but again his actions are to no avail. This time, Efimov is arrested, imprisoned, and tried in court, but he is still found innocent of wrongdoing. There is this twist, though. As Netochka and the musician B. have it, Efimov has more than secular justice on his side: after admitting to perjury, the violinist dies of brain fever.

As with the first scuffle over the violin, both Netochka and the musician B. have a lot of explaining to do. They gloss over why Efimov's accuser is so obsessed with the violin, as well as why the accused man undergoes arrest, imprisonment, and trial. In marked contrast to Dostoevsky's speaker in *The Brothers Karamazov*, who relished the legal proceedings against Dmitri, Netochka and the musician B. do not reveal the dynamics of the judicial case against Efimov. They are silent as to how the violinist is unmasked as a fraud, and how he instigates an investigation and trial in the first place, especially since the man admits that he has concocted his case against Netochka's stepfather solely from supposition and guesswork. The affair grows increasingly disturbing as Netochka and B. add a host of anonymous voices to the polyphony by introducing gossip and rumor, indirect and reported speech, middle and passive voices. Passive and impersonal constructions create an air of uncertainty around the case: the qualifiers "it was pointed out," "it was suggested," and "it was reported" (144, 145) take their place alongside constructions such as "the matter was put into motion"; "Efimov was arrested and taken off to prison"; "the trial began"; and the "violinist was accused of false testimony and was sentenced to an appropriate term" (144).

In the increasing narrative disarray, though, Netochka and the musician B. make two things clear. First, forces, worldly or otherwise, are keeping Efimov safe. The man escapes disaster repeatedly. He survives an evil conductor and a violinist; he triumphs over the landowner, the Count, and the courts. Second, the bond between master and man becomes stronger and increasingly codependent. As if sensing the new aura about Efimov, the landowner now looks upon his charge as "his own son" (145). When Netochka's stepfather is in prison, he comforts the accused and showers him with money and cigars. Further, when Efimov is acquitted of the charges against him, the landowner is so delighted that he gives his orchestra a day off.

A filial relationship with the landowner, though, is the last thing Efimov wants. A year after the incident with the violin, he bolts from the estate and a new complication arises. Suddenly Netochka's stepfather is billed as a musical genius: an extraordinary man. Almost immediately after Efimov disappears, the landowner receives a letter from a famous—but again unnamed—French violinist who declares his outrage that the landowner has abused Efimov: he has had "under his control... a genuine artist and the best violinist that [the Frenchman] has ever come across in Russia" (145). Adding insult to injury, the Frenchman notes that both he and Efimov are at the home of the Count, and that, as quickly possible, all parties need to resolve an important, but unspecified matter.

When Netochka and the musician B. relate this new turn of events, they build upon previous images and ideas and again create an air of uncertainty with the passive voice. When Efimov vanishes, Netochka notes: "A search was begun, but not a trace [of Efimov] was found" (145). To this, she adds that her stepfather's "talent has been ignored and that he has been forced to play another instrument" (145). Again, gaps abound. The identity of the Frenchman remains unknown, along with the story of how the man met Efimov and came to acknowledge his alleged genius, or how the two wound up at the Count's. Other, darker issues that are up for narrative grabs center on Efimov's alleged giftedness and the landowner's control over him, as a result of which Efimov flees the estate. Regarding Efimov's flight, Netochka's readers may well sense something amiss in the landowner's renewed outrage over his reputation and the charges against him. The landowner is "profoundly mortified" (145) by the Frenchman's letter. He wonders how Efimov "could slander him so mercilessly and unscrupulously . . . especially to a European artist whose opinion [the landowner] regards so highly?" (145). After all, the man continues, was this the very "same Efimov for whom he had gone to so much trouble and shown so much kindness?" (145). Déjà vu: outraged parent and ungrateful child.

As is their wont, Netochka and the musician B. not only overlook much of the dynamics in the meeting at the count's home; they also defy expectations as to what should occur there. By all rights, Netochka's readers have every reason to trust that the landowner is to be tried for his alleged abuse of Efimov. Such is not the case. Efimov is the one who again is under indictment, but this time for his own malfeasance. Standing by the "truth" (145) of everything he has told the Frenchman, Netochka's stepfather is even more rude than previously; and for a straightforward reason. If earlier Efimov asserted his own musical greatness as a means of escaping the landowner and seeking patronage and protection from the French violinist and the Count, he now sees the consequences of such a claim. This observation sheds new light on Frank's claims that Dostoevsky "takes pains to underline that Efimov's incomprehensible behavior has no simple social cause"; and that the character is "evidently the prototype of all of Dostoevsky's later 'dreamers' and intellectuals whose frustrated idealism (whether in relation to themselves or to humankind as a whole) will be allied to delusions of grandeur and similar inhumanity."[6] Again, as will be the case with Raskolnikov in *Crime and Punishment* and other self-styled extraordinary men in Dostoevsky's mature fiction, Efimov finds the idea of genius more seductive and powerful than reality.

Like his later fictional colleagues, Netochka's stepfather intuits that such a flattering self-concept also has this advantage. Efimov becomes a legend in his own mind: a star is born.[7]

Given this new outlook, Efimov enters an adversarial relationship with his former allies the Count and the French violinist. If only days before, the two sided with Efimov against the landowner, the reverse is now the case. Even before the landowner's arrival, Efimov is detained for slander against the Count. Matters become clearer when the landowner hears Efimov bring unsubstantiated charges of perfidy against his neighbor. "I know you well enough," Efimov rages against the Count, "Thanks to you, I came within an inch of being sentenced to death. I know that it was you who persuaded . . . your former musician to trump up a charge against me" (146). Such an allegation infuriates both the Count and the Frenchman, who brand Efimov "[a] rascal and a liar . . . fit for nothing but the most ignominious punishment" (146). Charged with malice and libel, he is again arrested and imprisoned. Efimov does not flinch, though. He tells the Count that "any trial, any punishment would be better than the existence [he] has experienced until now," (146) that is, his life on the landowner's estate as a member of the orchestra and his inability to leave because of his extreme poverty. In or out of prison, he is a self-styled condemned man.

As rendered by Netochka and the musician B., the interchange among Efimov, the Count, and the French violinist does not bypass the landowner. Rather, in the fury of charge and countercharge, he adds his own take on the codependent mix. The landowner challenges Efimov's claims to "genuine talent . . . since [he] has never proven himself to be more than a mediocre clarinetist" (146). More to the point, the landowner takes issue with Efimov's professed inability to seek a better life since, he asserts, his employee has always been free to leave the estate. To Netochka's readers, therefore, Efimov is guilty of more than slander and libel. In what will be seen as key themes in Dostoevsky, Netochka's stepfather has chosen confinement over freedom; he has agreed to a skewed tie with the landowner; he has lied about his greatness and liberty; and because of all three, he has no one to blame but himself for his unhappiness. Before the Count, the French violinist, and the landowner, Netochka's stepfather may indeed be "barely recognizable" (146); but the change results from psychological strain. Not unlike the nocturnal encounters in Dostoevsky's later novels, in which two men bare their souls, Efimov and the landowner meet for a final time. Here the relationship addiction between them takes an intriguing turn. However incongruous the reality, with no proof whatsoever, and having just opined publicly to the contrary, the landowner accepts Efimov's claim to musical greatness. The fleeting support of the Count and the French violinist to the side, he has become his employee's most enduring fan. Further, sleepless from "tormenting worries . . . [and] a strange sort of grief" (146), the landowner bids Efimov return to his orchestra. Such a desire, of course, is a selfish one. With Netochka's stepfather restored to his former glory, the landowner can enjoy even greater fame as a patron of the arts. His offer to renew ties is indeed seductive. The landowner offers to forgive Efimov "everything"; he will make the man his "leading musician"; he will "pay him more than anyone else" (146) in the group.

Efimov rejects the offer and breaks with his patron, now armed only with specious assertions of talent and facing an uncertain future. Still, his desire to cut all ties with his mentor is so strong that he claims to have satanic connections through the Italian conductor, whom he calls a devil. "I really cannot go on living with you," Netochka's stepfather tells the landowner. "The devil himself has gotten inside me" (146).[8]

In his alleged tie with the devil, Efimov adds new strands to his web of deception. As a professed tool of otherworldly darkness, the man achieves several objectives. He shores up shaky claims about his own genius and talent; he escapes both responsibility and the onus of freedom; and he develops a plan to wreak havoc on the world. In fact, Netochka's stepfather threatens the landowner as his first victim. "I will set fire to the house or something if I stay," he tells his former employee, "I might really go and do something to you which would put me away for years and that would be the end of it" (147). What Netochka's stepfather lacks as an artist, he makes for up as an actor. Melodrama is his newfound forte. Presaging the unhappy Smerdyakov in *The Brothers Karamazov*, who rues his entry into the world,[9] Netochka's stepfather confesses: "There are times when I am overcome with such terrible despair that I wish I had never been born. Just now I cannot be responsible for my actions; so you had better leave me alone, sir" (147). Efimov is no Faust, though. The story of how this friend (and fiend) has brought about his "ruin" (147) is long on emotion, but short on facts. "It would have been better for me to have lost my hand," he continues to the landowner, "than to have learned the things" (147) the conductor has allegedly taught him. The nature of such instruction, though, is anyone's guess.

Netochka and the musician B. strain credibility even further with two additional items. The first is Efimov's claim that he has taught himself to play the violin; the second is the landowner's willingness to believe such an avowal and to demand to hear a musical piece that Efimov ostensibly played once for the French violinist. As quoted by Netochka and the musician B., the landowner is every bit as capable of melodrama as his employee. "For God's sake, play something," the landowner begs Efimov. "I beg you, with tears in my eyes. . . . I do not think I can live unless you play for me the piece that you played for the Frenchman" (147).

The landowner's plea is important not only because of his unfounded willingness to believe in Efimov's greatness but also because, as is typical in codependence, it reverses the relationship between the two men. Now Efimov is the master and the landowner is the man. Whatever his tie to giftedness, Netochka's stepfather now has the freedom and respect for which he has yearned. "I am not ordering you [to play the violin]," the landowner tells his former hireling. "I am not forcing you. You must do it willingly" (147).

Efimov acquiesces to the landowner's request; but as Netochka and the musician B. tell it, the concert is all style and no substance. Netochka's stepfather agrees to play the violin with the sham grandeur of a broken vow. "I swore to myself," Efimov tells his former employer, "that I would never ever perform in front of you. . . . I will play you something now, but it will be for the first and last time. After this, you will never hear me play again, not even for a thousand rubles" (147). Further, when the would-be virtuoso, at long last, picks up the violin, he allegedly plays "his own variations on Russian songs" (147)—whatever those are. Indeed, so fearful is Netochka over a revolt by her readers given the growing haze over her stepfather's talent that she appeals directly to the musician B. for assistance. "B. said," Netochka writes, "that these variations were my stepfather's first and best pieces for the violin, and that he never played them so well or with so much inspiration" (147). But the fact that B.'s voice is rendered as indirect discourse undercuts the statement about Efimov's musical talent. There is a related issue. According to Netochka, when the landowner hears Efimov play, the performance reduces him to tears. Whether such a response is from ecstasy or from anger and frustration is unclear. In fact, the latter is more plausible because, without a moment's hesitation, the landowner issues his own oath to Efimov: he never wants to see the man again. "Now be on your way, Egor. I am releasing you," he tells Netochka's stepfather, "But you will not see me again. There is a wide road lying ahead, and it would be painful for us both if we should meet. So, farewell" (147–148). Whereas all critics of *Netochka Nezvanova* accept Efimov's claims to talent, the landowner applauds the man with one hand.[10]

Still, even in the final moments between the two men, the landowner acts like a codependent in his relations with Efimov. Regaining the upper hand in the relationship, he speaks to the would-be prodigy like a "father to a son" (147). His advice to Efimov is not only to study, but also to remedy his many faults (e.g., his conceit, his flirtation with evil, and—in a new and heretofore undisclosed wrinkle in the man's narrative blanket—his penchant for liquor). "Once you start to drown your sorrows in drink," the landowner tells Efimov, "and mind you, there will be plenty of sorrow, you are as good as finished. Everything will be lost to the devil, and you will most likely die in the ditch like that Italian friend of yours" (147). After an embrace from his former employer, Netochka's stepfather "steps out into freedom" (147).

EFIMOV AND THE MUSICIAN B.

Efimov's first taste of liberty is a disaster. According to Netochka and the musician B., it is the man's intention to "study, find a good job, and develop his talents to the full" (148). Netochka's stepfather, though, only adds new clouds to his already dark horizon. He falls in with the "most disreputable and sordid gang of hooligans ... [as well as with] a miserable band attached to a provincial traveling company" (148). As a true son of Dostoevsky, what suffers most is Efimov's "pride" (148), not his talent. Initially, the man seeks to remedy matters by resuming his codependence with the landowner. His letters to his former employer—the first one written in arrogance, the second, "in the most cringing language, hailing the landowner as his true benefactor and as a supreme connoisseur of the arts" (148)—results in a one-time sum of a hundred rubles, nothing more. After six years of wandering, Efimov "fears a loss of talent" (148). At long last, he moves to Russia's northern capital and a relationship with the musician B.

With B., Netochka is again up to her old tricks. As she has done with Efimov, and even with the musician at her narrative side, the girl still does not disclose where B. is from, who his kith or kin are, when he arrives in Saint Petersburg, or how he knows Efimov. As per the Count and the Frenchman, she does not even grace B. with a name. Further, when Netochka considers Efimov and the musician B. together, she is on the same shaky ground as previously. All she notes is that the two are young with similar hopes and dreams.

Dostoevsky's heroine is more credible when she notes the differences between the two men. Not unlike the skewed relationship between Golyadkin Senior, a failed clerk, and Golyadkin Junior, his successful alter ego in Dostoevsky's *The Double*, the musician B. is everything Efimov is not. The new friend is the archetypal German: cold, methodical, and persevering. He has suffered little hardship or sorrow. More important, perhaps, the musician B. has no delusions of grandeur: he knows both the "limits of his ability ... and the degree of his attainable success" (148–149). Unlike Netochka's stepfather and, one might add, most of Dostoevsky's central characters, the musician B. accepts his limitations. He does not curse God or fate; rather, as a "humble laborer in the field ... [he makes] the best of everything [he] has" (150). In a manner that is also unusual in Dostoevsky characters, the musician B. is "secure" (150) about his future. He "does not bury his talent," since he knows that success comes from "unending work; a voluntary subordination of self; and a constant struggle against complacency, laziness, and arrogance" (150).

By contrast, Efimov presents a pathetic picture. For the first time in her tale, Netochka tells the truth about her stepfather. The thirty-year-old Efimov is hardly a musical paragon. He is tired and weary. Worst of all, and as will be the case with later monsters in Dostoevsky, Efimov's avowal of greatness has succumbed to "a vague and rather obscure idea, that is, a sort of irresistible inner calling which, over the years, had lost most of its original clarity" (149). Like a zombie or automaton, he "acts almost unconsciously, simply following an old and familiar habit of constantly dreaming and brooding" (147)—with harmful results. Seeking to "deceive himself... with convictions that his energy, vigor, inspiration, and fire have not burned out" (149), Efimov manifests an "enthusiasm... that is spasmodic, erratic, and jaundiced... [like] fits of rapture" (149). His addiction is not only to people, but also to ideas.

In contrast to the Golyadkins, as well as to other dueling doubles in Dostoevsky's later writing, Efimov and the musician B. are bosom buddies. In fact, they get along too well, codependently. Whatever problems or inequalities they have, they surmount in the addictive needs of each other. Initially, B. is so "blinded" by Efimov's seemingly otherworldly spasms that he worships his friend as a "great musical genius" (149). Almost immediately, though, B.'s eyes open to the truth. His assessment of Efimov is even harsher than Netochka's recent judgment of her stepfather. B. sees clearly that Efimov's distress draws from despair over a wasted life and discerns that his friend's talent is the stuff of "blindness, vain complacency, and premature self-satisfaction" (149).

Allowed by Netochka to speak for the first time in his own voice, the musician B. provides new information about her stepfather. Not without fascination, and again presaging the tragic dualities of Dostoevsky's later characters, B. notes Efimov's "strange temperament... [born of] a desperately feverish contest... [between] inner omnipotence and violently overstrained will" (149). In fact, for B. the two poles of Efimov's being could not be further apart. On one hand, his friend has rejected the "most elementary mechanics of art" (149). On the other hand, he is consumed with the "most colossal plans for the future... [his wish] to be a first-rate genius... a composer... and one of the premier violinists in the world" (149). Simply put, Efimov has wanted to be an extraordinary man in art.

The musician B., though, commits the same crime against Efimov as the Count, the Frenchman, the landowner, and Netochka herself have done. Without any basis in fact, and contrary to all sensibility, sense, and knowledge of the truth, B. sets Efimov apart from mortal men. Despite the fact that Netochka's stepfather "never has read or studied anything... [and] speaks in a crude and rather simple tongue," he concludes that Efimov is nevertheless "a sympathetic, natural critic... [with] a deep, lucid... and instinctive understanding of art... [taken from] profound truths... which he has worked out by himself" (149). The musician B. hails Efimov as teacher and guide and acknowledges his "profound debt [to him] for his own progress and growth" (149).

Notwithstanding Terras's claim that Efimov has "a rare gift of understanding art . . . in a way that is both sophisticated and profound,"[11] B.'s encomiums to the man are in praise of folly. Just as Netochka's flawed fragments leave gaps in her portrait of her stepfather, so too the musician B.'s statements about him leave much to the imagination. He never details the nature of Efimov's alleged instincts or truth, or how he serves as a teacher and guide. Indeed, not the slightest hint of mentoring occurs between the two men. In what perhaps foreshadows the relationship between Alyosha and Zosima, for example, the musician B. relates to Netochka's stepfather as a groupie or disciple would to a guru or a god: wide-eyed and with his heart rather than his head. No other conclusion is possible when B. "marvels" at Efimov's wisdom; is "astonished" at his insights; and is "struck dumb" (150) at his understanding of music and life. Finally (and this is a key point), the musician B. sees Efimov as a theoretician, not a practitioner of music. Never does his friend's alleged prowess with the violin ever come into play.

As was the case with the landowner, the musician B. wants a relationship with Efimov to enhance his own stature in life. The tables between the two are turned when B. addresses Efimov's shortcomings, particularly his reticence as a performer. More to the point, he advises Netochka's stepfather not only to practice the violin, but also to play publicly at parties hosted by merchants, Germans, and petty officials.

It is a measure of how fragile the aura is about idols in Dostoevsky that as soon as B. asserts primacy in the relationship, Efimov goes into free fall. In need of a second look is Frank's claim that Efimov is "entirely free of Golyadkin's timidity and servility."[12] Questions, even doubts, pose a near-mortal threat to his being. Challenged by the musician B., Netochka's stepfather moves from "apathy, boredom, and grief . . . [through] gloomy and savage depression . . . [to] utter cynicism and almost moral collapse" (150). He resumes drinking and "succumbs to every vice" (150). The codependent equilibrium is offset further by Efimov's abuse (overt and covert) of his friend. At times, Efimov flies into rages, declaring that even if "someone will go down on his knees" (150), he will not touch the violin again. Further, he insists that, unlike B., he is an artist, not a "street musician . . . [who] would sink so low as to play for vulgar tradesmen quite incapable of appreciating his talent" (150). At other times, Netochka's stepfather ignores B. completely, disappearing for days on end until he returns to continue the codependent status quo.

The musician B. knows that Efimov is exploiting him personally and financially; but, addicted to his colleague, he endures the abuse. To quote a popular song, he finds that breaking up is hard to do. It is B.'s "friendship . . .

attachment . . . and compassion that bind him more closely" to his Efimov. With understated irony, Netochka notes that the "two men go on living as before" (151).

Eventually, Efimov and the musician B. cannot bear their "ghastly life" (151) together. What ends the bond is simple: B. moves toward success; Efimov, to failure. He is a "ruined man" (151). The final encounter between Efimov and the musician B. recalls the late-night confession between Efimov and the landowner. B. gives money to Efimov and begs him to return to his senses and talent. They weep and embrace.

The differences between the two meetings are considerable. Whereas earlier Efimov affirmed his genius, he now, "sobbing . . . [and] pale as death," utters a sober truth: he is "finished" (151) as a musician and a man. Here, though, the musician B. commits the ultimate act of perfidy against his friend: he resurrects the idea that Netochka's stepfather is an extraordinary man. "You do have talent," he says, "as an artist, you are a hundred times greater than I . . . achievements far greater than mine await you" (151). No doubt about it, B. continues, Efimov can understand and appreciate music. His "entire life is proof" (151) of his giftedness.[13]

Without blushing, the musician B. rewrites Efimov's personal history, absolving him of all sins to date. In this reconstructed past, it is the Italian conductor who bears the guilt for his friend's misery since it is he who aroused in the man "vague yearnings" (151) for better things in life. Even the six years that Efimov spent wandering have been a period in which he "studied, thought, and became aware of himself and his strengths" (152). For the musician B., Efimov's present could not be better. His colleague is endowed with "fire and feeling"; he "understands art and his vocation" (152). All that is needed, B. concludes with appalling ease, is for Netochka's stepfather to make a new beginning in life and to achieve greatness through courage, stamina, and patience.

The musician B., however, does not grant Efimov the freedom any idol or god would want or need. In a rare moment of honesty, he outlines the difficulties his friend will face ahead. One is external: the mob "will poke [Efimov] like a pincushion . . . [with] envy . . . stupidity . . . petty meanness . . . contempt and disdain" (152). The other is internal: "the strange ways . . . [and] coarse and glaring defects" (151) of Netochka's stepfather himself. As does the adult Netochka, the musician B. knows that his idol is no saint. In his view, his colleague suffers from a "kind of sickness" (151), the mark of all extraordinary men in Dostoevsky. Efimov is too "vain . . . impatient . . . conceited . . . [and] proud"; he "thinks too much . . . [and] frightens easily"; he is "bold with words . . . [but] feeble" (152) with deeds. Again, the musician B. seeks to help Efimov forget his own path. His friend should not "turn up his nose at humble work . . . [but] chop wood . . . at evening parties" (152). He should study, pursue his passion, and believe in a benevolent universe. "It is a wonderful thing," B. tells Efimov, "to trust in fortune!" (152).

However flawed B.'s affirmation of Efimov, it resurrects the would-be genius. Whereas previously Netochka's stepfather was listless and chalky-white, his cheeks now flush red; his eyes sparkle with fire and hope. Sadly, though, his shortcomings also reappear: "Deep self-abasement and humiliation . . . [moves first to] noble courage . . . [but then to] arrogance . . . impertinence . . . [and] defiance" (152–153). Efimov is his old self. Without anyone's help, he tells the musician B., he can make his way through the world, even to break a key taboo. Efimov promises to give a concert that will bring him instant fame and money. In response, B. recalls the landowner: shrugging his shoulders, he bids a final farewell to his friend.

Or so B. thinks. Even after the two men go their separate ways, he gives Efimov money a "second, third, and fourth time" (153). In fact, it is only on the tenth (!) request that B. finally loses patience with the man. Still, the addictive relationship continues. Several years later, the musician B. encounters Efimov in a tavern. Unsurprisingly, his friend falls short of anyone's idea of a genius-idol. Whatever arrogance and superiority the man showed his colleague previously is now gone completely. Externally, Netochka's stepfather shows the "permanent effects . . . [of] a dissipated life" (153). His face is yellow and puffy; his hair is thin and gray. His tattered clothes feature a frayed shirt with wine stains. Efimov speaks like a "madman"; he acts puppet-like, "superficial . . . pleading . . . [with] drunken lurching . . . and flamboyant moves" (153).

Internally, too, Efimov displays signs of deterioration and bifurcation. On one hand, the idea of success is still a mental "line of defense" for him. Netochka's stepfather "believes in the truth" of his greatness, that he has "nearly reached perfection" (154) on the violin. On the other hand, there is the reality of failure. As if in a "deadly nightmare," Efimov "struggles convulsively with a terrible conviction"—that "irreversibly and long ago," he has lost his chance at art, at "everything that gave meaning to his life" (155). Even when Netochka's stepfather "opens his eyes for a minute . . . [he is so] overwhelmed by reality . . . [that] he almost goes crazy with fear . . . [and] drowns his sorrows in the intoxicating fumes" of drink (155). Efimov berates B. for "strumming dance tunes to ballets"; but he also acts "like a groveling servant" (154) before the man. Accepting vodka from his (facilitating) friend—the last thing he needs—he is "so beside himself . . . that he almost begs to kiss the hand of his benefactor" (153). In a word, Efimov's behavior is "extremely repulsive" (154).

FAMILY UNHAPPINESS

In a sign of the enduring codependence between the two men, despite Efimov's abuse, the musician B. greets his friend with joy and resumes the skewed tie exactly where they left off previously. In this new encounter, the musician B. learns that Efimov has entered into a new and more intense union: a marriage to Netochka's mother. Efimov's latest venture into addictive relationships differs from his previous attachments in several ways. If Netochka's stepfather saw the landowner as a father and B. as a brother, he is now tied to a wife. Unlike his other hosts, the latest object of his codependent affection lacks status and stature: she is for him a "peasant, a cook [and] a coarse uneducated thing" (153). Also, with the lure of a thousand rubles, the woman has "grabbed by the neck . . . a starving man" (153), thereby making Efimov her captive codependent own. Finally, the resumed codependence between Efimov and the musician B. is no longer one-on-one; rather, as the two head for the man's apartment, it now embraces a family.

As her daughter notes, Netochka's mother is an unhappy soul whose gray past informs an equally bleak present. But she is not the coarse, vulgar being Efimov has made her out to be: attractive and well-educated, she once worked as a governess. She is also an "enthusiast and a dreamer" who, following in the footsteps of the landowner and the musician B., has seen Efimov as "some kind of genius . . . [with] arrogant talk of a brilliant future" (154). Like Efimov's previous disciples, Netochka's mother sees in him a means of gaining a spot in the limelight for herself. "Flattered by a glamorous image," she, too, has sought to be the "firm guiding hand" (154) in her husband's imminent success.

Her hopes dashed cruelly, the woman encounters the same abuse (overt and covert) that Efimov meted out to the landowner, the French man, and the musician B. Efimov sits idly by, forcing his wife to be responsible for the home. More seriously, he blames the woman for the demise of his talent, for "having ruined him . . . in a stuffy room face to face with a starving family" (154, 155). Once again, Efimov finds "an external cause . . . for his bad luck and disaster" (155). Indeed, it is hardly an understatement when Netochka writes: "I do not think that my stepfather ever realized how necessary his wife was to him at that time" (155).[14]

Netochka's mother does not suffer her loss lightly. Like Efimov, she, too, is a "true dreamer . . . [who] breaks down at the first contact with reality" (155). Still another contrast in this addictive relationship is that whereas the landowner and the musician B. suffered in silence at Efimov's capers, Netochka's mother does not. Irritable and shrewish, she seeks every pretext to quarrel with her husband and to badger him about his talent and work. Efimov gives as good as he gets. In fact, he takes sadistic delight in tormenting his wife. He steals money. He "lets all hell loose" (155) by inviting riffraff into the home. He tells his wife that he will not pick up the violin until after her death, thereby denying her any hope for her dreams of happiness, liberation, and success. Efimov's "blind obsession, irrationality, and mental wanderings" render him "almost unfeeling and inhuman" (155). They also give rise to a new addictive "idea" that once he buries Netochka's mother "everything will be put to right" (155). A final and key difference between the ties to the men in his life and the bond with his wife comes into play. Whereas Netochka's stepfather does not harm his previous hosts—the landowner continues life at the estate and B. moves on to a successful career—in his relations with his wife he becomes a destructive monster.

Still, addicted emotionally to Efimov, Netochka's mother kisses the hand that strikes her. As Dostoevsky's heroine writes: "Despite everything and right to her dying days, [the woman] still loves [her husband]" (155). She pays a high price for her affection. As the breadwinner, Netochka's mother washes linen, remakes old clothes, and prepares food for others. She also becomes "chronically ill and lives in perpetual torment and suffering" (155).

His heart again ruling his head, the musician B. becomes a "benefactor" (156) to Efimov and his family. But as the relationship is a codependent one, he causes more harm than good. The mother refuses the money, but Netochka, when pressed by B., does not. Her first encounter with the outside world is tainted by inequality and dependence. When the musician B. asks Efimov to play the violin, he obfuscates further unresolved issues about the man and his greatness. Efimov's wish to be a composer, together with his alleged theories of art, are cast aside when B. ignores an exercise book, supposedly containing original musical pieces written by his friend.[15] The musician B. also feeds one of Efimov's addictions with another, again agreeing to the man's demand for (more) vodka before he plays the violin. Further, B. enters into new complicity with Netochka in that the two render Efimov's musical performance not only with renewed indirect and reported speech, but also with utterances that defy credibility and truth. Everything that Netochka has just said about her stepfather's decline is called into question when she bolsters the musician B.'s resurrected admiration for his friend, that is, his statement that "Efimov really had been studying, and ... despite his boast of not having touched his violin since he married, he had made considerable progress since their last parting" (156). Further suspending disbelief is Netochka's own claim that with Efimov at the violin, his wife has rejoined the living. "It was such a joy to see my poor mother's face," she writes, "she felt proud of him again" (156). Further, Netochka offers no details about B.'s plan to present Efimov to society and find him a job. All she notes is that he has outfitted her stepfather with new clothes (i.e., implying that Efimov is being changed from without, not within).

Even more outlandish is Netochka's new image of Efimov as a model citizen who responds to B.'s offers of work and rehabilitation with gratitude and gusto. Without a moment's hesitation, Netochka's stepfather "promises to behave": he realizes that he is "being set on the right path"; and he is only "too pleased" (156) to follow B.'s proposals and advice. Overnight, the man gives up drinking, sets aside hatefulness, and even gets an (unspecified) position in an orchestra. Former vice transmutes to present virtue when Efimov, faithful to a vow to be "honest and meticulous in the performance of his duties," regains in one month "all that he has lost in a year and a half's worth of laziness" (156).

Implausibly, Efimov has solved all problems but one: his codependence. He is no freer of his ties to his wife and the musician B. than previously. Indeed, it is almost with relief that readers of *Netochka Nezvanova* greet the return of Efimov's addicted self. This time, though, the man sinks to new lows with both his family and society at large. Netochka's stepfather contributes nothing to the upkeep of his wife and stepchild. He spends his money on theater attendants, chorus singers, and the like who, for food and drink, make him "feel superior" (156).[16] Those who are not with Netochka's stepfather are necessarily against him. "Inspiring his friends with special respect for himself" (156), he damns his wife and workmates—musicians and managers, conductors and composers—for their stupidity, incompetence, and neglect. His loss of his job only energizes his malevolence. Netochka's stepfather reappears in his former rags, "indifferent as to whether his former workmates are pleased to see him" (157). He "spreads spiteful gossip, babbling nonsense and bemoaning his miserable predicament" (158). He even invites people to his home to "see what a diabolic wife he has" (157). Efimov gains a reputation in the theatrical world, but not the one he wants. Again, he is defined by superlatives, but now they are ones that brand him a louse, not a lord. To one and all, Netochka's stepfather is now "the most troublesome . . . the most cantankerous . . . and the most worthless of men" (157). Most importantly, perhaps, Efimov alienates the two people who, whatever their motives, believe in him the most. He subjects the musician B. to gossip and slander. He also isolates the adult Netochka, who despite her continued affirmation of her stepfather's "unhappy, ruined talent," (155), is tired of his behavior. "Indeed it was very strange," she writes in a rare moment of truth, "to see such an insignificant man, such a stupid and useless performer, such a negligent musician, full of such vast pretenses, boasts, conceits and ugly manners" (157).

If Netochka and the musician B. give Efimov a great deal of leeway in his conduct, his false disciples bring him up short. In fact, they can be as cruel as their supposed leader. The down-and-outers in Efimov's retinue force him to perform not as a gifted violinist but, rather, as an "unfortunate madman... a crackpot fool... and a home-grown Thersites" (157), the rank-and-file soldier in Homer's *Iliad* who, marked by a pointed head and crooked shoulders and legs, is dull, vulgar, and obscene, particularly in his mocking of Achilles and Agamemnon. Efimov's false friends also delight in the "clever things he says about his rivals... his intelligent and audacious caricatures of the musical celebrities of the day... and his witty talk... filled with caustic quips and cynical digressions" (157). They rouse the man with bawdy jaunts and jibes; they ply him with drink to speak rubbish; they watch how his "face falls" (157) with talk about respected musicians, particularly the world-famous (and unnamed!) violinist S., who is coming to Petersburg. More to the point, Efimov's would-be fans watch in fascination as the "real, permanent madness sets in," the split brought about by Efimov's "unshakable belief that he is the finest violinist in Petersburg," on one hand; and on the other hand, his equally staunch conviction that he is "misunderstood... persecuted... [and] left in obscurity... [by] ill luck... [and] intrigue... [an archetype] of the humiliated and injured who complain aloud [about their fate], but who find secret comfort in gloating over their unrecognized genius" (157). Small wonder that once again, Netochka's stepfather escapes in the only way he knows how: he "disappears like a fish in the ocean, never to be seen again" (158).

Or so Netochka's readers might wish. As witness to her own codependence, she brings Efimov out of hiding to replay an earlier scene. Once again, the musician B. finds Efimov on the street; once again, his "compassion prevails over his repugnance"; once again, Netochka's stepfather acts like a "lackey... obscene, silly, and revoltingly offensive" (158); and once again, the two go their separate ways. There are also cryptic remarks that a catastrophe will end her stepfather's "miserable, morbid, and delirious existence"; but not before he causes her mother's death and leaves a "torturous mark" (158) on her own life. Storyteller that she is, though, Netochka deems it necessary to fill in the lacunae in the story from her own time with Efimov and her mother, before tragedy struck all three of their lives.

Given the union between Efimov and her mother, it is not surprising that Netochka draws an initial scene of confusion and darkness. Her earliest recollection is at dusk, in a room littered with brushes, rags, bowls, and broken bottles. Her narration, as usual, is high on drama but low on cause and effect. In the language of codependence, Netochka's family is disengaged. In their attic apartment, a "death-like silence reigns for weeks on end," with her parents taking refuge behind boundaries of "vague but permanent antagonism ... [and] permeating auras of disorder and grief" (164, 165). The only interaction between husband and wife takes the form of ill-defined scenes that "last a couple of hours" (159). Flying bowls and brushes accompany Efimov making "some sarcastic remark," his wife "being terribly excited ... [and] crying about something," and Netochka "shaking in anticipation ... [and] trying as hard as [she] can to guess the outcome" (159).

In the narrative haze, two points come to the fore, both of which are typical of codependence. The first is that Netochka sees herself as the reason for the familial discord. What other conclusion is possible when with every blow-up, her mother points to her in heated and bitter tones? The second is that in the struggle, Netochka sides with Efimov, whom she wrongly considers her biological father, a belief that she sustains through the work. The assertion by Terras that in their early time together, Netochka gives "moral support" to Efimov does not even begin to tell the story between the two.[17] The reality, rather, is that when Netochka's "clings" (159) to Efimov, she foreshadows a tie that is tactile, desperate, and sexually suggestive. The strained physicality underscores the idea that life for the girl is a matter of terror and chaos on one hand, and power, control, and sacrifice on the other.

"Bursting into tears ... [and] in a terrible panic," Netochka seeks to "protect" (159) Efimov from her mother. Also, however illogically, the girl yearns to suffer chastisement for the sins she insists the man did not commit. "Goodness knows why," Netochka tells her readers, "but I felt that my mother had no other reason to be angry with him, that he was not to blame, and that I wanted to beg forgiveness for him and bear whatever punishment by myself" (159). Netochka gets an immediate opportunity when, rushing to Efimov's defense, she is grabbed by her mother, dragged behind a screen, and (inadvertently) knocked against a bedstead. Willingly, the girl suffers on her stepfather's behalf, not even "wincing" (157) at her mistreatment.

Important here, also, is that for the first time in her tale, Netochka finds herself alone with Efimov. With "her mother out somewhere" (159), Netochka sets the stage for what is to come. Efimov, as if grateful for Netochka's clinging defense of him, calls her to his side, kisses her, and strokes her hair. He then sets her on his knees and allows her to "nestle close to him" (160). Such a display of affection is seen as novel by both stepfather and child. For Netochka, such intimacy is, additionally, the dawning of memory, if not consciousness. "I suppose that [this meeting] was the first time I had received any caress from my parents," she writes. "Perhaps, that is why from that moment on, I started to remember everything so distinctly" (160).

Even worse, perhaps, Netochka transmutes Efimov's caresses into a mental construct that will destroy both her parents and take her to the brink. It is Netochka's "idea" (160) that her father is a saint worthy of love and her mother is a sinner deserving of contempt. Such a concept, however dubious, has this result: from this moment forward, she moves to a false maturity with adult-like stances and roles. Netochka now sees herself as Efimov's equal: a "fellow-sufferer" (160) at the hands of her cruel mother. Moreover, the cuddling gives rise to yet another "idea" (160): Efimov is a victim like herself. He is a "crushed creature . . . a martyr . . . and the unhappiest man in the world . . . so pitiful, so unbearably tormented . . . [and] so full of suffering" (160). Not unlike Ilyusha Snegiryov in his defense of his humiliated father in *The Brothers Karamazov*, Netochka assumes ascendancy in the relationship. "Having won [Efimov's] favor" (160) as his defender, she styles herself also as his champion, guide—and parent. Terras tells only half the story when he asserts that Netochka "derives her satisfaction from selflessly surrendering herself to her beloved."[18] More accurately, in the dynamics of codependence, Netochka is not daddy's girl, but daddy's mother. Foreshadowing such characters as Nellie in *The Insulted and the Injured* and Kolya Ivolgin in *The Idiot*, Netochka stands up for what she takes to be her family's honor and a wronged parent. For Efimov she experiences a "strange sort of love . . . boundless . . . compassionate . . . not childlike . . . [and] *motherly*" (160).

The slide of the child into morbid codependency also has this outcome. For the first (but not last) time in the account, the mature Netochka asserts her presence. The multiple ideas of the child persona are such that she cannot stand idly by. Soundly, the adult Netochka criticizes the addiction consuming her alter ego's being. "Whatever could have inspired the idea [of Efimov as a martyr] . . . [of my] strange devotion to him?" (160) she asks in embarrassment and sorrow. "How could I, a child, have had any understanding of his personal misfortunes? . . . Even today I cannot conceive as to how I came to these impressions" (160, 161).

Like any "false confession," though, such remorse is short-lived. The adult self lets the child self continue boldly and even exudes a sense of righteousness when she re-stakes her claim to the man. "It would have been horribly unnatural," the fledgling Netochka continues, "not to have loved my father passionately, not to have comforted him, not to have been tender toward him, and not to have done everything possible for him" (160).

IDOLS AND UTOPIANS

For her readers and mature self, the child Netochka seeks to validate her idea of Efimov. Hearing an offhand remark by her mother concerning her stepfather's alleged greatness, she confirms the man an "artist . . . and a man of genius" (162) with this incident. Coming home from the market at night, Netochka slips and breaks a cup holding yeast, after which she is pummeled by a boy. When the girl rises to her feet, she staggers and sways, as if intoxicated or drugged. With the yeast—metaphorical leavening for herself and ideas—the unsteady Netochka sees Efimov alongside a house with red curtains: "splendidly illuminated . . . [with] strains of music drifting down the street" (161).

Against this bright and magical background, Netochka establishes Efimov as her sole security. Again, she "clutches" the man, believing that he "loves her more than mother does" (161). In the "strange devotion" (161) to her stepfather, Netochka also asserts codependent tit for tat. Just as she defended her stepfather from her mother, so now does she expect that he will rescue her from punishment over the spilled yeast. "I felt sure that my stepfather would stand up for me" (161), she writes. In her mind, an alliance has come into being, with her mother the odd person out.

Initially, the coalition is successful. Efimov takes Netochka by the hand and then lifts her high in his arms. As a sign of things to come, though, the bond hits a bump. Efimov holds Netochka by her "bruised arm . . . hurting her terribly" (161). As was the case with the bedstead and her mother, the girl represses the pain. "I did not cry," she recalls, "for fear of offending him" (161). Just the reverse, Netochka is "particularly happy . . . that events have turned out so well" (161). The source of her joy is twofold: her tightening bond with Efimov and, more important, perhaps, her latest addiction: the house with red curtains, which she "dreams of . . . throughout the night" (161). Places now join with people and ideas as the objects of Netochka's addictive affection.

When Dostoevsky's heroine wakes up the following morning, her first "thought and concern" (161) is for this house. Unlike her attic dwellings, Netochka's edifice breathes not only clamor and commotion—but also danger and destruction. It stands out menacingly against phantasmal lights. It receives "sumptuous carriages with multicolored lamps . . . [and] a flow of visitors, dressed in heretofore unseen refinement and elegance" (162, 163). As the music plays, "shadows flit . . . across crimson-red curtains . . . [and] street-lamps gleam with a peculiar blood-red glow" (162, 163). Quickly, the house with red curtains "inflames [Netochka's] imagination" (162). It conjures up for her an "image of regal magnificence and fairy-tale enchantment... doubly magical and intriguing... [the source for] the most incredible thoughts and suppositions" (162). In Netochka's imagination, the house with red curtains becomes "a realm of paradise and eternal joy" (162, 163).

The house with red curtains is also the impetus for Netochka to set up her own utopia, her own Crystal Palace. The latter vast exhibition of glass and iron, built in London for the Great Exhibition in 1851, was the object of scorn for the hero in Dostoevsky's *Notes from the Underground*. Not for Netochka. Using superlatives, Netochka shares her dreams of "adorning her abode with the most brilliant, the most luxurious, and the most splendid things that [her] mind could conjure" (162). Having created an Eden for herself, Netochka needs an Adam (Efimov). The two are rich, well-dressed, and enveloped in "uninterrupted peace and comfort" (163). For the moment at least, and with a simplicity and quickness that would astonish Ivan Karamazov, Netochka has a perfect world.

However, like all utopias, Netochka's mythic garden comes with thorns.[19] Her paradise lacks a physical time and space. "But where [would my stepfather and I go]?" Netochka wonders aloud. "Not even my fantasy could find an answer to that" (162). The problem is fleeting. Just as Netochka seizes upon her mother's offhand remark about Efimov's alleged genius, so now does she latch onto a chance comment by her stepfather concerning his own idea about life. In the morbid codependence between man and child, two themes of the mature Dostoevsky come together: If Netochka envisions a pseudo-utopia with her house, Efimov asserts an equally spurious resurrection from the dead. "The time will come," he tells the girl, "when I shall no longer live in poverty, when I shall be a gentleman. When mother dies, I shall be born again" (162).

Initially, Efimov's comment fills Netochka with such sorrow that she sees her mother as already departed from this world. Horror-stricken, she runs into the chilly hallway, "buries her face in [her] hands... [and] sobs" (162). The coolness of the place, however, does little to temper the girl's inflamed idea. Her heartache over the presumed loss of her mother is shockingly short-lived. Her "wild imagination coming to her assistance," Netochka becomes "reconciled to [her] father's terrible wish" (162). Just as thirty years later, the Karamazov brothers will be judged guilty of patricide, so now is Dostoevsky's heroine charged with matricide.[20] Further akin to the moral monsters in the writer's mature fiction, Netochka thinks not only that she can leave the (mental) scene of the crime with impunity, but also that she can take her accomplice with her. To her growing list of wayward images and thoughts, she "fastens on to this [new] idea" (162): when her mother dies, Efimov and she will leave their attic home.

The more drawn Netochka becomes to Efimov, the more detached she is from her mother. "The more attached I grew to my father," she notes, "the more I came to loathe my mother" (161). Specifically, Netochka comes to see her mother as the sole obstacle to her happiness. When the woman orders the girl away from the window that looks out onto the house with red curtains, Netochka sees the admonition as interference in what she calls "our happiness" (162), her edenic life with Efimov. From that moment on, Netochka looks at her mother "intently and suspiciously" (162).

Like Efimov, Netochka knows that her mother is not the ogre she has made her out to be. For one thing, the woman is ill, physically or mentally. Her lips and cheeks are pale; her face is tear-stained. Her head shakes; her hands tremble. "Sunk in a kind of a stupor," Netochka's mother "keeps repeating something ... in a low monotonous voice, the words falling out of her mouth by themselves" (163). Pacing the floor, she "flings her arms into the air, folds them across her bosom, and wrings her hands in an expression of dreadful, exhausting grief ... [before] she collapses in a state of total oblivion" (164). For another thing, Netochka's mother is sweet, vulnerable—and maternal. In fact, hers is the only human touch in the novel. The woman often lifts her daughter's downcast head; strokes her hair; engages her in conversation; and "glows with such a warm motherly smile" (164). Most significantly, perhaps, Netochka's mother addresses her daughter as "Annetta" (164), denoting her as a person in her own right, apart from the "*nyet*" or nothingness of her existence.

Initially, Netochka does not resist her mother's advances, but disturbingly, she responds to the woman's love in much the way she answers Efimov's affection. As was the case with her stepfather, the child's tie to her mother is tactile, desperate, and sexually suggestive. It is also morbid and morose. Netochka's heart "throbs violently" (164) at her mother's attention. She feels a "strong urge to hug ... and weep with the woman" (164). Even more revealing is the fact that Netochka cannot "help loving her mother in secret ... [when she] closes her eyes tightly ... wriggles up ... [and] clings firmly to the woman" (164).[21]

Netochka's addictions are such that she cannot love two people equally or at the same time. Her allegiance to her idea of the future with Efimov voids all opportunities for reconciliation and love with her mother. She reopens the breach by noting, implausibly, that "the poor woman strokes [her] hair almost mechanically, without knowing what she was doing" (164). Further, with almost superhuman effort, Netochka "refuses to let go and display her feelings [toward the woman] ... controlling the tears that stream down her face" (164).

The child's "unnatural cruelty" (164) toward her mother once again brings the adult self into focus. Again, the adult Netochka not only sets the record straight as to her relationship addiction with Efimov, but she also calls the child Netochka to account for her wrongdoing toward the other member of the household. Remorsefully, the mature Netochka laments her mother's life at the hands of fate. It is only now, she writes, "that I begin to think what a misery her life was and that I cannot think of her tortured existence without feeling pain in my heart" (163). In question-and-answer, she moves to her own youthful part in the unhappiness. "How did I develop such cruel feelings toward a creature who suffered so eternally as my mother?" (163), she wonders. In what is seen as the finest moment of the mature self to date, the response is honest, simple, and direct. Her troubles with her mother, the adult self-confesses, draw from "abnormally feeling . . . love for one person . . . her fantastic, exclusive love for her father" (164). Further, as will be the case in later works by Dostoevsky, the sword of confession is invariably two-edged. With a nudge from the adult Netochka, the child persona acknowledges "misery . . . distress . . . self-reproach and pangs of conscience" (163) for her injustice to the woman.

Again, though, the confession is false. The joint sorrow leads nowhere; indeed, it vanishes as quickly as it appears. With her mother out of the picture physically and mentally, the adult Netochka has the child Netochka redouble the codependent knot with Efimov through reading, conversation, and fairy tales. Revealingly, no light—physical or symbolic—ever shines on these gatherings. Man and child always meet "in the evening . . . as soon as it begins to grow dark" (165). Whatever the intellectual promise of such tête-à-têtes, also, Netochka and Efimov take no steps forward, but many steps back. Reading breaks off when Efimov "strokes [Netochka's] hair and kisses her . . . [as she] almost weeps for joy" (165). The two converse for hours on end, "never growing weary of each other" (165). Unlike the formative ties between teachers and students in Russian gentry fiction,[22] Netochka "frequently fails to comprehend a word of what [Efimov] tells her"; but she "laughs and laughs . . . doing everything possible [to understand] . . . [and] hoping to please . . . and cheer him by doing so" (165). Even worse, perhaps, Efimov's fairy tales leave Dostoevsky's heroine "spellbound . . . greatly excited . . . [and] quite ecstatic . . . [about] the truth" (165) of what she has heard. Such yarns also "give her free rein to an elaborate dream-world . . . [in which] Efimov appears as a character . . . [and] her mother doing something or other to prevent her stepfather and her from going off together" (165).

It is only a matter of time before the charged Netochka seeks to realize her dream. She longs to "speak to her father about what the future holds for

[them]" (165). Since she is "quite sure that [their escape] is imminent," the girl "worries and suffers over ... what [the man] is waiting for, and where is he going to take [her] once [they] finally abandon [their] attic room" (165, 166). All she needs is a "furtive wink from her father ... to creep past her mother ... [and] to run off with [him] ... never to see the woman again" (166).

Like many dreamers in Dostoevsky, though, Netochka finds that her fantasies are dashed by the very people upon whom she has counted for support. When Netochka, at long last, queries Efimov as to their future life together, the result is a disaster. In truth, signs of catastrophe are evident even before the interrogation. Netochka overlooks that her stepfather has been drinking. Although she "makes [Efimov] laugh ... [and] embraces him warmly," she soon becomes distressed by the "alarming things [she] is about to say ... [and speaks] in a muddled and confused manner" (166). Her questions burst forth volcano-like in confused images and ideas: "When and where would they be going? What should they take with them? How would they live? And would their destination be the house with red curtains?" (166). Worse, perhaps, Netochka reminds her stepfather of his "promise"—when her mother dies, he will "take [her] somewhere where [they] will be happy and rich"—even though she realizes that such assurance is hardly assured. "In trying to convince Efimov [of my dream]" (166), Netochka confesses, "I managed to convince myself that this was what he had actually said, or at any rate what I believed him to have said" (166).

Netochka sees her dream destroyed. Like a blind Samson, Efimov knocks down the two pillars of her fantasy temple. "House? Red curtains? ... What nonsense is this? ... Mother dead? ... When is mother dead?" (166). Even worse, perhaps, Netochka hears what all of Dostoevsky's characters dread to hear: she is a "silly one ... a poor, foolish thing ... [who] understands nothing" (166).

It is a measure of Netochka's addiction to Efimov that amidst the rubble of her plans for the future, she still affirms her stepfather as an extraordinary man. As before, though, her claim to the man's greatness is vague and confused. Whatever Efimov tells her in the ensuing conversation, both Netochkas obscure with impunity. "I cannot remember all my stepfather told me (166), the senior Netochka writes. "I did not grasp a word," the child Netochka confirms, "everything was very unclear" (166, 167). In fact, it is only by means of unidentified "sentences and phrases" that Netochka "is forced to conclude all [her stepfather] must have been trying to explain to her ... [that] he is a great artist, [that] no one understands him, and [that] he is really a remarkable talented man" (167). Even more disturbing, perhaps, is that when Netochka renders an (equally nebulous) "satisfactory reply" to the things Efimov has allegedly told or asked of her, she brings her stepfather only to "laugh a bit" (167). As will be seen, such mirth is at the expense of both man and child.

KARL FYODOROVICH

Netochka and Efimov find diversion from their codependence with the entry of Karl Fyodorovich Meyer, a talentless dancer. It is one of the many defense mechanisms in *Netochka Nezvanova* that Netochka and Efimov see Karl Fyodorovich as a whipping boy for their own distress and doubts. Only by projecting their skewed selves on another fragmented being can the two find momentary relief.

Karl Fyodorovich has little to recommend himself physically. Small, thin, and gray-haired, he appears as a Petrushka. His nose is red-hooked and stained with snuff; his legs are unsightly and bowed. Karl Fyodorovich has come from Germany to join the ballet; but, despite his vaunted dedication to art, he has found work only in bit dramatic parts in which, in ironic comment on Netochka's worshipful stance to Efimov, he shouts: "We will die for our king!" (167). More revealing, perhaps, is the man's time offstage. When not dying for the king, Karl Fyodorovich drowns his sorrows in the company of the (ubiquitous) musician B., who erodes his credibility further with his own complaints about failure and fate. So much for B.'s—and Netochka's—assertions about his own success in life. In no way, therefore, does the musician B. exemplify Robert Louis Jackson's comment that he is a "simple, striving limited man of talent [who] receives a firm nod of respect from Dostoevsky."[23]

Karl Fyodorovich is Efimov, writ small: a double who, to paraphrase Gogol, is the crooked mug that the faux genius—and Netochka—would see if they dared look in a mirror. Initially, Efimov keeps Karl Fyodorovich at arm's length. But his own confusion and pain are such that in the case of his doppelgänger, he goes in for the kill. Knowing that Karl Fyodorovich's weak spot—his love of ballet but his lack of talent therein—is uncomfortably close to his own, Efimov takes such merciless aim at the man's doubts and fears that he forces Karl Fyodorovich to be the puppet-jester-buffoon he himself resembles so markedly. It is as much commentary on Efimov's Petrushka-like stance to life as it is on his double's that Karl Fyodorovich seeks to win artistic approval from both man and child first by jumping about the room; next by standing poised with his hands to the audience; and finally, with tears in his eyes, by throwing himself at their feet, demanding that they "decide his fate . . . [and let him] know if he is an artist" (168, 169).

Karl Fyodorovich is scorned by his audience. It is symptomatic of Efimov's own paralysis and wavering as a musician that "as if unable to pronounce judgment" on Karl Fyodorovich, he freezes his puppet-colleague "in a pose, swaying from side to side to maintain his balance" (168). Further, when, at long last Netochka's stepfather pronounces that Karl Fyodorovich "has not done it"—the "it" being more than mere dancing—he knows that he is "uttering the bitter truth" (168) also about himself. Such honesty is fleeting, since Efimov will not admit to shortcomings either in himself or in his colleague. In a "relentless and despondent way," Netochka's stepfather extends codependent kinship with Karl Fyodorovich by affirming that "fate" (44) has voided the man's dreams (and by implication, his own). Even more suggestive of the addictive tie between Efimov and Karl Fyodorovich is that when the two read from a second-rate play—most likely, Nestor Kukolnik's 1839 tragedy, *Jacobo Sannazaro*[24]—they see that the hero, a self-absorbed Italian painter who, with equal vigor, both asserts and denies his talent, "bears a striking resemblance to themselves" (168).

In the abuse of Karl Fyodorovich Netochka is a willing accomplice. Just as the girl sided with her father against her mother, so now, with equal fervor, does she take up arms against Karl Fyodorovich. In rapprochement, stepfather and child work hand in hand to vanquish the unfortunate man. A wink and a barb from Efimov over Karl Fyodorovich's dance brings Netochka to "bursts of merry laughter"; an upheld hand from her stepfather regarding his colleague signals that she "regain control . . . and be an impartial witness to his judgment" (168). Neither allays Karl Fyodorovich's "genuine groans" (169) over his doubt; just the opposite, they drive the man to frenzy by demanding that he dance to exhaustion.

It is a further sign of Karl Fyodorovich's addictive tie to Efimov and Netochka that although angry at the abuse initially, he accepts his diminished state at their hands. At times, Karl Fyodorovich is like Efimov in that he answers the disdain of his audience with a face that "flushes scarlet with indignation," eyes that "fill with tears," and a voice that quakes "with absurd emotion" (169). He, too, storms off the scene, vowing never to return. At other times, Karl Fyodorovich recalls Netochka's injury caused by her mother when, in a pirouette, he bangs his head against the ceiling, "bruising himself quite painfully . . . [but] bearing his pain like a Spartan" (169). Karl Fyodorovich's codependent state also calls to mind Efimov and Netochka. He ends his time in *Netochka Nezvanova* in the same way as he entered it, as a Petrushka, begging "with outstretched arms and a smile across his face" to be "taken seriously . . . as a true friend . . . and without mockery and jeers" (169).

TIGHTENING THE VISE

The renewed closeness between Netochka and Efimov extends beyond words. "I was so familiar with [my father's] facial expressions," the girl writes, "that I could recognize his smallest wish at a glance" (169). Sadly, Efimov's countenance often shows a wish for alcohol, chemical dependency keeping pace with emotional addiction. "The thing that vexed [my stepfather] most frequently," Netochka writes, "was not having any money... to get a drink, a thing that had become a habit with him" (169). Netochka comes to the rescue when on an errand for her mother, she bumps into her stepfather with several coins in her hands. When Efimov, in "inner conflict... [and] extreme confusion," asks Netochka for the money, she refuses. Unable to "hide her feelings" (169) for the man, however, the girl crosses an ethical divide by not only giving the coins to her stepfather but also offering to lie on his behalf. "I will say that I lost it," Netochka tells Efimov, "that the children next door stole it from me" (170).

In what will be the ultimate moral imperative in Dostoevsky's mature fiction, Netochka sees that necessarily, crime means punishment. Guilt, fear, pity, and eroticism consume her being. Netochka's cheeks burn; her heart "throbs with new and unpleasant sensations"; her mind and soul are "full of compassion... overwhelmed with shame... [and] seized by panic" (170). At long last, Netochka sees Efimov for who he is. If earlier the man had dashed her dreams, now he does the same to her being. Netochka backs away from Efimov physically and emotionally. No longer does she delight in tags as an "angel... [and] a good... and clever girl" (170). She also does not allow her stepfather to kiss her hand as his patroness and protector. In fact, she runs away from him altogether.

Just as Efimov returns to musician B. and Karl Fyodorovich revisits Efimov, Netochka comes back to her stepfather. Recalling their meetings over books, man and child again meet at dusk, without the light of day to show to them their addictive wrongdoing. As previously, also, emotions both within and between Netochka and Efimov run high; but with a new twist: they are now partners in crime. Although the theft of the coins seems trivial initially, the consequences of their misconduct are so momentous that the two might have just as well murdered the woman outright. Anticipating Raskolnikov in *Crime and Punishment* almost twenty years later, Netochka has "agonizing pangs of conscience" (170) over her deed. In a singular moment of honesty, Efimov also tells his stepdaughter that what she has done is "shameful and bad" (170). After all, he continues, Netochka "ought to feel sympathy for [her] mother, who is so sick and poor, but who still takes care of us" (170).

Such joint morality—and confession—is only momentary. No sooner does Netochka see Efimov, than she experiences "extreme joy" (170) in his presence. Efimov is also insincere. Symptomatic of his own ethical constriction, he not only whispers his admonition in a dark corner of a building; but he also seeks to bribe his stepdaughter for her good behavior with pieces of cake. More seriously, perhaps, Efimov travels down his usual self-justifying path by taking no responsibility for the theft. In his distorted mind, it is Netochka who has done wrong, not he. He also advances further to the dark side when he proposes returning the coins with another lie. "I could say that I found the money again" (170), Netochka recalls her stepfather telling her. Efimov's perfidy strikes like a poleax. Whatever joy the girl had at seeing the man dissipates into enduring "terror" (171). During the day Netochka "cannot utter a word or move an inch" (170), her body wracked with fever and cold. At night, she is wakeful, weeping, and weak, with "morbid nightmares" that leave her "bitter" (170) about her stepfather. Once again, the two part company. Netochka does not look at or go near her stepfather; Efimov avoids his stepdaughter's eyes.

When Netochka tells her mother that she has lost the coins in the snow, she gets yet another opportunity to suffer on Efimov's behalf. Netochka is spared the "expected beating" from her mother, but she must hear her mother's reproach that the girl "obviously does not love her" (170). As Netochka herself admits, such a claim hurts her "more than any beating would have done" (170). Caught in the undeclared war between mother and stepfather, she is abused by both.

A mother is still a mother. Awakened by Netochka's distress over Efimov and knowing "too well . . . [her daughter's] morbid irrationality" (170), the woman rushes to comfort her. There is no hidden agenda. The woman kisses her daughter, moves to her bed, covers her with blankets, and lulls her to sleep. Like any criminal in Dostoevsky, Netochka is so "unbelievably tormented" by her crime over the coins that she is "on the verge of telling" (171) her mother everything that has transpired between her and Efimov. Like other wrongdoers in Dostoevsky, however, Netochka resists confession, reconciliation, and remorse. Just as the girl avoids the gaze of her stepfather, so she also cannot "bear to look at her mother" (171). The result is that Netochka is condemned to the lot of any stiff-necked sinner in Dostoevsky's corpus: enduring isolation and punishment. "Never before," she tells her readers, "had I ever suffered such excruciating heartbreak and pain" (171). Such torment is understandable. After all, the "desire for the mother," which the famed French psychiatrist Jacques Lacan sees as the first, if primal need for any child,[25] not only comes late to

Netochka—but because of her codependency with Efimov, she represses it throughout her young life.

Unable to stand alone, her pain less searing with Efimov than with her mother, Netochka returns again (!) to her stepfather; but with consequences that are even more serious than previous ones. If earlier man and child crossed an ethical line, they now transgress a sexual one. Seeking to "please ... [and] delight" her stepfather, Netochka talks about everything other than "what transpired on the previous day" (171). Such a seemingly forgiving attitude triggers an explosive response from Efimov. Initially, he experiences a "sort of joy... [and] a childish satisfaction" (171) at his stepdaughter's false reconciliation. Matters turn physical, though, as the simmering eroticism between the two comes to the fore.[26] "Unable to restrain himself any longer," Efimov arouses Netochka to climax. He kisses his stepdaughter until she "laughs and cries at the same time" (171). The tryst does not stop there. A surprising move by Efimov invalidates Terras's claim that one "finds no trace of morbid sexuality in the works of the young Dostoevsky"[27]—he pulls out his violin. Readers of *Netochka Nezvanova* are correct to question why he would engage in such an action at this time. Whereas the violin figured prominently in the first part of Netochka's narrative, it has all but disappeared in the later chapters. It also defies logic and credibility that Efimov would kiss Netochka passionately one moment and the next present her with the problematic instrument which, disturbingly, he is also moved to kiss.

One thing is clear: the eroticism between Efimov and Netochka is such as to suggest that, with the violin, there is more to the encounter between adult and child than meets the eye. With Netochka, Efimov is nothing less than a pedophile, and that what now transpires between the two heralds the sexually charged and abusive scenes between man and female child in Dostoevsky's mature works.[28] Evidence for such a view, for what Guerard aptly calls the "very openness of the incest-pedophilia fantasy ... the gross phallic exhibition of a sinister violin," abounds.[29] Netochka's stepfather "unbuttons his waistcoat" (171). His face is "transformed ... grave but triumphant" (172). Efimov "looks mysteriously into [Netochka's] eyes as if searching for the pleasure he expects [her] to be feeling" (171). He holds the violin "carefully and reverently in his hands," regarding it as "something very special and beautiful ... his instrument" (171). "Nervous ... and terrified" (171), the man moves Netochka to the bed and hands her the object also to kiss.[30]

Her response is similarly suggestive. Netochka sees the violin as a "strangely shaped object ... something quite unfamiliar ... [which] she has never seen before ... but [which] she also wants to look at more carefully"

(171). The girl takes the instrument into her hands; but frightened by what she is doing, she hands it back hastily to her stepfather.

Even more despicable, perhaps, is not only that Efimov, after playing with the violin, deems Netochka as a good and clever child, but also that he again proclaims his greatness as an artist and resurrects the dream of escape. The girl may not "understand [Efimov's] conversation"; but she grasps "phrases she already knows," that is, her stepfather is an "artist and genius who, one day as a performer, will make them rich and happy" (171).

In response, "tears pour down [the girl's] cheeks" (171). To both man and child, the violin "offers mutual consolation" (172). Despite an "anxiety . . . [that is] morbid . . . anguished and overwhelming," Netochka has "love . . . [and] passion" (172) for Efimov. Her "only one true pleasure . . . [is] dreams and thoughts" (172) about her stepfather. Her "only one true desire . . . [is] to do anything that might please him" (172).

With grandstanding appeal to addictive self-sacrifice and victimization, Netochka tells her readers: "How many nights did I stand on the stairs waiting for him to come in . . . shivering and blue with cold, in the simple hope that I might catch sight of him one second sooner?" (172).[31] The price, though, is for her well worth the suffering and pain. Unashamedly, with perverse boasting and delight, Netochka confesses that she "becomes almost delirious with joy whenever [Efimov] offers [her] the slightest caress" (172). The "strange devotion" she has for the man "develops into quite a romance" (173).

Irrevocably, also, Netochka opts for Efimov over her mother. "I could not be indifferent to the everlasting hostility [between my parents]," she tells her readers, "so I had to choose between them . . . to side with one or the other" (172). Her decision, however spurious, is for the lesser of two evils: she sees Efimov as "less gloomy . . . morbid . . . and fearful" than her mother; she is "attached [to him because] . . . he has aroused her fantasy" (173).[32] Although, with the nudging of her adult self, Netochka is "[torn to] shreds with pity and despair" (172) over her decision, she does not confess her sins. Rather, Netochka again rejects her mother for an artist-genius stepfather on her own terms. In redefining the tie between herself and Efimov, she brings her stepfather "nearer to her level" (173). Almost immediately, however, the girl resumes her ascendancy over the man. Efimov is for her "a buffoon-child," one moment, but the next, "broken . . . pitiful . . . and almost mad" (173).

This manner of struggle for dominance is typical of codependence. Netochka enjoys her new sense of power and prestige. She is again Efimov's mother. "Gradually I felt myself rising about him," Dostoevsky's heroine confesses boldly, unashamedly. "I sensed that he needed me and that I could dominate him a little" (173). In true Dostoevskian fashion, though, push soon comes to shove. Netochka the girl adds: "I was so proud, I so gloried . . . in realizing how necessary I was [to my stepfather] . . . that I even played with him at times" (173).³³

SOUNDING THE DEATH KNELL

Setting the stage for "a most terrible catastrophe still haunting [her] memory" (173), Netochka notes the arrival in town of a famous musician. Once again, smoke obscures fire. As will be the case in Dostoevsky's major novels, "rumor . . . sensation . . . and effect" (173) raise more questions than answers. They also tell a story hauntingly close to that of Efimov and the musician B. Despite the fact that the famous musician—known typically as S.—performs rarely in public, he maintains a "lasting freshness of talent" (173). The only certainty is Efimov's response. "The poor madman," Netochka writes, "really believed that there was only one musical genius in the entire world and that genius, of course, was he" (173). Even worse, perhaps, Netochka's stepfather not only faces new taunts from his erstwhile friends who insist that once he hears the musician S., his "life will not be worth living"; he also has an even more inopportune encounter with the musician B. and Prince X., "a well-known dilettante with a deep understanding and love of the arts" (174) and, it will be recalled, the very man who wanted to buy the ill-fated violin earlier in the story.

Be he a success or (more likely) failure, the musician B. is in no mood to restore Efimov to his pedestal. The change of heart is striking. Out of earshot of his former colleague, Efimov leads the charge against him. B. tells X. that Efimov's story is "ghastly . . . hideous . . . and heartbreaking" (174). More directly, he indicts Netochka's stepfather as a "madman . . . [guilty] of three crimes," ruining his wife, his stepdaughter, and himself. Efimov's "peculiar . . . life-time idea . . . [as a] visionary and poet" is bankrupt; it has "forced him to realize that he is nothing, a nobody . . . not in the least bit an artist" (174, 175). Still, like any troubled would-be genius in Dostoevsky, Efimov still harbors dreams of glory that evolve into a desire to rule the world. Ever the "dreamer," B. continues, Netochka's stepfather believes that "suddenly, with the wave of a wand . . . [he can] become the most famous person in the world . . . a Caesar" (175). The musician B. predicts disaster for his former friend. "Prove to Efimov that he is not a musical genius," he tells Prince X., "and I assure you that he will be thunderstruck and die on the spot" (175).

Yet even after the summary verdict and execution of his former colleague, the musician B. still holds fast to what he wants Efimov to be. As will be the case with the disciples of Myshkin in *The Idiot*, Stavrogin in *Devils*, and Zosima in *The Brothers Karamazov*, he will not let the man go. Notwithstanding his harsh verdict of the man, B. so wants an idol in his life that he insists that Netochka's stepfather has a "genuine vocation" as an artist and that his genius "rests on solid foundations" (175). B. even asserts that Efimov's "madness is stronger than the truth . . . [and that] quickly he will invent some counter-argument [to survive]" (175). Such is the legacy of codependence, of relationship addiction.

The belief in Efimov squares even less with the reality than previously. As B. and X. "draw level" (175) with Netochka's stepfather, they find that the man is uncertain, evasive, preoccupied, and ready to flee.

From the musician B., Prince X., and others, Efimov can run, but he cannot hide. No sooner does he leave his erstwhile supporters, than he runs into Karl Fyodorovich, who, as if taking revenge for his earlier abuse, presents Efimov with a poster of the upcoming concert by S.

Although Netochka understands little of the interchange between the two men, she reports not only her stepfather's flippant dismissal of S. but also his distress over the man's impending performance. Her response is unfounded but typical of codependent relationships. Believing that she "alone is responsible for all the anxiety and commotion . . . on [her] father's face" (176), Netochka acts as his parent-protector, worrying that he has been "crushed completely" (176). It is Netochka's first and enduring life-lesson, though, that when her stepfather again kisses her, calls her "darling," tells her that she is a "good and obedient child," and affirms that "she loves him enough to do whatever he is about to ask her" (177), he is up to no good. "I knew that [my stepfather's] words and endearments were insincere" (176), Netochka tells her readers. She is not prepared, though, for what is to come. When Dostoevsky's heroine is asked by Efimov—"silent, gloomy and distraught"—for the location of the twenty-five rubles his wife has brought home the day before, Netochka is "frozen with horror" (177). The girl is even more dumbfounded when "exactly as suspected" (177), Efimov exhorts her to cede to him the coins her mother has given her to buy sugar and tea. Knowing that again she is "stealing from Mama" (177), Netochka is beside herself with guilt and fear. She screams, whines, and cries; she wrings her hands; she tugs at Efimov's waistcoat. She even "falls on her knees" (54) before the man.

Her suffering does not stop there. Resisting Efimov's demands, Netochka falls victim to new overt and covert abuse. Called a "wicked girl" (177) by the man, she is also threatened with abandonment (and by implication, the end to what is left of her dreams). Like other pseudo-extraordinary men in Dostoevsky, Efimov may not believe the visions of others, but he has no difficulty in manipulating them to his own ends. "All right, I will leave you right now," Efimov tells his stepdaughter. "You can stay with Mama. I am going away and I will leave you behind. Do you hear me?" (177). Netochka is battered further when her stepfather not only charges filial infidelity but also jeopardizes the parental bond. "You love more mother than me," he says, "I am not your father. I do not wish to be your father. In fact, I do not want to have anything more to do with you!" (178).

"Wounded" not only by Efimov's threat of desertion but also by her own unresolved wish "to see her mother dead" (177), Netochka is potentially what any codependent child dreads to be: an orphan. She stands in a "sort of stupor, rooted to the spot and shaking all over" (177). Feeling as if "[her] heart will burst... [she is] hardly conscious... screaming... crying... and unable to see or hear anything" (178).

Netochka is sufficiently aware, terrified, and codependent to give Efimov "anything" (178) he wants. "God knows how much" (178), she writes. Together with new affirmations of loyalty and love, she not only furnishes Efimov with the coins, but she also tells him the location of the rubles, promising to get additional funds for him at a later date. Agreeing to steal again for her stepfather, Netochka proceeds down the path of all Dostoevskian heroes and heroines: having committed one crime, she readily commits others. "Papa, dearest Papa!" she pleads, "I do love you more than mother. Take the money, take it!" (178). As a morbid codependent, also, the girl asks nothing for her trouble. Routinely, she turns down the doll and the "sweets... which [Efimov] will bring her every day" if she continues to be a "good girl" (178).

Although Efimov does not take the coins—he beats a fearful and hasty retreat from the scene—the damage is done. "Wounded forever" by Efimov, Netochka "herself a child, understands [the man] thoroughly... to be a child himself" (178, 179). As is typical in Dostoevsky, also, Netochka's experience with her stepfather makes her wiser, but also sadder. Of its own emotional weight, the bond between them verges on collapse. For once Netochka has a valid "idea": since she "no longer loves [Efimov] as she did previously... she fears... [that] she has lost [her] former Papa" (179). No longer can the girl relish her stepfather's "ecstasy" over her acquiescence. Efimov's promise that they will "leave mother and go away that very day" (179), the stuff of her "eternal dream," now inspires her "rebellion" (179).

Netochka has even more to bear from the "stranger... [and] madman" (179) she now sees Efimov to be. Waiting for her mother to give her the money she has promised to her stepfather, she feels as if under a "sentence of death . . . counting each second . . . in the most agonizing and unforgettable hours in her life" (179). The girl does what the man asks, though. With an "icy hand gripping her heart" (180), she again gives the funds to Efimov.

Under such duress, Netochka does something reprehensible and totally out of keeping with her character. Having separated herself from Efimov physically and emotionally, she also claims the higher moral ground by casting herself as an innocent victim of people and events. Even worse, perhaps, is the fact that she accomplishes this whitewash with a psychic appeal to her adult self. In one of the lowest points in Dostoevsky's first novel, the adult Netochka, rather than calling the child Netochka to account for her wrongdoing, assists in the falsely confessional mystification. In the reconstruction, lie follows lie. The child is sweetness and light; Efimov is not. The man may not be a musical genius, but undoubtedly, he is an evil one. Efimov, both Netochkas agree shamelessly, "has prompted [his stepdaughter's] better instincts into misconduct" (179). Time and again, he has "led her into sin . . . [sacrificing her] defenseless childhood and running the risk of disturbing her unstable mind still further" (179–180). Because of Efimov, the Netochka doubles affirm even more blatantly, the child is host to "new sensations, yearnings and doubts that crowd her mind and torment her thoughts" (180).

The adult Netochka soon realizes that such finger-pointing compromises her parental position in the story. Quickly, she seeks to regain her narrative authority for both sides of her persona by professing to have not only perfect hindsight but also a worldly wisdom that is way beyond her formative years. "How difficult it is to deceive someone of my temperament," the senior self boasts, especially for "someone who already, at an exceptionally early age, had experienced and comprehended so much [that is] good and evil" (179). The damage undone, she returns the child to the limelight.

The "convulsive fit of grief" (180) that the fledgling Netochka experiences not only over the money she has given to Efimov but also over her mounting losses (physical and mental; past, present, and future) does not lead to moral clarity. Instead, it precipitates new encounters with her mother. When her shamefaced husband enters the room, it takes the woman only a moment to grasp that with the stolen coins, her family has been conspiring against her. For the first time in the narrative, Netochka's mother assumes a major and frightening presence. Years of addictive codependence and anger consume her being, and she responds like a caged animal to her self-imposed keepers. The metaphor is more than apt since, in what is seen as Dostoevsky's first *scène de scandale*, Netochka's mother flies to the door, locks it from the inside, throws away the key, and charges her tormentors. Efimov is for her a "murderer... a godless creature... [and] the curse of her life!" (180). More to the point, perhaps, the woman does not realize how close she is to the truth when she asks her husband: "Do you want to ruin her too... and a child to boot!" (180).

Netochka expresses confusion over the row but also engages in self-protective disassociation from the goings-on. "I was barely able to understand," Netochka tells her readers, "what my mother and stepfather were doing or what was happening to me" (180). As before, though, the girl remains sufficiently conscious to stand by her man. Codependence affirms itself anew. Even as her mother grabs her hands, Netochka "vows to remain silent and not say a word about her father" (181). She also extends to Efimov what will be his final chance to resume their addictive bond. It is still the case that despite all the fuss and harangue, all the pain and angst, and all the lies, half-truths, and broken promises that have riddled the relationship, Netochka has always seen her stepfather as her one and only. In the current situation, any response from him, no matter how trifling or prosaic, is all the girl needs for enduring affection and love. "For the last time," Netochka writes, "I raised my eyes to my father.... One look, one word from him expressing what I had been hoping and praying for and, despite my suffering and torment, I would have been happy." (181) It does not happen. Again, Netochka's hopes and dreams are dashed, her body and soul vanquished. When Efimov "intimidates... [Netochka] with a cruel and threatening gesture," she has an "attack of nerves" (181) before falling senseless to the floor.

When Netochka comes to her senses, she encounters an event that contrasts markedly with the previous scene. In an almost Cinderella-like aura, a footman dressed in sumptuous livery enters the attic home, bewildering the "musician Efimov" (181) with a long-desired (and feared) item: a complimentary ticket from B. and X. to attend the concert by S. However doubtful (and most likely, perverse) their motivations, the two set off a chain of events that underscore the codependence of all involved. Needless to say, Efimov does not rejoice in the fortuitous turn of events. Not unlike Raskolnikov in *Crime and Punishment* in his anguish over his crime of murder, Efimov becomes faint and in need of water. The ticket-bearing footman, though, makes a "great impression" (181) on Netochka's mother. To the deluded soul, he offers a codependent fairy tale, the "faintest glimmer of hope... [in her] crazy husband's self-assurance... [as well as in] a complete change in his fortunes" (181). Netochka is not the only one addicted to Efimov. Her mother, after "eight years of never-ending misery and suffering... still loves her husband" (181). In an instant she manages to offer the forgiveness and reconciliation that prove so elusive in Dostoevsky's mature fiction. She figuratively wipes the slate clean. "In a burst of new hope," the woman is "prepared to reconcile herself to Efimov . . . [and] to forgive him for all that he has done to her life" (181). Even more shocking, perhaps, is the fact that Netochka's mother is willing to "overlook his last crime, the sacrifice of her only child . . . [and] to reduce it to a mere shortcoming, to an act of cowardice induced by poverty, the degradation of his life, and his desperate situation" (181). Like her daughter, Netochka's mother loves with an endless, unequal, and ruinous love. For her husband she, too, knows only "infinite compassion" (181). It is a further sign of the addictive relationship between husband and wife that "impulse . . . [and] enthusiasm" bring Netochka's mother to "concoct a thousand and one plans" (181) for her spouse. Without batting an eye, she comes up with a silver ruble for Efimov to tip the messenger. She also prepares her husband's toilet and dress, tying a cravat around his neck in what can be seen as a reaffirmation of their codependent tie.

Such good cheer is fleeting. No sooner does Efimov leave the attic than Netochka's mother returns to her old self. She not only resumes "hostile feelings . . . [and] cooling enthusiasm" (182) over her husband; she also continues with her own self-willed demise. Her lip trembles, her body shakes, and her "ashen face glows suddenly . . . [with] sobs, lamentations, and complaints" (182). Like Dostoevsky's heroine, Netochka's mother assumes the blame for Efimov's shortcomings. In her disordered and codependent mind, it is she, not Efimov, who has brought to the family disaster and disgrace. "It's me, it's me who is to blame for everything," she says, "miserable woman that I am!" (182). The woman is not above doling out her own covert abuse when, like her husband, she terrifies her daughter with talk of abandonment. "Netochka, my poor darling! My poor unhappy child!" she says, "Who will take care of you when I am gone, when even now I cannot educate you, look after you, and care for you as I should?" (182). Unsurprisingly, though, tears, hand-wringing, and "frantic displays . . . of convulsive kisses" (182) do not bring about an eleventh-hour reunion. When coupled with Netochka's "bursting heart . . . and clasping hands" (182), such actions only underscore the torment the two have inflicted on each other. Even worse, perhaps, is the new "rush of acute misery . . . and the groan from her [the woman's] chest" when Netochka, innocently or otherwise, asks her mother "why [she] does not love papa" (182). In one fell swoop, the unhappy woman sees the entire horror of codependence. "My poor child!" she says, "I never noticed how she has grown up . . . and knows everything, everything! My God! What ideas we have given her, what examples have we set!" (182). Not unlike the torment of Katerina Ivanovna and Marmeladov over Sonya and their other children in *Crime and Punishment*, she berates herself and Efimov for the unhappiness of their daughter. Never, Netochka adds, has she "seen such suffering" (182). Again moving to dissociation, Dostoevsky's heroine enters into "semi-consciousness," caught between "horrible dreams" when asleep, and a "numbed stupor" (183) when awake.

As before, though, Netochka is sufficiently aware to see Efimov reenter the attic, pale, distracted, inert, and, child that he is, in a regressed, fetus-like state. His head is bowed into his chest; his hands are pressed rigidly against his knees. Notwithstanding such a state, the man does what everyone in *Netochka Nezvanova* has begged, cajoled, and demanded that he do: he confronts the violin. In a gesture hauntingly reminiscent of Peter's denial of Christ, Efimov picks up the instrument three times. Recalling Christ's agony and crucifixion, he plays to a codependent audience: Netochka, who hides behind a curtain; and his wife, who is dead.[34] To the latter, Efimov responds "breathing freely . . . with a horrible pale face . . . [and] a flickering smile" (183). His feelings are an apparent mixture of relief that his wife is gone; an attraction to the lure of freedom and the road; and most significantly, perhaps, bitterness at the joke that has been his life.

It is, perhaps, the ultimate irony in *Netochka Nezvanova* that Efimov plays the violin not only to honor the woman who has stood by him and his dream but also to express his grief at his loss as well as his fear at the abyss yawning before him. To what Guerard sees rightfully as the "one of the most macabre configurations in Dostoevsky,"[35] the man gives the concert of his life, but the inspiration is from codependence, not music.[36] Efimov is "hideous, monstrous . . . distraught, agonized, and pale" (183). "With a gesture of despair" (184), he begins to play. What emerges, though, is not the "notes of a violin" (184). Rather, Efimov gives vent to something far more elementary, searing, and in its own addictive way, truthful. He fills the room with the "cries of a human voice . . . the groans . . . [of] complete despair . . . [and] a last awful note . . . a cry, the agony of torture and the misery of hopelessness" (184).

Netochka's reaction is equally ironic. She is moved by her stepfather's performance, but also not in a creative or life-affirming way. Joined by the adult self, she recalls that as a child she found herself caught between "senses that are so thrown off by all [she] has witnessed . . . [and] impressions which are dubious and incorrect . . . agonizing and frightful" (184). With Efimov's playing, also, Dostoevsky's heroine confronts again the thought-induced murder of her mother. As before, crime moves to punishment. Seeing "the still, sharp outline of her mother's limbs . . . a terrible thought flashes like lightning through [Netochka's] mind" (183). With a terrified shriek, she rushes from behind the curtain and in a desperate attempt to recapture the bond with her stepfather, grabs him by the hand. Such a move almost leads to her own end: the startled Efimov brandishes the violin over her head. Another minute, Netochka recalls, "and he might have killed me on the spot" (184). Almost immediately, however, Netochka's lunging leads to returned codependence. "Oh, so there's still you! It is not over yet!" Efimov tells his stepdaughter. "You are still with me!" (184). That is all the two need to start again. To Netochka's plea that they flee as soon as possible, he answers: "Yes, we will run away. It is high time. Come along, Netochka. Hurry, hurry!" (64).

Like all such escapes in Dostoevsky, this one is doomed to failure. The relationship no longer oscillates between adult-child and child-adult. Rather, it moves to something even more perverse when as a follow-up to the sexually charged incident over the violin, Efimov shoves the disputed money into the top of his stepdaughter's dress. What may have been lost on the child Netochka is not lost on the adult self. Feeling the "silver against her body," the senior Netochka recalls that she "shuddered . . . since for the first time, she understood the meaning of money" (185). There is also the issue of the dead woman lying before them. Efimov insists on atonement for Netochka's mother, but he takes no responsibility for his spouse's demise. "*It was not me, Netochka,*" he tells the child, "*Remember, Netochka, I am not guilty of this*" (186).[37] His actions take a turn for the even worse when he shifts the guilt to Netochka by forcing her to fall on her knees before the now cold and blue corpse. He also leaves the girl in the dark as to what has happened, physically and metaphysically, to the woman. To Netochka's question, "What's the matter with Mama? Where is she?" (186), he remains silent. It is unclear precisely to whom and over what the two make artificial amends. The appeal for relief is physical, not spiritual. God is absent from their minds and hearts; remorse, reconciliation, and reintegration are also far from view. "Pray, my child, pray," Efimov bids Netochka, "You will feel better. . . . Yes, really it will make you better" (185). From ignorance or fear, also, Dostoevsky's heroine does not dare hope for eternal life. Rather, whether Netochka understands death or not, she moves to join her mother in the nether world. "Exhausted with anguish," Netochka lies on the floor "like a dying person" (186).

Still, even in these dark and desperate tones, the codependent fantasy of man and child does not die. "In terror," Netochka whispers to Efimov, "Papa, let's go. It's time!"(186). Gripping Netochka's hand, the man agrees: "Thank God, it is all over now!" (186).

Netochka's long-awaited fantasy comes to be. "Everything I had been dreaming of for an entire year had come true," she writes. "We left our miserable lodgings" (186). The girl soon realizes, though, that her dreams for the future have been shattered. "But was this what I was expecting?" the girl continues, "was this what I had dreamed up, was this what I had created in my childish fantasy when I conjured up the happiness of a man whom I had loved in such a non-childlike way?" (186). The answer is no. The elements sound a warning when Efimov and Netochka step out into darkness and snow, down a sloping pavement toward a dark canal with ice holes. As has been the case throughout their relationship, the bond between man and child is cold, unequal, and forced. "Chilled to the bone," Netochka "clutches [Efimov's] coat-tails in a fitful way" (186). She is "overcome by terrible feelings" (186), thoughts of her abandoned mother holding sway. Together with the adult self, the child wonders: "Why had she and Efimov left her mother alone? . . . Why had they abandoned her body like some useless object?" (186).[38]

Even in death, the mother ultimately drives the final wedge between Netochka and Efimov. It is one of the ultimate ironies in Dostoevsky's first novel that Netochka, having done her utmost to isolate the woman from both her present and her future, now seeks to have the woman join her and Efimov on their journey. "Papa, why have we left Mama there?" Netochka inquires. "Let's go home and fetch her" (187).[39] Understandably, such a proposal for the crazed Efimov is the last straw. His pain unbearable, he breaks the tie once and for all. "Yes, Netochka, it is no use," he tells his stepdaughter. "You must go back to mother. She is getting cold there. . . . Fetch someone for her and then come back to me. You go alone and I will be waiting here. . . . I will not go away" (187). Such is the final farewell to the girl. When Netochka sets off for home, he runs in the opposite direction.

To the already moribund Netochka, such a move "stabs her in the heart" (187). Screaming, and gasping for breath, she rushes to catch her stepfather, but to no avail. Efimov disappears from sight down a series of winding side streets, which serve as an apt metaphor for the twists and turns of addiction. His hat, lost in the flight, is the sole memento of his being. Slipping on the pavement, her face "bathed with blood" (187), Netochka again enters into disassociation. She experiences "something indescribable," as if she is running away from an unidentified pursuer until, "her legs failing, she loses consciousness" (187).

Dostoevsky's heroine returns to her senses but still remains Efimov's parent-protector. Her heart "bleeds . . . with pity" (187) for the man. She makes the best of a bad situation when, not without the falsely confessional grandstanding courtesy of her adult self, she grants to her stepfather the faux freedom he craves so desperately. Even as his "most beloved child" (187), Netochka wants to overtake Efimov "simply to kiss him warmly once more, to tell him not to fear me, and to calm and reassure him that I would not run after him if he did not want me to, but that I would return to mother alone" (187).

Learning later the details of Efimov's demise—he soon dies in a hospital in a fit of madness—the child Netochka joins with her adult self to be remarkably nonchalant, even philosophical about the man. Like prosecuting lawyers, the two summarize the case against their stepfather. In so doing, they fashion schemata for the pseudo-geniuses and extraordinary men in Dostoevsky's later fiction. As the two Netochkas see it, Efimov's death is the logical outcome of an illogical life. The man began life with a "sustaining . . . but incorporeal and empty dream"; he ended it seeing his fantasy "disintegrate before his eyes . . . crumbled and faded like a ghost" (188). Efimov suffered from "delusions and tortures of dreams"; he knew "terror . . . convulsive anguish . . . [and] instant madness" (188). With "presentiments" of the future, the man masked with "protective lies . . . [hopes for] escape" and a blindness that "refused to recognize light for light, darkness for darkness" (188). For the would-be genius, such defense mechanisms proved ineffective. Like all verities in Dostoevsky, the "naked and crystal clear truth" moved like "unbearable light . . . a lightning stroke . . . and a fatal blow . . . [from] an ax that always hung over his head"; and which, painfully, testified to his "weakened bow" (188) as a musician and as a man.[40]

Both the adult and child Netochka still attest to the "musical phase of a genius" (188) for Efimov, but they limit such an assertion to the requiem he plays for his dead wife. In so doing, they transfer what had been their hopes and dreams for the man from an artistic point of view to a psychological and codependent one. What Efimov played over his spouse was from his heart and soul, true, but what issued forth was not music but something far more elemental, genuine, and searing: the anguished cry of a man whose codependence has led him to ruin himself and others.

CHAPTER THREE

ALL IN THE CODEPENDENT FAMILY (II)
Netochka and Katya

A DREAM COME TRUE?

The now nine-year-old Netochka is saved from Efimov's fate by a fortuitous event. When she awakens, she finds that fate has smiled upon her. Indeed, as the girl looks about her new surroundings, she wonders whether, even without her stepfather, she has realized her fantasy dreams of a red-curtained house. Lying in a soft bed and attended by a young girl and her parents, Netochka "awakens to another existence" (187). Her new hosts are none other than the family of Prince X., the individual who appeared intermittently in her story of Efimov and who, after the Dickensian "coincidence" (188) of encountering Netochka as an abandoned orphan, has taken her into his home.[1]

Terras's assertion that Netochka "adjusts well to her new environment" needs reexamining.[2] The girl continues in the same physical and psychic angst as previously. Her face is buried in her hands, her brain is in a torpor, and her heart beats furiously. With her "immature mind" (193), the child perceives both present and past as a dream from which she longs to awake. Netochka does understand one thing, however. If in the first part of her tale she lived with family, now she is alone and living with strangers.

Almost immediately, she becomes disenchanted with her surroundings. The place is formal, monochromatic, and austere: gloomy and grim. Netochka is lost amidst long hallways, sweeping staircases, and (in a sign of the familial borders and the disengagement to come) disengaged, elegantly attired men who do nothing but stare at each other. A true daughter of Dostoevsky, Netochka feels "perfect harmony ... [with] the majestically tormented dwelling" (189) she now calls home.³ Paranoia again takes hold of Netochka. Indeed, she is even more alienated from her second home than from her first. For no apparent reason, Netochka has a strange mistrust of everyone around her. Not unlike the situation when her mother orders her to stay away from the window, Prince X.'s insistence that she stay in sight of family and staff strikes her as an attempt at persecution rather than solicitude. Typically, Netochka never specifies the agents, times, or circumstances of the alleged interference in her new life. She notes only moments when members of the household look in on her without saying a word, seeing herself as a hostage. As was the case in the first part of *Netochka Nezvanova*, middle and passive voices underscore the lack of agency. "It seemed to me," Netochka tells her readers, "that I was being taken care of for some purpose, and that they wanted to do something to me later" (191). Like a prisoner facing execution, Netochka "is dressed" in linen and "put" (190) in a dress. After her hair "is brushed," she is first "taken" to Prince X. and his family and then "taken" (191) back to her room. On the following day, the "entire procedure is repeated . . . when she is taken to the [family] again" (191). Further, Dostoevsky's heroine is "pestered thoroughly" by an anonymous "they" who teach her how to bow, speak, and be gracious and cheerful. In the girl's distrust, even the statues "hide deliberately in secluded niches to frighten and spy upon her" (189, 193).

Intuitively, Netochka sees flaws in her new family. Her new rich clan is even more disengaged and bordered than her old poor one. In marked contrast to the tortured family gatherings in *Crime and Punishment* and *The Brothers Karamazov*, no gathering of the Prince, the Princess, and their child Katya takes place.

An aura of menace and fear also informs the group. The nominal head of Netochka's new household is something other than the "mystic," "guardian angel," or "the first of Dostoevsky's perfectly good men"—"warmhearted and generous," "kind and unselfish," and "of a religious turn of mind"— that Malcolm Jones, Grossman, Frank, and other critics deem him to be.⁴ Just the opposite is the case. Recalling such later Dostoevskian princes as Valkovsky in *The Insulted and the Injured*, Myshkin in *The Idiot*, and Stavrogin in *Devils*, Prince X. knows that he is "very odd and quite unlike other people" (189). He speaks little and abruptly, without "so much as a trace of a smile on his lips" (189). Nowhere does he utter or issue what Lacan sees as "societal imperatives—the Father's rules, laws, and definitions."⁵ Also missing is the patriarchal law, order, and conservatism that defined Russian gentry fiction.⁶ To Netochka's further consternation, Prince X. lives in complete solitude, so much so that his family sees him as a "strange man" and behaves as if "he were never there" (189).⁷

The difficulties Netochka has with X.'s wife, the (also unnamed) Princess, mirror her problems with her mother. Like the unhappy soul in the first part of the tale, the Princess wants nothing more than to embrace her charge heart and soul, to "take the place of [her] mother" (190). Perversely, though, the new ward's response is again a self-imposed (and codependent) border of silence, rejection, and rebuke. As a codependent, and with a nudge from her senior self, Netochka admits that she is incapable of appreciating such good fortune and that she has only herself to blame for her troubles. At times, her resistance to the woman is passive: Netochka does not "summon the strength" (190) to answer the Princess's questions. At other times, she resists actively, as is the case when the Princess asks her to sit on a stool like any ordinary child "lacking any naïveté" (191).

Netochka makes a public display of her borders. When the Princess, at a gathering of guests, becomes affectionate and attentive with the girl, Dostoevsky's heroine figuratively bites the hand that feeds her. Hostile that her past provokes sympathy from the group, Netochka keeps her boundaries intact. She backs away when guests attempt to see or kiss her. Her eyes tear-filled and lowered, her face alternately crimson and pale, Dostoevsky's heroine "longs to run away, to be alone, and to disappear" (190). Her distrust of the Princess recalls her unjust suspicions toward her mother. Indeed, the sudden transformation of the Princess from white to black—so typical in the bivalence of a codependent—defies credibility. When the two are alone again, Netochka alleges that the Princess looks at her crossly, speaks to her abruptly, and frightens her with (heretofore unnoticed) compressed narrow lips and piercing black eyes. The response is typical, if by now reflexive. Falling asleep in a fever, Netochka wakes up crying over (undisclosed) bad dreams.

Given her difficulties (real and imagined) with the Prince and Princess, Netochka moves to new isolation and diminishment. Her favorite way of passing the time is to retreat to a corner behind furniture, and to scout out new hiding places "in case of need" (191). Nowhere does she find peace. Internally, Dostoevsky's heroine is still haunted by her past. Mental images of Efimov, her mother, and the violin bring on quakes and ravings in which she "begs forgiveness for something" (193).

Externally, Dostoevsky's heroine encounters in her new home a third (and for her, more pernicious) adult: the (generic) old aunt. In the old aunt Netochka is host to an individual who, like Father Ferapont, the rigid law-and-order monk in *The Brothers Karamazov*, not only wears her law-and-order faith on her sleeve but also seeks to impose it on others. The reclusive old aunt remains confined to the upper floor of the house, clothed in plain black woolen dresses with pleated and starched collars. Her daily existence is filled with rosaries, masses, fasts, holy books, and visits by ecclesiastical dignitaries and pious people. The old aunt inflicts her religiosity on the household, requiring that everyone follow monastic etiquette by talking in whispers, walking on tiptoe, and keeping conversation brief and business-like. Whatever the old aunt foregoes in penance and mortification (e.g., high-heeled shoes) must also be eschewed by the others. Indicative of her seignorial sway, no one rebels against the woman's self-styled theocracy.[8] Immediately, the old aunt seeks to bring Netochka into the religious routine. If the girl is to be believed, the initial meeting is less than successful. The old aunt looks upon the girl as a savage in need of physical and spiritual conditioning. Annoyed that Netochka is, however incredulously to her readers, too noisy and active, the woman bids her to be still. Horrified that the girl lacks religious awareness, the old aunt also insists that she attend liturgies. More often than not, though, the hermit-like aunt orders Netochka out of her sight. The girl's response is typical. Along with the usual shaking and tears, she does her best to put her worst foot forward. Breaking a cup at the precise moment that the old aunt issues yet another restriction against her, Netochka creates a panic throughout the household and must retreat to a remote room until the storm blows over.

Caught between what she perceives as a rock (the Princess) and a hard place (the old aunt), Netochka has little choice but to opt for the Prince as her protector. From experience, she knows that codependent beggars cannot be choosers. Seizing upon his remark that she is a poor orphan, Dostoevsky's heroine plays the man like a harp. With a gaze that is unhappy and crushed, she falls on her knees before him, clutching and kissing his hand, and drenching it with her tears. Netochka receives an unexpected response to this melodrama. For the third time in her tale, she is told to trust in God. Being ordered to pray over her dead mother by Efimov was one thing; being pressed to attend liturgies by the old aunt was another. Now Netochka is led by the Prince to a chapel, with predictable results. Gloomy and mysterious, the place fills her with dread. Netochka can muster no faith in God, his Mother, the angels, or the saints when standing before the icons in their glistening settings. Further, when the Prince, like Efimov, bids Netochka to kneel and pray, flashbacks of her dead mother bring on a nervous fit and worse. "I lay delirious for goodness knows how many hours," she tells her readers. "I almost died" (194, 195).

The self-styled role of orphan, Netochka does not confine to the Prince. Rather, in a moment of screen memory and spontaneous regression, Netochka breaks her isolation in an angst-ridden, psychotic way. In the surrounding darkness, Netochka hears hypnotic music that starts out soft and then grows louder, drawing her toward its source. What Dostoevsky's heroine finds is nothing less than the realization of her house with red curtains, her "paradise" (195). Again, in contrast to her second bout of drab and dreary life, everything is hyperbolic lights, noise, and action: a veritable feast for her strained senses. Once again, Netochka "ignites [her] imagination" (195). Once again, dream and hyperbole override reality and sense. Dostoevsky's heroine is spellbound by joyful faces, pretty dresses, and eyes sparkling with pleasure. Aroused physically, she "sheds tears of ecstasy" over a staircase that is "illumined brilliantly"; a ballroom that is "ablaze with thousands of candles"; a perfumed air that "blows like warm wind"; voices that move from "thousand . . . [to] millions"; and a "sea of light . . . [that] floods . . . and blinds with its brilliance" (195, 198). Without a doubt, Netochka notes in triumph, the "place where [she] had wanted to go with father . . . the place which she had in her dreams and fancies . . . was not a dream at all!" (195).

Netochka, though, does not feel the slightest inclination to join the festivities or the cast of thousands. She is neither the societal-seeking Golyadkin Senior nor Golyadkin Junior in *The Double*. Just the opposite is the case. Whether from motives of fear or guilt, Netochka again seeks codependent diminishment, hiding in corners and behind curtains, her heart beating so strongly that she can barely stand.

Like any Eden in Dostoevsky, Netochka's latest vision of paradise has a fatal flaw: a guest musician she imagines to be Efimov enters the dream. To her disoriented mind, no fewer than three miracles have occurred: her stepfather has risen from the dead; he has become reconciled with society; and, for the pièce de résistance, he is a violinist who performs willingly in public. Codependence, readers of *Netochka Nezvanova* learn, extends beyond the grave. To her already sexually inflamed state, Netochka adds a heart that "throbs with anticipation" and a breath filled "with infinite yearning" (196). Heralding the seismic shock to come, Dostoevsky's heroine can "scarcely breathe from excitement" (195). Not for her lack of trying, Netochka's fantasy flashback is not cause for insights into her past. The performance is for her more raw than real. In the psychic merging of Efimov and the musician, what Netochka hears is not music but her own enduring conflict over her parents. In the violinist's performance, also, she relives the grief of her stepfather in his requiem for her dead mother: a "wail of despair, a lament, [and] a prayer uttered in vain . . . and dying down in sorrow" (196). Further, Dostoevsky's heroine is privy to an "increasingly familiar voice from within" (196), her growing awareness of her guilt toward Efimov and her mother.

Like all men, women, and children in Dostoevsky, Netochka is reluctant to accept the truth or give herself over to heartfelt confession. Her heart refuses to believe what her soul is telling her, and the results are predictable. On one level, the suffering is physical: Netochka clenches her teeth to hold back the pain. On another level, the agony is spiritual: Netochka has a vision of hell, the price for her codependence. In a perverted *sobornost'*, or "spiritual union," everyone in the room shares in her sin and suffering. They, too, "want to scream at the ghastly moans and wails that torment their souls ... and that flow on, more anguished, plaintive, and prolonged" (196).

A final cry from the violinist's instrument "pierces [Netochka's] heart and wrenches apart [her] insides" (196). It also forces the girl to stage an entrance that is as disturbing as any of Dostoevsky's mature scenes of scandal. Throwing caution to the wind, Netochka pulls back the curtains and dashes into the room. Pushing her way through the astonished crowd and believing that she is embracing Efimov, she throws herself at the violinist with an anguished shriek.

Netochka's brash, crazed attempt to resurrect and reconcile with Efimov is a disaster externally and internally. Externally, the people whom Netochka saw as comrades in spiritual suffering now become her enemies. Like a many-headed hydra, black eyes fixate on the girl as if they wish "to consume [her] with their fire" (196). To Netochka's further sorrow, long bony hands lift her amidst laughter "that rings out ... [and] reverberates ... in a concentrated roar" (196). The internal disaster occurs when Netochka, simmering with anger and guilt, decides that the violinist she took for Efimov was in fact his murderer. In a final frenzy, Netochka loses consciousness.[9]

KATYA

When Netochka comes to her senses, she is startled to see the face of a child bending over her. The child is Katya, the Prince's daughter, who has just returned from Moscow. With Katya, Netochka immediately resumes her penchant for idols, fairy tales, and dreams. This time, though, the relationship addiction is not with an adult, but a child like herself. (It is yet another indication of the Prince's unhealthy aura that Netochka does not seek a tie with him.) Although Netochka sees Katya as a girl of her own age, she does not pursue equality or friendship. Rather, from the moment Dostoevsky's heroine lays eyes on the Prince's daughter, she moves to new codependence. Her response to the girl is a feeling of happiness and a "sweet premonition filling her soul" (197). Infused once again with otherworldly bliss, Netochka has little trouble in elevating Katya to an angel-guardian who, for what she lacks in physical features, more than makes up for in brilliance and light. Like the initial portrait of Efimov, not to mention other alleged supermen in Dostoevsky, Katya is extraordinary and perfect in every way. Indeed, unlike Efimov, the object of Netochka's addictive affection exhibits a beauty that she seeks to possess in a compulsive way. Try to imagine, Netochka tells her readers, "a face of idyllic charm and stunning, dazzling beauty" (197). Katya's visage "transfixes in sweet confusion ... [and] trembles with delight" (197). It "makes [one] grateful for its existence, for allowing [one's] eyes to fall upon it, for passing [one] by" (197).

Foreshadowing what is to come, it also engenders new eroticism. With Katya, Netochka feels her "frail nerves ache with sweet ecstasy" (197). Simply put, she follows a path common to many characters in Dostoevsky. She opts for what both Jackson and Ksana Blank identify as Dostoevsky's later meld of true, higher beauty and a "low order of aesthetic sensation."[10] If Netochka is overawed by Katya it is because, in a replay of the addictive bond between Efimov and the musician B., she sees the young Princess as a polar opposite: a double for codependence. Unlike her lethargic low-flying self, Katya is constant noise and motion. The girl stays only for a few minutes, Netochka tells her readers, because "she could not sit still" (197). Soon, though, Dostoevsky's heroine invests the young Princess's restlessness with a dark and disturbing cast. Specifically, Netochka sees Katya as so willful and compulsive that her normalcy comes into question. An inner darkness seems to lurk just beneath her external light. "To be always on the move, running, skipping and making a commotion about the house," Netochka continues, "was for Katya an absolute necessity" (197).

An intrusive adult, Netochka adds further dissonance to Katya's portrait by noting that the child's upbringing has been as problematic as her own. Steiner's claims that Katya is "outgoing and cheerful" and Grossman's comments about her unclouded past and her "healthy and graceful" present need reconsideration.[11] Particularly disturbing are the mature Netochka's hints of something amiss between father and child. With memories of the charged relationship between Netochka and Efimov still fresh, the mature self sounds an alarm with her comment that the greatest influence on the young Princess was her father, whom she "adored ... [in a way that was] open, frank, and unarmed" (206, 207). The key words here are "adored" and "unarmed." To the senior Netochka's taste, the nominal head of the household is shadowy and remote only intermittently; as Efimov with Netochka, he looms uncomfortably large in his daughter's imagination. The potential for codependence is present.

Equally problematic for the adult Netochka is Katya's tie to her mother. Neglect and boundaries affect rich families as well as poor ones. Between the two girls and their mothers, though, there are differences. If Netochka was allowed by her mother to do as she pleased in the privacy of her internal and external worlds, Katya is at the mercy of a parent who impedes and confuses her daughter at every turn. It is hardly surprising that the young Princess has inherited her mother's power, willfulness, and pride. After all, in what is the domino effect of codependence, the girl has been subject to the same "moral tyranny" (206) of her mother that the woman (and everyone else in the household) has experienced at the hands of the old aunt. Even worse is the instability of Katya's upbringing. The love between the young Princess and her mother is judged by the adult Netochka as "morbidly excessive" (207). Justifiably, the young Princess is "outraged" by her mother's parenting, which the adult Netochka calls a "strange combination of pampering and ruthless severity . . . [in which] what was permitted on one day was, for no given reason, forbidden the next" (206). Although Katya's formation (or lack thereof) differs markedly from that of Netochka, the result is the same. The young Princess, too, has no clear idea of right and wrong; she, too, must figure out morality and ethics unaided, in bruising trial-and-error.

A second difference between the childhoods of Netochka and Katya is that, whereas the former includes moments of filial closeness, the latter does not. Not once in the narrative do Katya and her mother embrace, kiss, or talk in a meaningful way. Rather, in the stratified and frigid atmosphere of the home, the two remain behind well-established barriers. Katya's obedience to her mother is formal and direct, but also manipulative. She and her mother enter into a bargain, not a bond, with each of them seeking only self-styled gain from the other. Indeed, given the state of affairs between the older Princess and Katya, it is not surprising that like Netochka, the young Princess opts for her father over her mother, despite the potential dangers therein.

BINDING, BONDING

Apropos of Katya's flawed upbringing, it is logical that initially, the young Princess has only pity and scorn for Netochka.[12] Further, the young Princess rejects outright the role of poor orphan that Netochka stages so successfully with the Prince. Almost to the applause of readers of *Netochka Nezvanova*, Katya's recurring demand is that Dostoevsky's heroine quit being sick, boring, and bewildered. Daily she batters Netochka: "Well, are you all right now? . . . Didn't I tell you to get better? . . . Still thin as ever?" (197). Delivering her remarks in a relentless staccato, the young Princess zeroes in on Netochka's reticence, her indifference to games, and her penchant for thinking. Katya also keeps the upper hand with Netochka by deflecting the girl's questions about the Prince and the other members of the household. Boundaries remain safe and secure. In fact, to the new ward, the only thing that the young Princess discloses is already patently clear: Katya talks too much and thinks too little.

Netochka responds to Katya in a typically passive-aggressive way. When visited by the young Princess, Dostoevsky's heroine appears pale and thin. Her face is doleful "with a nervous smile"; her body "cowers as if guilty of something" (197). Netochka takes full measure of Katya's body, speech, and mannerisms. Particularly intriguing are the young Princess's piques of temper. Dostoevsky's heroine delights when Katya frowns and shakes her head. She is even more taken when the young Princess stamps her feet or fixes her dark eyes on Netochka for hours on end.

It is only a matter of time before, as was the case with Efimov (and despite similar covert and overt abuse), Netochka makes Katya the focus of both her external and internal worlds. When the two meet, Netochka cannot take her eyes off the girl. When they go their separate ways, Netochka continues to gaze, spellbound, at the spot where the young Princess had been standing. For Netochka also, parting from the young Princess is not only sweet sorrow but also the catalyst for new fantasies and dreams. To her taste, she does what all Dostoevsky characters do in the clash of reality and ideal: she fashions her own Katya. When Dostoevsky's heroine is not inventing lengthy conversations with the young Princess, she envisions playing pranks with the girl, after which the two weep together when scolded.

Netochka so obsesses over Katya that she wishes to possess her, body and soul. As was the case in the morbid codependency with Efimov, eros comes to the fore; but this time, Netochka is the aggressor. Days, Dostoevsky's heroine awaits the girl's visits with "tremendous excitement . . . still longing to kiss her" (189). Nights, she dreams of the young Princess "as if we were in love" (197). Curiosity and boredom also move Netochka closer to Katya. When the young Princess queries her playmate about how she spends her time, she is intrigued by the girl's reply. "I think about you" (198), Netochka responds. It is indicative of Katya's own penchant for codependence that she first kisses Netochka and then gives her cake. Immediately, though, the innocence of such a move assumes a darker cast. To Netochka, the young Princess makes it clear that "it is [her] cake . . . something forbidden" (199). Not unlike the Edenic snake, she bids Netochka to "eat it all . . . eat more, eat more" (199), recalling the cake that Efimov offers Netochka as an enticement for stealing money from her mother.

Faithful to her codependent narrative mode, Netochka does not specify who has forbidden whom to have cake and why. She is more concerned with Katya's stance over the perceived infraction. After Netochka eats the cake, the young Princess is frenzied and giggles with glee before she becomes impetuous and brusque. She also displays sexuality beyond her years. A breathless voice attends eyes that sparkle, cheeks that are aflame, and curls that are in wild disarray. Again, the question arises: From whence the frenzy?

In the disturbing portrait of Katya, one thing is certain: Netochka will have the girl as her codependent own. Claims by Edward Wasiolek, Grossman, Terras, Mochulsky, and others as to the girl's submissiveness toward the young Princess need a second look.[13] Seeing the young Princess as irresistible, consumed by the thought that she cannot be separated from Katya any longer, and "burning with new feelings . . . [and] unable to restrain herself" (199), Netochka attempts a new type of clinging. She throws her arms around Katya and kisses her.

Immediately, Netochka senses that she has done something wrong; however, in a manner typical of Dostoevskian characters, she avoids thoughts about the ethics of her actions. Rather, she seeks to restore codependent bivalence and the vertical status quo. Katya is good; Netochka is bad. Katya is high; she is low. Katya is also nimble and strong, but Netochka is "exactly the opposite . . . completely lacking in all the qualities that appealed to the [young Princess]" (200). Suspending disbelief, Netochka even portrays Katya as naive and open, with a "true and noble grace" (200).

In the codependent black-and-white bivalence, also, Dostoevsky's heroine delights in self-abasement. She accepts the young Princess's verdict that she is quiet, thoughtful, and sick. She also "blames herself" (199) for her many peculiarities, real and imagined. Netochka's perceived inability to forge ties with her world is particularly subject to "tormented doubt" (199). Her belief is that she is displeasing to everyone, particularly to Katya not only from the beginning, "but also once and for all" (199). At every hasty word and doubtful look from Katya, Netochka is ready to cry. Her uncertainty over the young Princess mounts not only by the day but by the hour. It brings on "gloom . . . tears . . . sinking spirits . . . dark thoughts . . . contempt . . . repugnance . . . [and] disdain" (199, 200).

Katya's reaction to Netochka's kiss is similarly telling. Initially offended, the girl frees herself from her playmate's embrace, but (and this is an important point) she also grabs her playmate's hands in the process. The young Princess does not end matters there, though. Katya shrugs her shoulders and compresses her lips, but in the strained silence, she stares at Netochka for a long time.

Although Katya believes, rightfully, that "one can do nothing with Netochka" (200), she acquiesces to a demand by Madame Leotard, the governess, that she engage her playmate in games and other activities. Again, though, the young Princess finds Netochka desiring further intimacy. Extending her hand to the girl, Dostoevsky's heroine asks forgiveness—and more. "Do not be cross with me, Katya," Netochka says, "because I like you very much" (201). The ensuing question-and-answer is straightforward. "Perhaps you would like me to kiss you?" (201), the young Princess asks Netochka. "As you like" (201), is the girl's response.

The kiss Katya gives to Netochka is disturbing for several reasons. It has been bestowed seriously, "from obligation" (201). Pressing her lips against Netochka's, the young Princess enters into an emotional tit-for-tat with her playmate. More serious, perhaps, is the fact that after Katya kisses Dostoevsky's heroine, she does something quite untoward. Initially cheerful and content, she moves to quasi-orgasm: she laughs and shouts to such an alarming degree that, exhausted and out of breath, she throws herself on the sofa to rest. Again the skewed cause-and-effect only adds to lingering suspicions of something not quite right in the young Princess's life.

The strained closeness between Netochka and Katya takes an unexpected turn during school lessons with Madame Leotard. A chance remark by the Prince, that at times Katya is like Netochka, has a grain of truth. Both have a tendency to embrace polarities, appearing subtle and intelligent one moment but silly and naive the next. Katya also mirrors Netochka in this "idiosyncrasy" (201): she views academic problems and challenges as "humiliating" (201). Also, like other self-professed intellectuals in Dostoevsky, the young Princess has little use for formal education. She can sit before books but learns little. Dull and scatterbrained, she drives Madame Leotard to distraction.

By contrast, Netochka does well in her studies. Mastering the French alphabet in one sitting, she readily makes up for lost time as a student. Netochka's newfound love of education, though, shows key shortcomings. As her readings with Efimov demonstrated, Netochka's abilities as a student stem not from her intellectual curiosity or prowess but, rather, from her desire to please her teacher. Also, Netochka's success in her studies leads to conflicts with Katya. In a manner that recalls the early codependent relationship between Efimov and the musician B., Netochka progresses in learning, but the young Princess stagnates and even regresses. Madame Leotard exacerbates tensions between Netochka and Katya when she champions the former over the latter.

"Look at Netochka," the governess chides Katya, "a sick child, but in her first lesson she has done ten times more than you. Are you not ashamed?" (202). The governess praises Netochka not only intellectually but also morally. As she sees it, the ward in their midst is smart and sober. She also harbors an honest heart, one that Katya would do well to emulate and (however ironic it might seem in the context) even to "love" (203).[14]

The response accords with other disturbing facets of Katya's personality. Annihilation of Netochka is the desired option. The young Princess so "burns beet-red with shame . . . [that she wishes] to chew [her playmate] to pieces" (202). In no way will Katya cede primacy to Netochka, physically or mentally. Silence and indifference give way to scorn and taunt. To Netochka's hesitancy over her ability to dance or to play the piano, the young Princess responds: "I can. . . . [Such things] are very difficult" (202). School is another cause of disagreement. If there is one thing that the young Princess (or for that matter, any character in Dostoevsky) cannot tolerate, it is ridicule. "Madame Leotard says that you are cleverer than I," the young Princess continues, "Are you going to make fun of me now just because you are so?" (203).

After Madame Leotard chides her repeatedly for boasting about being a princess, Katya becomes furious and abusive. Her cheeks glowing scarlet, Katya now seeks to humiliate Netochka at every turn. Elements of her playmate's past—her unstable parents, the lack of clothes and toys—are ammunition for the volleys of overt and covert abuse that she fires at the girl. Indeed, so outraged is the young Princess by what she sees as Netochka's challenge to her position in the household, in her "troubled equilibrium . . . [and] antipathy" (207) for her playmate, she becomes sickly, pale, and thin. Only a threat by Madame Leotard to inform the Prince of her behavior causes Katya to cease her abuse of Netochka and herself.

Netochka parries Katya's verbal blows in several codependent ways. She lapses into silence; she keeps a stiff upper lip; she excuses the young Princess's behavior—Katya is "not to blame for the governess's words" (202), she says. Again, the girl even throws her arms around her playmate, all to no avail. Figuratively punch-drunk by Katya's assault, Dostoevsky's heroine goes down for the count. Trembling, "her heart pierced and bleeding" (204), she breaks her silence and confesses her past to her playmate. Recalling her time with Efimov and her mother, Netochka admits that she lived with them in one room. Netochka would not be Netochka, though, if she did not embellish her alleged confession with false or exaggerated detail. Seeking to rise in Katya's estimation, the girl tells her playmate that she was the glue that held the family together, the one who did all the chores such as shopping and housekeeping. Even more mock heroically, perhaps, Dostoevsky's heroine lies that her parents loved her, and that the two even taught her to read.

As is the case with all the humiliated and oppressed in Dostoevsky, and as her periodic revolts against Efimov demonstrate, Netochka can be pushed only so far. Anger seizes her being. "Blushing in indignation . . . trembling with new and unbelievable sensations . . . [and] bursting into tears of heart-felt anguish" (204), Netochka returns Katya's questions with queries of her own. Her own grilling is even more rapid-fire and hard-hitting than her playmate's. "Why are you asking me such things?" Netochka assaults the girl. "Why are you making fun of me? . . . Why are you asking me about my father and mother . . . in this way? What have they ever done to you?" (204). On a roll, Netochka calls in the troops. When the Prince enters the room, the girl does what she does best: she plays the ultimate victim. Grabbing the man's hand, she covers it with her tears.

Initially, Katya is bewildered by Netochka's outburst; but she does not yield to the Prince. Stonelike and pale, she acknowledges her ridicule of Netochka, but that is all. The young Princess resists with all the force of her being her father's demand that she ask her playmate's forgiveness. In fact, Katya wants nothing less than Netochka's expulsion from the household. "I do not want to ask her forgiveness," she shrieks. "I do not like Netochka and I do not want to live with her any longer" (205). For such a response, the young Princess is hauled by the Prince into his study. When she returns, her eyes are red and her cheeks puffy. Despite new admonitions by her father and Madame Leotard, Katya banishes Netochka from her physical and mental sight. She decides to "act as though [the girl] was not even living in the house" (207).

Netochka yields totally. As she did with Efimov and her mother, the girl assumes "utmost blame" (205) for the quarrel. When the Prince orders her to leave the room, she appears "frozen and half-dead with fear" and collapses on the sofa, her head buried in her hands.

Just as she had done with the increasingly abusive Efimov, the morbidly codependent Netochka overlooks Katya's abuse and continues to uphold her as an ideal. Indeed, the lengths to which Netochka goes to champion her abusive playmate far exceed what she was willing to undergo for her stepfather's sake. With the same uncritical posture she took toward Efimov's genius, she now touts Katya's moral and aesthetic superiority. The young Princess's admission of guilt before her father is more than sufficient for Dostoevsky's heroine to prove her case: Blithely, Netochka overlooks the fact that the girl has shown no remorse over her actions and portrays Katya as someone otherworldly and angelic. She is not alone in her view. Everyone, Netochka insists, loves and admires Katya. Even passersby "utter exclamations of delight" (207).[15] Netochka begins to create an idol. As she sees it, what radiates from without also does so from within. The young Princess, Netochka tells her astonished readers, cannot lie because "her instinct . . . sense of justice . . . [and] sweet and generous little heart always lead her in the right direction" (205, 206). Recalling her specious support for Efimov, Netochka even attributes metaphysical sensibilities to Katya. Just as, in her eyes, Efimov possesses a profound instinctual understanding of art, so too does the young Princess display an "aesthetic appreciation . . . an exquisite sensation of awakened beauty" (207).[16]

As was the case with her stepfather, the codependent Netochka excuses and even justifies Katia's behavior. Netochka's defense of Katya is also an *apologia* for herself. The girl's shortcomings, Dostoevsky's heroine asserts, are that she "enters into enthusiasms with too much passion . . . [and] egocentricity" (207–208). Shades of Ivan Karamazov and his wish for a perfect world in *The Brothers Karamazov*, contradictions cause Katya "anger and offense" (202). In fact, nothing chagrins the young Princess more than when people and events are other "than what she wishes [them] to be" (202). The remedy for such failings, the child Netochka insists, is simple: the young Princess must be "led . . . [to] the correct path by experience and example" (208). Of course, Netochka explains precisely neither who is to lead and mentor Katya nor the nature of this path.

In the rehabilitation of Katya, Netochka makes one thing perfectly clear: the young Princess is not to blame for her own shortcomings. Rather, the girl is the pawn of someone or something that has sullied her Edenic innocence and naïveté. Katya's original beauty, Dostoevsky's heroine writes, has, in time, "acquired a false form" (207). Her playmate's aberrant behavior is not innate; rather, it has been "implanted in her . . . in moments of conflict" (207). Again, what Netochka means by such claims, particularly the reference to conflict, is anyone's guess. It is certainly not the case that, as Jackson asserts, "the beauty of Katya is corrupt [and] evil is a part of her nature."[17] Netochka sees Katya as perfect, not only in the present but also in the future. The young Princess "glows with gratifying hope . . . and heralds splendid days to come" (207). Like other deities, she will make straight her path. "Even at the cost of continual deviation and error," Netochka concludes, Katya is "born for happiness . . . and will be beautiful and sincere" (208).

Given her renewed codependent stance—her "increasing love" (207) for Katya—it is not surprising that Netochka seeks to restore the tie as quickly as possible. "A thousand times I wanted to go to Katya," she confesses to her readers, "but a thousand times I hesitated, not knowing how she would react to me" (205). So desperate is Netochka for a truce with Katya that in ultimate (vertical) subservience, she yearns to do what she has already done with Efimov and Prince X.: throw herself at the young Princess's feet.

Three days after their quarrel, Netochka gets her wish. To her dismay (and, most likely, to her delight as well), she finds that Katya is also suffering greatly, so much so that others fear for her health. The young Princess—silent and pale one moment, blushing and crying the next—extends to Netochka an olive branch, but not without complications. When Katya asks Netochka to pardon her, she makes it clear that she does so only after coercion by the Prince. She also manipulates forgiveness to her advantage. Switching agents and objects, she says to Netochka: "Papa says I must kiss you. Will you give me a kiss?" (206). In other words, Katya signals to Netochka that she is open to the physicality her playmate has been wanting, but Netochka must make the first move.

Netochka responds to Katya's overtures with charged eroticism. Nowhere is there a shred of innocence or shyness, or a sense of wrongdoing and guilt. "Breathless with excitement" (206), Dostoevsky's heroine throws her arms about her playmate. It is not Netochka's codependent way merely to peck Katya's cheek. Rather, the girl first kisses her playmate's hands; then she "smothers them with tears" (206). Katya answers in kind. Her lips and chin quiver; her lips are moist. She "overcomes her agitation" (206) with a smile. With almost orgiastic abandon, the tomb-like house is rent with laugher, shouting, and the "clatter of something falling over and breaking . . . of books flying to the floor . . . and of [Katya's] hoop spinning across the room" (206). The ecstasy is mutual. Under the pretense of Katya's having reconciled with the Prince, Netochka's heart "begins to throb with joy" (206). Despite the lacerations of confusion and embarrassment, the girl is in Katya's thrall. Netochka "can barely understand what is happening to her" (207). Within her are "new and unfamiliar emotions . . . which tear her apart . . . in suffered agonies" (207). Indeed, so searing is Netochka's codependent obsession with and possession of Katya that she even begs her readers' forgiveness for what she is about to say, that she "loves Katya with a love that is genuine, passionate, and with all its ups and downs" (207).

For the time being, and to Netochka's chagrin, Katya does not pursue the proffered bond. In fact, she keeps her distance, physically and emotionally. The codependent attraction continues to exist, though. Indeed, as Dostoevsky's heroine would have it, fate has brought them together, even if the truth of the situation is that Netochka is actually stalking the girl. It is with feigned naïveté, along with a dash of chutzpah, that Dostoevsky's heroine writes that

Katya cannot understand how Netochka "has more than once crossed her path when she had absolutely no wish to find [her playmate] there" (206). Fate be damned, it is Netochka's constant presence that causes Katya to stare at her "with increasing intensity" (206).

DUELING WITH A DOG

The tortured relationship between Netochka and Katya takes a momentary but significant turn with a confrontation between the young Princess and the household dog, Sir John Falstaff. Falstaff may be an animal, but, as rendered by Netochka, he shows the same traits as other relationship-addictive individuals in her narrative. Indeed, he is seen as human. Bereft of any moral sense whatsoever, he exemplifies codependency in dangerous and dramatic ways. Indeed, the animal is so bereft of moral sense that he is capable of murder.[18] Falstaff has a checkered history. Although he is a bulldog with an excellent pedigree, he has had a rough street life. Like Netochka, the dog has known neither security nor love in his youth. Also like his counterpart, Falstaff has been found, sick and dirty, by the Prince and saved from an almost certain death. Falstaff further mirrors Netochka in that his first days in the Prince's house are a disaster. Societal rules and codes of conduct are even more alien to him than they were to the other orphaned ward. In fact, the newcomer to the household behaves so coarsely that he is tied to a rope and consigned to the backyard.

Again like Dostoevsky's heroine, the human-like Falstaff is unhappy with his status as a second-class citizen; and, as seen by Netochka, he, too, plots to improve his standing there. An opportunity comes when Sasha, Katya's heretofore unmentioned brother, falls into the Neva. The screams of Katya's mother, her wish to jump into the water after her son, the attempts of the family to save the woman from her certain death, and the efforts to secure a boat—all do little to rescue the boy from the currents. Falstaff wastes no time in serving his masters. He plunges into the water, grabs the child between his teeth, and swims triumphantly to the shore.[19] Falstaff earns the recognition he craves so desperately, but with a perverse, Dostoevskian twist. Like any perverse codependent in the writer's corpus, he maintains his boundaries. Even more so than Netochka, Falstaff does his best to make himself unwelcome and unloved. When the Princess throws her arms around the dog and kisses him in ceaseless gratitude, Falstaff does what any Dostoevskian face- and space-saving character would do. Indeed, the animal proves wrong the later comment by Ivan Karamazov that a beast can never be as cruel as a person. As Netochka tells it, Falstaff so hated being kissed by anyone that he responded by biting the woman's shoulder.

The dog is not punished for his actions. Indeed, in what is seen as a recurring theme in *Netochka Nezvanova*, the more Falstaff abuses others, the more he is loved by them. Although the Princess suffers from Falstaff's wound for the rest of her life, her affection for the animal is "boundless" (214). In fact, after Katya, the woman sees the dog as "dearer than anyone in the world" (214). (This begs the question as to the Prince's rank in her affection.) In line with addictive behavior, the Princess raises Falstaff as an idol. The dog is moved inside; he is adorned with an intricately carved silver collar and "enthroned" (214) on a magnificent bearskin rug. His name is changed. Whereas Netochka is doomed to endure the negative aura of how she is known to the world, Falstaff enjoys a more fortunate fate, his initial name being the lower-class Friska. Like Efimov, the dog is even accorded the status of genius: without explanation or proof, the Prince senses in the animal a "phenomenal voracity of mind" (214).

Unlike Efimov, the human-like Falstaff enjoys his status.[20] Aloof, proud, and cold, he is a "true Englishman" (214). Unlike others in the narrative who are depicted as disembodied voices, Falstaff glories in his physicality. He is not Zhuchka-Perezvon, the life-affirming dog in *The Brothers Karamazov*. Rather, Falstaff is "fierce as a tiger . . . and strong as a bear . . . enough to defy his master" (208). Like a master-potentate, the dog is also singularly selective in his choice of a companion. He is not a clawing codependent; just the opposite, it is he who sets the parameters for addiction. The Princess is the only one whom Falstaff allows to enter his royal presence. She alone receives the singular privilege of being allowed to stroke him without threat of "instant retaliation" (214).

Falstaff has two foes in the household. One is the old aunt. The second and more formidable one is Katya, with whom the lines of battle are drawn. The dog rejects the girl's demand for "dominance . . . authority . . . [and desire] to be loved and bowed down to" (208). The house in which Netochka now lives is too small for Katya and Falstaff. One has to go or submit to the other. Stinging from the stalemate with Netochka, it is the young Princess who throws down the gauntlet before the dog. She will show both who runs the domestic show.

Katya and Falstaff have scuffled previously. "Falstaff tried to bite me today" (199), Katya tells Netochka in an earlier conversation. Such animosity is a prelude to all-out war between the two. One afternoon, with Netochka pale and shivering, Katya attempts to bend Falstaff to her will. Initially, she entices the dog with coaxing gestures, fond names, and biscuits and cakes. The young Princess even violates the ultimate border-bending taboo: she seeks to pet Falstaff and persuade him to follow her.

Falstaff responds to these gestures with bemused tolerance. Stretched out and enjoying a nap, he is in no mood for a fight. The dog knows that he holds the upper hand in any contest. Just as Katya wishes to annihilate Netochka and gain primacy in the household, so, for similar reasons Falstaff shows no hesitation about "tear[ing] [the young Princess] to pieces" (208).

Undeterred, Katya seeks to transgress Falstaff's boundaries by moving in on him in a diminishing spiral, and with a predictable response. The dog, sensing that the young Princess has entered into his "sacred . . . [and] forbidden territory" (208), growls and bares his teeth. As she does with the frustrated sorties with Netochka, Katya becomes thoughtful and vexed. Stomping her feet, she moves to her usual line of defense: the sofa. As she also does when frustrated by Dostoevsky's heroine, the young Princess enters a state of quasi-erotic frenzy. In "extreme agitation" (209) over Falstaff, she stomps her feet. Her head "fills with blood"; her cheeks "flame like the sunset"; her eyes "brim with tears of annoyance" (209).

Heedless of Falstaff's powerful jaws, vicious snarls, and menacing glares, Katya "crosses the boundary" (209) into the dog's sacred space. In her death-defying stunt, so typical of codependents, she makes for Netochka a "wonderful picture" (209). Her feet stand their ground and her eyes are "joyful and giddy . . . flashing with victory" (209), she pets the dog three times. Unwilling to risk his position in the household, the dog does not put an end to Katya. He leaves the room.

Initially, Katya's victory seems a Pyrrhic one. Challenging death one moment, she figuratively dies the next. Having "staked out a position in [Falstaff's] conquered territory" (209), Katya has eyes that are strange, and cheeks that are deathly white. So overcome is the young Princess by her suicidal challenge of the dog that in a half-faint, she barely reaches the sofa. Falstaff aside, though, the young Princess gains an even more important win with Netochka; but with this difference. If Falstaff departs the scene with a modicum of dignity and grace, Dostoevsky's heroine loses both and more in renewed codependence on her playmate. With Katya, Netochka is "no longer in control of herself" (209). Readily, she admits that she "pines for love" for the girl; and that her "infatuation [for her playmate] . . . knows no bounds" (209). It is also part of Netochka's daily regimen that, whenever she sees the young Princess, her heart "throbs so painfully that [she] feels dizzy" (209). There is also a wish to strengthen the tie. "Thousands of times," she wishes to "throw her arms around [Katya's] neck" (209) and bind her to herself.

Netochka's love for Katya now "verges on the abnormal" (210): it has become morbid codependency. At first, she absconds with the young Princess's things. On one occasion, she steals a handkerchief; on another, a piece of ribbon.[21] She even appears to derive sexual pleasure from them. When Netochka is not kissing the handkerchief and ribbon, she is showering them with her tears. Such license soon moves to an even greater intrusion: Katya's body. In the dead of night, Dostoevsky's heroine tiptoes to her sleeping playmate and gazes upon her for hours on end. In time, silently and trembling in fear, she moves to kiss the young Princess's hands, hair, shoulders, and feet.

If Netochka thinks that Katya is oblivious to her renewed overtures, she is mistaken. The young Princess may remain unresponsive to Netochka at night; but she shows ample disorientation toward the girl during the day. Typical of relationship addiction, and mindful that Dostoevsky's heroine is in her cross hairs, the young Princess blows hot and cold. At times, she is disturbingly pensive and silent. At other times, Katya becomes irritable and demanding. She blushes frequently, loses her temper, and "raises unprecedented rackets" (210). A true Dostoevskian heroine, the young Princess also tests Netochka's affection in "little acts of cruelty" (210). There are sins of omission. Knowing "full well that [her playmate] pines for her" (210), Katya often spends entire days with her mother, even, for a period of time, moving into the woman's apartment in the home (yet another sign of the familial disengagement). There are also sins of commission. The young Princess Katya refuses to sit next to Netochka at dinner. Or, like a beast at its prey before the kill, she again paralyzes her playmate with intense stares.

Momentarily, she wins. Netochka is so stunned by Katya's harshness that she submits to "torment, sorrow, and grief" (211). In "heartbroken agitation," she "racks her brains" (211) over her playmate's moves. Bouts of "indignation . . . pride . . . [and] a sense of injustice" bring her to return Katya's stares with "serious and independent" (211) gazes of her own. What Netochka's eyes do, though, the rest of her cannot. Her heart "aches more and more"; her body "grows weaker and feebler than ever" (211).

BREAKING TABOO

At this point in the narrative, readers of *Netochka Nezvanova* are correct to ask whether the erotic codependency between Netochka and Katya goes unnoticed in the household. The answer is yes and no. Katya's parents sense something amiss between the two girls; but their responses also show an unwillingness to deal with the situation—or something far worse. When Katya complains of fever, the Princess responds in inappropriate ways. One wonders about the dynamics of the household, as well as the relationship between and among father, mother, and daughter when at such a complaint—normal in the life of a child—the woman's hair "almost turns white" (210) from fear. Additionally, as if to safeguard the prison- and tomb-like atmosphere of the household, the distraught Princess does not summon a doctor to the home. Troubling is not only the woman's (defensive) desire to look past Katya and herself and to find a scapegoat for her daughter's distress; but also her (equally self-protective) willingness to close her eyes to the emotional addiction before her. Netochka notes that the Princess ascribes these changes in Katya "to me and my sullen nature" (210).

Even more disturbing is the Prince's response to the morbid tie between the two girls. It is of interest to note that although the Princess had wished to separate Netochka and Katya earlier, she faced opposition from her spouse. In fact, the Prince was "very adamant" (210) that the two girls stay together, but without any explanation from him or Dostoevsky's heroine. The acquiescence of the Princess—she "understands the Prince completely" (210)—darkens the situation even further.

Madame Leotard is not so amenable. More and more, she watches in alarm at the tie between the two girls. The woman is particularly distressed by Katya's increasing tendency toward extremes: in the morning, the young Princess dances, frolics, and throws herself on her governess's neck with wild glee, but by evening, the girl becomes quiet and dreamy and "makes an unnatural effort to appear cheerful" (211) before bursting into tears.

The "unseen crisis brewing inside [Katya]" (211) convinces Netochka that all is not lost in their tormented relationship. In fact, just the opposite is true: the young Princess seems to be coming apart at the seams, bringing Dostoevsky's heroine to "throb with hope" that, in their "little romance" (211), the two can pick up where they had left off. She is not deceived in her wish. For reasons that Netochka never makes clear, the two suddenly come from behind their barriers and join in body and soul. The smoldering tension between the girls breaks out into open flame. When, again for undisclosed reasons, Katya leaves her mother's apartments to resume life in the household, she adopts a literally no-holds-barred attitude toward her playmate. To Netochka, she now shows a "long penetrating gaze . . . [and] a lovely sparkle in her eyes" (211). Indeed, so changed and charged is the young Princess's demeanor toward her playmate that *both* girls blush and lower their eyes, "as if ashamed" (211).

Katya and Netochka engage each other in what is recognized as Dostoevsky's classical approach to characters in addictive struggles for power and control. Just as Katerina Ivanovna and Grushenka in *The Brothers Karamazov* bow and scrape in mutual attraction and hate, so do Katya and Netochka assume mutual mock mortification and sacrifice out of similar motives and emotions. The pretext for the courtship between the two girls is the tying of a shoelace; and, again, it is Katya who makes the first move. "Your shoelace is undone," the young Princess tells Netochka, "Let me tie it for you" (211). Although Netochka herself bends down to attend to the item, she is stopped from doing so by the young Princess. Taking Netochka's foot "firmly" (211) in hand, the girl accomplishes the task. Katya is not content to let the bonding/binding rest there. Although both girls are warm and secure, she seeks also to touch and tie other parts of Netochka's body. "Your throat is not covered," Katya tells her playmate, "Here, let me wrap it up" (211). The girl even adds a personal touch. With a willing Netochka, the young Princess unties and reties the kerchief with "a mischievous smile . . . her misty black eyes twinkling merrily" (211). (Recall how Netochka's mother, revived in her bond with Efimov, also tied a cravat around the man's neck.)

Whatever innocence or goodwill readers of *Netochka Nezvanova* may hope for in such a move is set aside when Katya's finger touches her playmate's "bare neck in a gentle way"; and when, in response Netochka "sighs deeply . . . [and] blushes as red as a cherry . . . beside herself in a sort of sweet terror" (211). Throwing caution to the winds, the two engage in physical intimacy. Particularly disturbing here is that Netochka and Katya explore the flesh not as adolescents with a normal and healthy interest in sexuality. Rather, they get down to business like experienced lovers—or even worse. Although Netochka pleads innocence for herself and her playmate—"I did not know what was happening to me, or what had come over Katya"—she is well versed in preliminaries, kissing Katya's shoulder in a "stealthy way" (212). Even more darkly, perhaps, Netochka finds in her playmate an overtly ready and willing partner. Only the initial foray is needed to trigger in Katya an orgiastic response. The girl "quivers" before she experiences an "attack of nerves" (212). Even more gratifying for Netochka is the fact that, before the seizure, Katya had been thin and pale, but after, she is rosy, cheerful, "incredibly healthy . . . [and] full of whims and fancies that were not typical of her" (212).

It is not surprising that Katya, in this aroused and addicted state with Netochka, behaves even more recklessly than previously. If earlier she engaged Falstaff in a literal life-and-death struggle for control, she now takes on the old aunt in an even more potentially lethal conflict. The woman, it will be recalled, rules the household with an iron hand, but also with the same unsteady truce that marks Falstaff and Katya. Like the dog, Katya is also an "idol . . . [capable] of making even her mother cede to her whims" (212). To date, the unspoken compromise among the three would-be deities has established borders in the household. Falstaff has his rug; the old aunt, the upstairs quarters; Katya, the rest of the home.

All is quiet on the domestic front until the young Princess again decides to flex her muscles, her goal being renewed dominance in the tit-for-tat codependence with Netochka. Like all moves and countermoves in *Netochka Nezvanova*, Katya's appeal to the old aunt is couched in an allegedly innocent request for a visit with her rival.

Initially, the encounter between the young and old idols is fraught with dissembling and pretense. Katya, in much the same way that she sought to disarm Falstaff, presumes sweetness and light. She also watches Netochka for calculated effect. In a bow to the woman's sense of social and religious propriety, Katya falls on her knees to beg forgiveness for "all her misdemeanors, her noisy play, and her shouting and disturbing her aunt" (212). The impression management makes its mark. Indeed, it is a measure not only of the old aunt's own codependence on acceptance and love but also of her equally pressing yearnings for social and spiritual order that, with tears in her eyes, she accepts Katya's false confession—one of many in *Netochka Nezvanova*—and forgives the girl in a solemn way. The reconciliation lacks as much sincerity from the old woman as it does from Katya. The relationship remains vertical and power-driven. Her vanity flattered, the old aunt delights in the "prospect of victory" (212) over the girl.

She should be so fortunate. Having breached the old woman's boundaries, Katya goes in for the kill. To her rival's horror, she now confesses an entire list of imagined wrongs, "pranks which were as yet no more than schemes and projects for the future" (212). Her plans were to pin a visiting card on the old Princess's dress, to hide a pack of cards in her pocket, and to scatter bits of wool about the door. More darkly, the young Princess seeks additional false repentance for more destructive urges. She yearns to replace the woman's religious books with French novels; to break her spectacles; and, as the pièce de résistance, to hide Falstaff, her other enemy, under the bed.

Unsurprisingly, Katya drives the old aunt to the brink, from "red to white with rage" (212). In a burst of giggles, she adds insult to injury by abandoning the woman altogether. Although the young Princess is reprimanded by her mother for the ensuing ruckus—the old aunt threatens to quit the household and she forces Katya's mother to plead on her daughter's behalf and to punish the girl—the offender is not deterred in her quest for domestic dominance. In turn, the young Princess plots revenge against her aunt by entering into an alliance with Falstaff.

Katya's choice of Falstaff as her weapon of mass destruction is both seminal and strategic. With the arrival of the old aunt into the home, Falstaff has been kept on a tight leash. At her demand, the animal is not allowed in the upper floors of the house. He is also banished to a remote room whenever the old Princess wishes to grace the family with her presence. Falstaff's space and social position as an idol in the family are diminished in his eyes.

As rendered by Netochka, Falstaff seeks to annihilate the old aunt. Three times the dog has broken from his confinement and rushed to the woman's quarters. "Dreadfully insulted . . . [and] frantic with resentment" (213), he has even made for the old lady itself. So determined is Falstaff to end the woman's hegemony that members of the household must struggle to rescue her from the animal. His siege is a partial success. He so frightens the old woman that she screams every time she sees him, afraid he will devour her outright. Just as Falstaff is banished from certain regions of the house, so now does he seek to confine the old aunt to her apartments. Whenever Falstaff is "overcome by attacks of spleen" over his "irreconcilable enemy who . . . remained unpunished . . . for encroaching on his rights," he waits "craftily" (214) for an opportunity to attack his foe.

Falstaff is indeed a Dostoevskian creature. He is in no rush to exact revenge on the woman. Foreshadowing the Underground Man, he takes as much delight in plotting and waiting for his chance to strike as he does in shortening the old Princess's years. Like his fictional colleague, he is willing to lie in wait for as long as three days to fulfill his plans. Falstaff's fury at his domestic situation, which mirrors that of Underground Man, is unwarranted. Whatever his difficulties with both the young Princess and the old aunt, his position remains secure. More than once the old woman presents the family with the ultimatum that they choose between Falstaff and herself, but to no avail. Indeed, in a reflection of her addictive tie to Falstaff, Katya's mother refuses to part with the dog.

The smoldering enmity between Falstaff and the old aunt fuels the aroused Katya's need to reassume authority not only over Netochka but also over the household. The young Princess seizes the moment to strike terror in everyone's heart when, with the horrified Netochka in tow, she coaxes the animal up the stairs to the old aunt's quarters.

To Katya's dismay, however, Falstaff is too clever to fall for the ploy. Even as he, like Efimov, assumes the stance of a Caesar "prepared to leap across his Rubicon" (214), he shows only indifference to the girl. (Recall Efimov's appeal to Caesar in the first part of the work.) Like everyone else in *Netochka Nezvanova*, including the narrator herself, Falstaff is a master tactician. Even as the dog senses that Katya is about to open the door to the stairs, he puts his huge paws on the windowsill and gazes at the building across from him. The dog behaves as "disinterestedly as a man who has gone out for a walk and stops for a minute to admire the architecture of a neighboring edifice" (214).

Unlike Netochka, though, Falstaff does not need houses with red curtains to whet his appetite for fantasies and dreams. He is more than content to find satisfaction inside his home. Against Katya's enticements, though, Falstaff can maintain his defenses only momentarily. With his goal in sight, the dog can be as aroused erotically as anyone else in the work. If Netochka's soul pines in codependent obsession for Katya, so does Falstaff's "heart throb . . . in sweet expectation" (214) for similar possession of the old aunt.

Inner emotion moves to outer joy when by Katya, Falstaff is "beckoned, invited, and implored to go upstairs and to wreak his vengeance [on his foe] without delay" (214–215). In a highly singular moment in Dostoevsky, Falstaff moves from an entity of thought to one of action. In contrast to other personages in *Netochka Nezvanova*, Falstaff knows exactly what he wants and how to get it. Yelping and baring his teeth, he "shoots fiercely and triumphantly up the stairs" (215). So determined is the dog to get at the old aunt that "like an arrow . . . or a cannonball" (215), he overturns a chair, sending it flying into space. When Falstaff reaches the door to the woman's quarters, he is all but ready to dig a tunnel to his prize. "Scratching the portal ferociously," Falstaff howls "like a lost soul" (215).

The shrieks of both the old aunt and Madame Leotard thwart Falstaff's victory and bring about his final downfall in the household. The old aunt is not the only one who abhors the beast. Rather, akin to the way that Efimov's disciples turned on their erstwhile idol, an "entire legion of [Falstaff's] enemies" (215) muzzle his jaw, tie his paws in a noose, and drag him downstairs at the end of the rope. If Terras judges the scene as "very humorous . . . innocuous and tame,"[22] others take a different view. Whereas only moments before, Falstaff was seen as ruler of the roost, he is now "withdrawn ignominiously from the field of battle" (215).

SELF-SACRIFICE

Katya's mother knows that her daughter, fearful and pale, is responsible for what could have been the end of the old aunt. She does not call the young Princess to account, though. Rather, seeking a scapegoat, an "innocent person" (215) for the mayhem, she is willing to let Katya get away with murder. The woman's search comes to a speedy end when Netochka steps forward to take responsibility for the crime. "I let Falstaff in . . . by accident" (215), she tells the Princess.

Of course, like most self-sacrifice in Dostoevsky, Netochka's forfeiture has a fatal flaw. Jones's assertion that "Netochka takes the blame and accepts punishment for the misdeed so as to prove her affection for Katya" only begins to explain the motivation for her action.[23] Even more open to another view is Frank's claim that "Netochka's self-sacrifice, and Katya's response, already contain the emotive-experiential basis of Dostoevsky's Christianity."[24] The reality, rather, is that struggle, verticality, dominance—and codependence—continue unimpeded. To her perverse delight, Netochka "scores a victory" (215) on three counts. For one thing, she has vanquished Katya. Indeed, never before has Dostoevsky's heroine seen the young Princess in such a deflated state. Her face is downcast and pale, and her arms hang limply at her side. For another thing, Netochka claims even further triumph by suffering happily for her playmate. Banished to a remote room, she "[enters her] dungeon dizzy with joy" (215). Like all who sacrifice themselves in Dostoevsky, though, Netochka gets more than she bargained for. A set of circumstances—Madame Leotard visits her sick daughter; the maid thinks that Netochka has been released; Katya has been obliged to sit with her mother—results in the stipulated time of four hours becoming an "entire night in prison" (215). At four in the morning, Katya and others not only rescue Netochka from her plight, they also allow her to triumph again by gaining attention and sympathy. Awakened by others, Netochka reverts to time-honored and codependent patterns. "Flinging" (216) herself on Madame Leotard's neck, she weeps, shivers, and aches. The floor (physical and dramatic) is hers.

The calculated response is successful. For the first time in her narrative, Netochka emerges as the heroine for all to admire and applaud. Madame Leotard takes Netochka in her arms and begs her forgiveness. Katya raises a commotion and obtains Netochka's release. Even the Prince steps out of the shadows to express his ire and relief. Regarding the man's response, though, several points are important. The first is that the Prince appears to know a great deal about Netochka, such as the fact that she is "dreamy and imaginative" (216). How he knows such a thing, no one cares to say. The second point is that the Prince reacts violently to Netochka's incarceration, in a way that may be just but is nevertheless out of keeping with his overly quiet and reserved manner. His statement that Netochka's torment is "dreadful . . . barbarous . . . savage . . . [and] inhuman" (216) conveys a concern that goes beyond his understandable distress over the brouhaha involving the girl. Finally, with Madame Leotard, the Prince goes on the offensive. As he sees it, she is the problem, not the two girls. He attacks the woman for deferring to her "idol" (216): the great eighteenth-century writer-philosopher Jean-Jacques Rousseau. Rousseau is no authority on children, the Prince claims. What Katya's father has in mind is unclear. None of Rousseau's ideas on education and child-rearing find any resonance in the narrative. Nowhere in *Netochka Nezvanova* has there been a discussion or demonstration in reference to Rousseau's ideas that children are naturally good, that they seek reason for self-mastery and virtue, or that they learn morality from experiencing the consequences of their actions. Also absent from Netochka's narrative are Rousseau's claims about ideal men and women and about the moral superiority of the patriarchal family (particularly his idea that mothers bear the responsibility for their children). Indeed, what both the adult and child Netochka put forth in their collective life story could not be more antithetical to what Rousseau believed valid and necessary for familial ties. They, too, would agree that he is no authority on children.[25]

About Rousseau, though, the Prince makes one thing clear. In his view, the man did not practice what he preached, particularly in his personal and family life. Specifically, Rousseau is for the Prince an "evil man" in that he "renounced his own children" (216).[26] Although the Prince apologizes to Madame Leotard for his outburst, he does one more disturbing thing before he leaves the room. He first kisses Netochka "with great feeling" (217); then he makes the sign of the cross over her. Given everything readers of *Netochka Nezvanova* know and suspect rightfully about the man, both actions are open to question.

EROS UNBOUND

With Netochka finally in the good graces of the family and with Katya off the moral hook for her siege of the old Princess, both girls are left to their own devices to pursue physically what both have been wanting mentally: a consummation of their relationship addiction. Such an outcome is not surprising since the two, at long last, have achieved an emotional if perverse parity. They have met each other's challenges for power and control; they have exchanged positions of victor and victim so often that they stand mated in their addictive chess game. Jones's contention that the "affair between Netochka and Katya is full of pagan sensuality" only touches the surface of the addictive tie between the two girls.[27] Also, claims by Julius Meier-Graefe that the "struggle of the two children for one another ... has the melody of inimitable sweetness ... [and] the eroticism [and] simplicity of Greek pastoral poetry";[28] or by Frank that "the relation between Netochka and Katya is a paradigm for what Dostoevsky's greatest protagonists will later find so difficult to accomplish—the grateful surrender of pride to love and self-sacrifice"—fail to hold up under scrutiny.[29] An "extremely preoccupied" Katya sets up the liaison. "Quite flushed" and with a "laugh" (217) on her lips,[30] she makes for Netochka in a clinging way, grabbing the girl to suggest an assignation after dinner. It should be noted that, as in their earlier physical flirtations, both Netochka and Katya sense the moral quandary of their actions. To Netochka, Katya talks "hurriedly, as if ashamed of something" (217). When a servant walks past the girls, she turns away from her playmate quickly. Undeterred, though, the young Princess follows through with her plan.

The actual meeting between Netochka and Katya is rife with eroticism. "Profoundly disturbed ... [and] breathing heavily" (217), the young Princess first blushes, falls on the sofa, and buries her face in her hands.

Flushed and tearful, she then springs from her place and throws herself on Netochka's neck. Her arousal is so immediate and extreme that readers of *Netochka Nezvanova* wonder—rightfully—if somehow, somewhere, Katya has already known physical love. With no apparent shyness or innocence, the young Princess moves to consume Netochka in a way that recalls Falstaff's attempt to attack and devour the old aunt. From the moment Katya lunges at Netochka, her cheeks are moist; her curls are in disarray; and her lips are as "swollen as cherries" (217, 220).[31] With explosive violence, her heart races so quickly that Netochka can hear every beat. "Sobbing hysterically," Katya kisses Netochka "wildly [her] face, eyes, lips, necks and hands" (217). She finds a willing partner. Netochka is "overjoyed . . . [and] happier now than she has ever been in her life" (217). She returns the clinging, the two "embracing sweetly and joyfully . . . like two lovers after a long separation" (217). Being kissed by Katya "sweetly, silently, and fervently," she, too, "weeps for joy . . . [like] one resurrected from the dead" (217).[32]

The addictive eroticism between Netochka and Katya increases in intensity. Netochka, waiting for the next assignation, is so overwrought that she thinks her heart will burst. Indeed, she does not know how she will "survive" (217) the time apart from her mate. The young Princess is equally flurried, her heart also "beating so fast" (217) not only over Netochka but also over what is conceivably a second and heretofore undisclosed source: the servant girl Nastya, helping Katya to undress, kisses the girl's foot after removing her shoe. When Katya invites Netochka into her bed, the games begin anew, the two "embracing . . . crying and laughing at the same time" (216, 218). It would not be the early or mature Dostoevsky if he did not attend such physical trysts with philosophical confession and commentary on life and love. In between erotic bouts, Netochka and Katya discuss their tie with remarkable frankness and insight. To the chagrin of both, the two assert that in their initial time together, more occurred than met the eye. "Blushing pitifully" (208), the young Princess lays claim to mock confession. She admits to her sobbing playmate not only that she knew about Netochka's theft of her personal items, but also that she feigned sleep during the girl's physical advances. There also has been the problem of parity. Verticality is very much on the young Princess's mind when again recalling the image of the doppelgänger that plagued the addictive tie between Efimov and the musician B., as well as between Katya and Netochka early in their relationship. The young Princess confesses that she often cannot bear her playmate because Netochka is everything she is not. Confusion, embarrassment, guilt, and emotional distance take periodic hold of the young Princess because Netochka—"nice . . . meek . . . mild . . . [and] very clever"—sees her as "silly" (219). Even worse, perhaps, is Katya's codependent fear that love is an entity in short supply and that she has "hated and loathed" (218) Netochka because, in her view, the Prince has chosen her playmate over her. Katya, though, does not discuss her father further. Instead she frays already tangled narrative threads. The young Princess insists that the Prince is kind and good, but she does not specify in what way. She claims that she loves her father more than anyone in the world, but that Netochka also holds primacy in her heart. Then, too, there is this cryptic comment: "But what am I to do with him?" Katya asks aloud about the Prince, "He is always so . . . well . . ." (109). Like Netochka with Efimov, Katya raises more questions than answers, perhaps finding discretion the better part of valor.

Katya also acknowledges that like Netochka she, too, is a master of codependency games. At times, she engages in a cat-and-mouse with Netochka: "I looked at you and thought, 'What a sweet little thing she is. I will go and tie her shoelace and see what happens. . . .' I really wanted to kiss you" (219). At other times, Katya plays truth-or-dare and king of the mountain. Regarding her run-in with Falstaff, the young Princess confesses to Netochka that although she was terrified of the "monster" (219), she risked life and limb to gain parity with her playmate. "I knew you were watching me," she confesses, "but come what may, I had to do it. I scared you, didn't I? Weren't you afraid for me?" (219). Katya admits that, in Netochka, she has found a partner worthy of codependent contests. "It was not just that you were taking the blame that made me so happy," she tells the girl, "It was that you were ready to be punished for me. I thought: 'I expect she is crying now, but how I love her!'" (219).

Whatever the difficulties, though, and in sync with the ups and downs and back and forth that mark the addictive ties linking Efimov, Netochka's mother, the musician B., and other characters in *Netochka Nezvanova*, Katya holds fast to Netochka. "Kissing and kissing" the (codependent) object of her affection, she professes to love her playmate "terribly" (218). Fearing abandonment—"Don't leave me, Netochka," she says—the young Princess also tells her playmate that she "cannot live without her" (219). On the brink of mental and physical obsession, Katya dreams about Netochka "day and night"; she, too, wants to "move in . . . and sleep" (219) with her playmate in her room. Whatever "fear and shame" (219) the young Princess experienced earlier in their tie now vanish in a new conviction: "How lovely it is now" (219), she pronounces. Like other codependencies in *Netochka Nezvanova*, such good feeling is not without cruelty, even sadism. When Katya is not pinching Dostoevsky's heroine, she wishes to "squeeze [her] to death" (219). As is the case with Netochka, love for the young Princess is not an art, a belief, or a skill. Rather, love is codependency: a clinging and clutching that constricts genuine emotion and contact.

Netochka accepts Katya's mock mea culpas at face value and not only forgives her playmate for her transgressions, past and present, but also resumes her secondary position in the relationship. Aroused by the young Princess's "nervous giggles, feverish face, intent gazes... showering kisses... and tears that quiver like little gems on her long lashes," Netochka cares little that she is called "little orphan... stupid crybaby... [and] a pale, little thing" (220, 221). "Overcome with joy... [and] her heart breaking," she embraces Katya again, clinging to her "for three long minutes in silence" (219).

PARADISE LOST

If Dostoevsky's characters seek happiness in multiple spaces and times, Netochka and Katya are no exception. Evoking Netochka and Efimov in their hoped-for paradise, the two girls now seek to extend their Eden into the future. Together in bed, Netochka and Katya seek to settle "everything between them for the next twenty years" (220). Like all utopias in Dostoevsky in general, and particularly in *Netochka Nezvanova*, the ill-fated house with red curtains of the past and the equally problematic abode of the present—the mythic garden that Netochka and Katya bring into being—have serious shortcomings. For one thing, the two are notoriously vague about what, exactly, they need to resolve. For another thing, the one issue that Netochka and Katya agree upon underscores the codependent weaknesses not only of their relationship, but also of their ties between and among everyone else in the work.

Katya puts forth the plan for how the girls should live. As previously, the key issues are power and verticality, but with a new twist. In a plan that would do Ivan Karamazov proud, the young Princess proposes to advance the two concepts in a shared and scientific way. Her idea is that they will issue commands to each other, trading off every day, and those orders must be "obeyed unquestioningly" (221). Katya even includes a provision for forgiveness and peace. In her idea, the two girls must first argue for the sake of appearance, but then reconcile quickly. Such naïveté aside, Netochka and Katya are Dostoevsky's first social engineers, his architects for "eternal happiness" (221).

It is also revealing to note that when Netochka and Katya actually seek to realize their utopia in life, they only exacerbate their problems with existence in four ways. For one thing, they accentuate the idle purposelessness of their time on earth. The two are so "happy... [that] they hardly know what to do with themselves" (221). Another aspect of their difficulties is that Netochka and Katya are so obsessed with each other that they build borders, or barricades, against everyone else. "We kept hiding and running away from everyone," Netochka confesses to her readers. "Above all, we always avoided meeting anyone face to face" (221). Also, in their addictive love for each other, Netochka and Katya regress physically and mentally. Moved to tell her past to Katya, Netochka poses as a victim with such dramatic aplomb that she not only imbues the young Princess with pity-filled shock and tears but, recalling her time with Efimov, also casts her as her new defender. "Why didn't you tell me all this before?" the young Princess responds. "I would have been so kind to you. I would have loved you so much!" (221). She would have dealt with the boy who mistreated Netochka on the street by giving him a "sound beating" (221). An absence of air is readily apparent. Katya "almost stifles [her playmate] with her kisses" (216). That the two "must have kissed each other a hundred times" makes Netochka so "breathless from happiness . . . [that she will die] from joy" (221).

The eternal happiness that Netochka and Katya believe they have fashioned for themselves encounters a more immediate obstacle: Madame Leotard has been observing the two with increasing dismay. In accurate, if chilling detail, she reports to the Princess that, when together, Netochka and Katya are in a "state of frenzy" (221). They chatter incessantly, they kiss continually, they cry "like lunatics" (221). Although the governess is at a loss as to the reasons for such behavior, she draws upon her previous experience with Katya to assert that her charge is undergoing a "nervous crisis" (221). She also recommends that Netochka and the young Princess see less of each other. The Princess agrees readily. Jealous of the tie between the two girls, the woman again deems Netochka to be the root of all evil in the household. Dostoevsky's heroine is hardly innocent, but her unjust vilification by the Princess again raises suspicions of something untoward in the family. Katya's mother denies Netochka agency and choice; she casts the girl's shortcomings as genetic and environmental. "I knew that that peculiar little orphan would give us trouble" (222), the Princess claims. After all, the woman reasons falsely, Netochka's "breeding, habits, and morals" (222) are the legacy of her mother. "The things they told us about her, her background," the Princess continues, "Awful! Really awful!" (222). Once again, precisely who has said what about Netochka, or why such things should rear their heads at the end of the story and not the beginning, is anyone's guess. Equally telling is the fact that the Princess clears Katya of all complicity in the affair. She blames Netochka's "unnatural" influence exclusively for causing her daughter "to love" (222) the girl. As she sees it, there is no need for Katya to confess.

Although in a sudden turnaround Madame Leotard—and interestingly, also the Prince—defends Netochka, the two cannot stop the Princess's decision to separate the girls. The ruling, however, does little to impede or end the tie between the youngsters, since, peculiarly, the Princess insists that Netochka and Katya be parted only for a week! Even so, it is a measure of the escalated tie between the two girls that they receive the modest restriction in an extreme and typically codependent way. Over the news of the weeklong separation, Netochka becomes almost deathlike. She moves from being "aghast . . . [to] falling ill . . . [to] being overcome with sorrow and grief . . . [to] falling to a state of despair and misery . . . [and to] finding it difficult to breathe" (222). Similarly affected, Katya sustains the relationship with secret notes to her playmate. Like a fictional lover-in-hiding, she demands: "Write and tell me how much you love me" (222). The young Princess also refuses to submit to any restrictions concerning her playmate. "Embracing [Netochka] all night in dreams," she again promises sweets and new time together. "I keep thinking of escaping and reaching you," Katya writes to her playmate. "I will escape" (222).

Netochka and Katya do not suffer for long. After only three days, they are rescued from their plight by Madame Leotard and the Prince, who endeavor to rejoin them (even as they sense, however obliquely, the destructive nature of the tie between the two girls). Madame Leotard, seeing that Katya is "dreadfully pale" and Netochka is "certain to fall ill a third time" (222), demands that the youngsters be reunited. The Prince actually arranges a secret meeting between the two.

In Dickens such a happy reunion might have been portrayed as a stroke of good fortune or the result of a kind act; Dostoevsky's world is not so benevolent. "Panting" (222), Netochka races to her rendezvous. There she is grabbed from behind by Katya, who kisses her passionately. Amidst the laughter, tears, and the two girls "rushing into each other's arms" (223), stands the Prince, who does not impede the goings-on. The Prince's actions are even more disturbing when he joins in with the girls in their aberrant behavior. Whereas throughout the second part of *Netochka Nezvanova*, the Prince has been austere and aloof, he now engages in rough-and-tumble. On his knees and shoulders, Katya climbs like a "squirrel" before, "crying with delight," she crashes to the sofa with her father "falling down behind her" (222). Readers of *Netochka Nezvanova* are right to raise their eyebrows further when the Prince queries Netochka and Katya: "You little imps! What has happened to you both? What kind of friendship is this? What kind of love is this?" (223). He is dismissed summarily by Katya, who replies: "Be quiet, Papa. You don't understand our affairs" (223). Even more disturbing, perhaps, is that the Prince, "moved by the sight" (223) of the two girls reunited, promises that from now on, all three of them will meet every day.

The Prince's plans do not come to be, though, courtesy of a sudden and unmotivated event: news that Katya's (still absent and unnamed) brother has fallen seriously ill in Moscow (why is he in Moscow?) brings about the departure of the young Princess and her mother. (Interestingly, Netochka declines to say whether the Prince joins the two.)

Once again, the Prince is the one who arranges the final encounter of the two girls, who, predictably, are out of their minds and beside themselves with grief. Netochka, learning of the break-up only at the moment of parting, rushes to embrace Katya, "hardly aware of what [she] is doing" (223). In turn, the young Princess screams and faints, after which her playmate, in a replay of an earlier scene, kisses her allegedly unconscious body. When Katya comes to her senses, she moves to the ultimate codependent send-off. With the "strangest expression on her face," she whispers to Netochka "my life" as she "squeezes [the girl] convulsively in her arms" (223). With a final kiss, the young Princess disappears from Netochka's life.

It is interesting to note that when Netochka ends her story of Katya, she does not follow the same path she did with Efimov. She does not, lawyer-like, indict the young Princess for her failings or for the problems in the relationship. She also shows no regrets or remorse for their time together. Instead, without the slightest pretense of engaging in confession (whether true or false), she flaunts her addictive tie to Katya as she tells her readers that she has related the story "on purpose" (223). With the young Princess, she has had "pleasure" and closeness—so much so that their "stories are inseparable... [Katya's] romance also being [her] romance" (223). Even fate, the refuge of last resort that she, Efimov, and other personages in *Netochka Nezvanova* appeal to for their sins of omission and commission, is seen as enabling the union. "It seems that I was destined to meet Katya," Netochka tells her readers, "and she was destined to meet me" (223).

Clearly, for all that Netochka has learned from her association with Katya, she still has a great deal to ponder and resolve about her time with the young Princess. Like Efimov, the girl continues to loom large in her life and love.

CHAPTER FOUR

ALL IN THE CODEPENDENT FAMILY (III)
Netochka and Alexandra Mikhailovna

ALEXANDRA MIKHAILOVNA

Netochka's move into the third and last stage of her narrative features many of the same codependence-inspired lacunae and inconsistencies as the earlier parts of her tale. She does not explain why Katya and her mother postpone their return from Moscow indefinitely. She does not inform her readers as to fate of the problematic Prince. Did the man accompany his family to Moscow or remain in Petersburg? If the Prince accompanied the family to Moscow, then why, and with what thoughts and actions toward Katya? If he stayed, then why, and with what thoughts and actions toward Netochka? Netochka is also mum about the fate of Madame Leotard. For reasons unknown, the woman does not accompany Katya and her mother to Moscow, nor does she attend to Netochka in St. Petersburg. Like a stone, she, too, drops from the narrative. Netochka plays fast and loose with time and space in the last part of her story. After a "period of tranquility," which she compares to a deep sleep, she "wakes up again" (223) at age seventeen in the home of Alexandra Mikhailovna, Katya's older sister! The fast forward soon derails, though, when reports at various times from her third abode come from a purportedly younger Netochka. Additionally, Netochka as narrator extends to the final part of her tale the same biographical haze that surrounds the characters in the first two parts. Nothing is known about Alexandra Mikhailovna other than that she is the Princess's daughter by her first husband, "a mere leaseholder" (224). Netochka declines to give any information about the duration and quality of the marriage, the fate of the man, or the circumstances of the second union to the Prince. Netochka does not comment on the tie between Alexandra Mikhailovna and her stepfather.

Despite the lack of information, Alexandra Mikhailovna emerges as a new codependent type in Netochka's narrative. If previous characters in the girl's story relish immediate struggle and control, the twenty-two-year-old Alexandra Mikhailovna is rendered initially as such an epitome of perfection that she seems not to be of this world. She is not "externally glamorous," as Terras asserts.[1] Indeed, nowhere in Dostoevsky (early or mature) does a character approach the ideal that Netochka assigns to the woman. Reminiscent of visual representations of the Mother of God, and almost twenty years before the ideal image of Raphael's *The Sistine Madonna* captured Dostoevsky's imagination in *Crime and Punishment*,[2] Alexandra Mikhailovna has a face that is "angelic . . . child-like . . . [and] serene"; a smile that is "shining . . . placid and bright"; and eyes that are "bright . . . good . . . blue as the heavens . . . [and] childishly clear" (224, 225, 229).

In Netochka's initial portrait, Alexandra Mikhailovna seems to be at peace internally. An "air of freedom" wafts from a life that is "rosy . . . quiet and apparently calm," so much so that it would be "hard to imagine that any worries could trouble [the woman's] noble being" (225). Netochka extends the inner equipoise of Alexandra Mikhailovna to her outside world. It is unthinkable, she writes, that the woman could dislike anyone, since compassion was "always uppermost in her heart" (225).

The feeling is mutual. Netochka finds herself drawn hopefully, hopelessly, to Alexandra Mikhailovna, even more than she had been initially to Katya. Captivated by so much love and warmth, by "so much profound sympathy for all that was noble," Dostoevsky's heroine "surrenders [her] soul entirely" (229) to the woman. In fact, her enthusiasm for Alexandra Mikhailovna is such that in Netochka's perception Katya's sister merges with the vault of heaven. Gazing upon Alexandra Mikhailovna, she asserts, is like "[looking] at the blue sky . . . [at] the lofty cupola of the heavens" and spending "entire hours in secret contemplation . . . to bring freedom and tranquility to the soul" (229).

From Netochka's perspective, Alexandra Mikhailovna undergoes deific transfiguration. Periodically—the circumstances are typically unclear—Alexandra Mikhailovna attains near-mythic status. Color rushes into her cheeks; her eyes flash like lightning, "giving off sparks" (229). If earlier a "pure flame of beauty" guarded Alexandra Mikhailovna's being, it now "illuminates her, passing through eyes" (229). As such, Dostoevsky's heroine concludes, Alexandra Mikhailovna is what every philosopher and artist searches and sacrifices for in the name of beauty and truth. Any painter, she notes, "would give half his life to portray . . . that inspired face on canvas" (229).

As with other deities in *Netochka Nezvanova* (if not throughout Dostoevsky's entire corpus), Alexandra Mikhailovna is not at peace. Duality marks her being. On one level, the distress is physical. Jackson's comment that

Alexandra Mikhailovna "provides rich formulation of Dostoevsky's early ideal of feminine beauty" appears to ignore details of her appearance:[3] her frail body is "prone to tuberculosis" (224), and her thin, pale face creates a "sharp, severe outline" (229) against thick, black hair.[4] The woman's eyes are particularly bivalent. When not happy and calm, they are "heart-piercing . . . defenseless . . . [and] fearful of every sensation and outburst of emotion, of every momentary joy and frequently quiet sorrow" (229). On another level, the pain of Alexandra Mikhailovna is social. Like her new ward she, too, has been subject to people and events beyond her control. Because Alexandra Mikhailovna had a "modest" dowry and "little hope of a brilliant match" (224), the Princess and others (identified only as "they") married her off to the highest bidder, a well-to-do man.

As was also the situation with Netochka, Alexandra Mikhailovna's move from rags to riches has not been happy. She, too, has been very much on her own, physically and mentally. She, too, is ill at ease with her new world and society. She, too, finds her family fading rapidly from view. The Princess, "not knowing what to do with her elder daughter" (224), visits her only twice a year. In fact, the mother so resists bringing her two daughters together that the Prince again arranges secret meetings, this time for an "adoring" (24) Katya and her sister. Questions abound. The reasons for the Princess's opposition to the visits remain undisclosed, as does the nature of the tie between the two half sisters. (Has their mutual adoration become problematic?) Readers also remain in the dark about the content and form of these encounters and might well wonder why the meetings, which take place weekly, occupy no space in Netochka's story.[5] Like the old aunt in the second part of *Netochka Nezvanova*, Alexandra Mikhailovna, too, lives "a very reclusive, almost monastic existence" (224, 225).

Such isolation informs the entire household. Netochka's comment that in her new residence, more than eight years passed without a single undisturbed month does not mean that for the first time in her life the now almost eighteen-year-old girl has found domestic tranquility and peace. Rather, what she encounters is a third bout of *déjà vu*, a seemingly cursed fate to live in tomb- and fortress-like surroundings. With the exception of rare and unexplained visits by the musician B., Netochka writes, no one comes to the house. But there is one difference in the new living arrangement.

Whereas the boundaries of Netochka's first two homes brought restlessness and disquiet to its female occupants, the borders of Alexandra Mikhailovna's home gladden her for the "complete isolation . . . [and] seclusion" (225).

Alexandra Mikhailovna would not be a character in Dostoevsky if she did not harbor a self-consuming secret. Still waters run deep—and dark.

An unidentified someone or something casts an "austere shadow over her beautiful features"; fills her with "secret sorrow . . . and hidden heartache"; and startles her as "painful, dreadful, and inevitable" (227). Like other personages in *Netochka Nezvanova*, though, Alexandra Mikhailovna keeps her borders intact. "Guarding her heart constantly," the woman does not "forget herself, even in dreams" (225).

Like Netochka and her fictional colleagues, however, Alexandra Mikhailovna can be equanimous only for so long. She, too, embodies self-negating contradictions. "The happier [Alexandra Mikhailovna] is, the calmer and more tranquil her life," Netochka writes, "the closer she moves to depression . . . [and] nervous collapse" (225). Even as the woman tells her new ward that she is quite content, she dissolves into tears and experiences "a terrible and prolonged melancholy" (227).

Alexandra Mikhailovna is exemplar of codependence, not the paragon of stability and beauty that Terras and Frank claim her to be.[6] Her attempt to become Netochka's third mother is portrayed in the narrative almost as an act of desperation. Kissing and embracing the girl warmly, Alexandra Mikhailovna invites her new ward to "live with her as her daughter" (224). For the third time in the novel, Netochka treads lightly, remembering previous painful ties, rather than rushing to begin a new connection. Her boundaries secure, Dostoevsky's heroine responds to Alexandra Mikhailovna with the self-insulating pose of a "little orphan . . . [with] a throbbing chest . . . and a dull pain in [her] heart" (224). Further, the fact that her new benefactress has received letters from both the Prince and Katya rakes raw old wounds. Netochka "stifles her sobs" (224) at the Prince's wishes for her happiness. She is surprisingly stoic, though, when Katya, in a few (unspecified) lines, writes that she is now needed by the Princess and will never see her playmate again. Doors in life do not close, Dostoevsky's heroine realizes sadly; rather, they slam shut with erstwhile family and friends bolting the locks. Once again, Netochka writes, "I had to tear myself from all that had grown dear to me and to which I felt I belonged" (224). With Alexandra Mikhailovna, moreover, Dostoevsky's heroine lives her first days in much the same way she did with Efimov and the Prince: "completely exhausted and racked with mental suffering" (224). Much as the girl believes that for her "a new story begins" (224), readers of *Netochka Nezvanova* are right to suspect that the sorrow of the third part of her narrative will draw from the angst of codependent addiction in her first and second ones.[7]

Notwithstanding Netochka's reticence, Alexandra Mikhailovna rushes to possess the girl. Indeed, the urge is self-consuming. So delighted is

Alexandra Mikhailovna to welcome Netochka into her solitary existence, so comforting does she find the girl's presence, that the woman quickly "devotes her whole heart [to her ward], loving [the girl] as if [she] were her own daughter" (225). Netochka's remark, though, that Alexandra Mikhailovna does not distinguish between the girl and her own offspring must be taken *cum granis salis*. For one thing, recalling the mysterious brother in the second part of *Netochka Nezvanova*, readers cannot know with certainty whether Alexandra Mikhailovna has one child or "children" (229). No specific references to the names, ages, or number of children appear in the narrative, but the one child that does appear in the section attracts very little attention from either Alexandra Mikhailovna or Netochka. Every morning, the two "wake [the child], wash him, dress him, play with him, and teach him to talk" (230–231). After that they do what all parents do in *Netochka Nezvanova*: they leave the child to his (or her?) own devices.

The emotional siege that Alexandra Mikhailovna lays to Netochka is too irresistibly addictive for the girl to refuse. "With an aching heart and eyes still moist from parting with Katya," Netochka throws her earlier caution to the winds and resumes clutching and clinging. "Eagerly [she] throws herself . . . into [Alexandra Mikhailovna's] maternal embrace" (225). It is also a symptom of the sudden and skewed bond between Alexandra Mikhailovna and Netochka that neither desires anything or anyone beyond the other. Netochka's "warm love" for her new friend "never knows interruption" (229). For the tortured girl, what is not to like? Alexandra Mikhailovna fulfills a wealth of needs: the woman is not only a "mother . . . [but also] a friend . . . a sister . . . and a benefactress" (225). A red-curtained house come to life, Alexandra Mikhailovna "replaces [Netochka's] entire world" (225).

LESSONS IN CODEPENDENCE

Initially, the codependent relationship between Netochka and Alexandra Mikhailovna focuses on education. As was the situation with Efimov, Netochka is again the student of a teacher who has more than a professional interest in her. The lessons are also less than successful. Mother-like, Alexandra Mikhailovna sets about the girl's studies with such fervor and haste as to ensure disaster. Even simple communication goes awry. "We tried to do everything so precipitately," Netochka recalls, "that we could not understand each other" (230). Further, having failed to learn from her initial failures in instruction, Alexandra Mikhailovna does what every would-be frustrated teacher in Dostoevsky does: she exerts even more zeal, fervor, and devoted patience, but to no avail. Matters become even worse when Alexandra Mikhailovna declares herself to be opposed to any education whatsoever and expresses confidence that she and Netochka will "somehow find the correct method [for learning] as [they] go along" (230).[8]

Needless to say, the instruction is "strange" (231) for several reasons. Heralding the disasters of teachers and students in Dostoevsky's later works (the lessons between the bumbling Stepan Verkhovensky and Stavrogin in *Devils* is a key example), the nurturing is not grounded, rational, or timely; rather, it is grandiose, fevered, and eternal.[9] Alexandra Mikhailovna makes no attempt at training Netochka's mind in a rigorous way. Instead she aims for a vague, if fevered arousal of the soul. Her lessons lack logic, focus, or what she dismisses as "pointless... [and] dry information" (230) with which to negotiate life. As Andrew points out rightly, with education and reading Netochka enters into a "symbolic order,"[10] but the signs she learns are harmful and false. "There was everything in these studies, but nothing precise," Netochka recalls of her lessons with her benefactress. The two engage in "most fervid, passionate conversations" (231). Well past night, they embrace "art... reality, ideals, the past, the future" (231).

Unsurprisingly, teacher does student more harm than good. Recalling her readings with Efimov (and in contrast to the models of education in Russian gentry fiction), Netochka "shares [Alexandra Mikhailovna's] enthusiasm" (231). She "listens as hard as she can" and "laughs and is moved" (231) by materials, but she understands nothing. Dostoevsky's heroine also rebels against the more conventional, if rigorous teachers whom, however inconsistently, Alexandra Mikhailovna hires for specific courses of study. Given Netochka's faux sense of time and space, it is no surprise that she finds lessons in geography and history particularly irritating. With geography, the would-be student complains of "simply going blind" (231)—the adjective says it all—in searches on maps. She also bristles at self-styled verticality, or what she sees as her instructor's "maintained superiority in the precise knowledge of the latitude and longitude of any city, as well as its exact population in thousands, hundreds, and tens" (231). How much more fun, Dostoevsky's heroine asserts, is geography with Alexandra Mikhailovna. Facts and figures, after all, are the last things on their minds. Rather, arm in arm, the two "set off on such voyages, visit such countries, see so many marvelous sights, and experience so many magical and fantastic hours!" (231). How unfortunate the teacher of the subject, Netochka also laments, that he does not join them in their psychic trips, that he does not know as much about the world as they do about history. Netochka and Alexandra Mikhailovna also tackle times gone by "in [their own] way" (231). The two become so "absorbed . . . enthusiastic . . . [and] excited" over the materials that they read "more between the lines than is there" (231). They even begin to blur the lines between fiction and reality, as Netochka appears to do when she asserts that "all Netochka read about has actually happened to her" (231). The lessons between Netochka and Alexandra Mikhailovna reach a nadir, though, when the two turn to fiction. For once in *Netochka Nezvanova*, Dostoevsky's heroine tells her readers the title of a work under study. The choice is hardly surprising. Given their penchant for castles, maidens, and knights, Netochka and Alexandra Mikhailovna read Walter Scott's 1820 novel *Ivanhoe*, a swashbuckling tale of knightly life and love in twelfth-century England, "at least three times" (236).[11]

Like every codependent relationship in *Netochka Nezvanova*, the exchanges between benefactress and ward soon devolve into contests for dominance and control. Although Dostoevsky's heroine asserts that "from the beginning, the usual pupil-teacher relationship vanished entirely . . . [and the two] studied like friends" (231), this is clearly untrue. In her teaching, Alexandra Mikhailovna believes that she scores a "complete victory" (231) over Netochka. Her pupil, though (as she tells it), is more than up to the challenge. After making such "tremendous progress" in her studies that she can call her every observation "true" and her every impression "correct" (236), she gains increasing confidence and "vehemence" in her convictions . Unabashedly, the girl notes, "sometimes it seems as if [I am] teaching Alexandra Mikhailovna," and the poor woman does not "notice the crafty shift" (230) in power between the two. *Quod est demonstratum*. In Dostoevsky as well as in life, a little knowledge is indeed a dangerous thing.

The codependency between teacher and student is such that, as was true of the spats between Netochka and Katya, the two flirt as much as they fight. Possessively, Dostoevsky's heroine again "throws her arms around [Alexandra Mikhailovna's] neck and hugs her" (230). With her instructor, she "feels as lighthearted and happy as if she has had no misfortune in life" (230); under the influence of this god-like benefactress "everything . . . in [her] soul . . . is smoothed out and brought into harmony" (230). Recalling the addictive highs between Efimov and Netochka, the heroine expresses gratitude to Alexandra Mikhailovna "for making [her] love [the woman] more and more each day" (230).

As with every addictive relationship in *Netochka Nezvanova*, it is only a matter of time before Netochka and Alexandra Mikhailovna become attracted to each other physically. When reading, the two "grow [so] excited . . . [that] all constraints [between them] vanish" (236). They "speak freely—sometimes too freely" with the result that they are "ill at ease afterward" (236). Mercifully, though, Netochka and Alexandra Mikhailovna set limits to their behavior—they "limit the intimacy ... [to borders] beyond which they dare not go" (236).[12]

One such boundary is music. Just as a violin was the medium for sexual exploration in the first part of Netochka's narrative, so does a piano provide a similar venue in the last. When at the piano Alexandra Mikhailovna improvises on a theme from an Italian opera, she unwittingly sets the scene for an implicit tryst. A few played bars is all it takes not only to "captivate and arouse" Netochka, but also to spur her to make overtures to Alexandra Mikhailovna that the latter "has been expecting" (237). Dostoevsky's heroine is moved to sing, something she has never done before. Accompanied by Alexandra Mikhailovna, who "follows every note in a sensitive way," the two "become inspired" (237). Nature takes its course. Netochka is "stirred to greater energy and passion" (232). "Her voice rises" courtesy of Alexandra Mikhailovna's "delighted wonder ... [a feeling] she perceives in every touch of [the woman's] accompaniment" (237). In the climactic moment, Dostoevsky's heroine ends her song with "such spirit and power" that Alexandra Mikhailovna "seizes her hand in delight and gazes at her joyfully" (235). The woman is so "stunned by the unexpected event" that she lies in a "state of ecstatic happiness" (237). The time at the piano, Netochka asserts, has been for both a "moment of revelation, empathy, and closeness" (237).

Even more problematic, perhaps, after the encounter at the piano, Netochka's alleged talent is called into question by people and events. Like Efimov, Dostoevsky's heroine is not the genius she and others claim her to be, and as in Efimov's case, musician B. plays a central role in creating confusion about her talent, even though by this time he lacks all credibility. The now "old man" insists that "undoubtedly, [Dostoevsky's heroine] has a voice, possibly even talent"; but he does so "gravely, anxiously, and perhaps even a little mysteriously" (237). Further, B. joins with the now also backtracking Alexandra Mikhailovna to assert that "on second thought ... it is too risky to praise [Netochka] too much at the beginning" (237). Recalling how Netochka and Efimov ridiculed the dancing of Karl Fyodorovich, the musician B. and Alexandra Mikhailovna "go out of their way to point out the defects" (238) in Netochka's performance. Also problematic is the girl's stance toward the two. On one hand, their about-face triggers in Dostoevsky's heroine new paranoia. Seeing that B. and Alexandra Mikhailovna "exchange glances and plot on the sly," Netochka senses an "entire conspiracy" (237) against her. On the other hand, the girl is so fazed by their response that she "laughs for the rest of the evening" (238).

Further shades of Efimov, Netochka waxes eloquent about an imagined "artistic life" (249) and her superiority over everyone she meets. Like her stepfather, she disdains people outside her home as "trivial . . . petty . . . everyday . . . frustrated and busy"; living in "huge buildings crowded from top to bottom" and having "nothing whatsoever to do with art" (249). Again like Efimov, she refuses to study. Formal training is not for her. She scorns her current instructor D., the best and most famous teacher of voice in the city, as "a queer fellow . . . pedantic and mean . . . [the source of] laughter . . . [and] entertainment" (249). (Like B. and Alexandra Mikhailovna, the man is nonchalant about her musical gifts.) Mirroring her stepfather further, Netochka claims that her talents are "only two steps away" (249). Such giftedness, she also asserts, leads her to "a passionate and diffident hope . . . to dream happily . . . transported by fantasies . . . [of] a marvelous future . . . and castles in the air" (249). Unsurprisingly, Netochka does not continue her lessons for long. When Terras, Frank, Fridlender, Grossman, and other critics of Netochka Nezvanova accord to Dostoevsky's heroine the same giftedness they see in Efimov, they overlook her shortcomings as a singer.[13]

PORTRAIT OF A CODEPENDENT MARRIAGE

As with all addictive ties in *Netochka Nezvanova*, two is company, but three is a crowd. This time the odd man out is Alexandra Mikhailovna's husband, Pyotr Alexandrovich. This husband differs from the hapless Efimov in the first part and the shadowy Prince in the second in that he makes his mark in life. People "show a special liking for him"; he has "luck and good fortune everywhere" (225). He joins the ranks of other professionally successful males in Dostoevsky who are angels in the street but devils in the home. Seen (on one end) by Konstantin Mochulsky as "meriting a place among the ranks of Dostoevsky's most terrifying, demonic heroes"[14] and (on the other end) by Frank as being "in line with the self-complacent, self-assured Russian bureaucrats whose greatest incarnation is the knuckle-cracking husband Alexei Karenin in Tolstoy's *Anna Karenina*,"[15] Pyotr Alexandrovich impresses Netochka as someone who occupies a middle ground—an individual without body and soul. (Revealingly, his name and patronymic never come up until late in the story). Tall and slim, taciturn and cold, Pyotr Alexandrovich conceals his face behind large green spectacles: the snake in the Eden of codependency. On the rare occasions when he is home, Pyotr Alexandrovich is like the Prince in that he, too, opts for a hermit-like existence.

Not surprisingly, and more cruelly than Efimov in the case of Netochka's mother, Pyotr Alexandrovich restricts Alexandra Mikhailovna physically and psychically. Nowhere does he allow the woman equality, independence, or growth. Rather, Pyotr Alexandrovich treats Alexandra Mikhailovna as a "child" (227) to be seen, but not heard; to speak only when spoken to. More so than at any other time in *Netochka Nezvanova*, codependent oppressor and oppressed is the order of the day. For his wife, Pyotr Alexandrovich has only stares and smiles of pity and contempt. He also makes the most of the secret eating away at them. What Alexandra Mikhailovna has done and what Pyotr Alexandrovich suspects (or knows) remain unclear. Still, the husband delights in making his wife suffer and squirm. When Alexandra Mikhailovna becomes silent and pale, Pyotr Alexandrovich does not inquire why. Rather, relishing the "awkward and depressing moments . . . that go on forever" (227), he exacerbates his wife's shame and guilt. First, he rises from his chair and walks back and forth; then, heaving a deep sigh, he mutters a few abrupt words. Finally, for the coup de grace, he takes his leave of the woman but not before making the sign of the cross over her "as if she were a child" (227), and a sinful one at that!

Quite successfully, Pyotr Alexandrovich keeps his wife on and off her guard. It is the daily regimen of Alexandra Mikhailovna to "persuade herself that [Pyotr Alexandrovich] is pleased with her, and that she has no cause for anxiety" (226). So "intimidated" is the woman by the man, though, that Alexandra Mikhailovna does not "dare initiate a conversation" with her spouse; rather, she listens "timidly . . . and self-consciously as if she were his slave" (227). Her only responses to her mate are to turn pale when Pyotr Alexandrovich is "stern and depressed" (226) and to blush when he talks with an edge. Even worse, perhaps, are the rare instances when husband actually addresses wife. Conversation is never conversation between Alexandra Mikhailovna and Pyotr Alexandrovich; rather, text cedes to subtext as the woman "weighs each word . . . [and] searches for other meanings" (227) in whatever her spouse has told her. She even has Netochka to parse out hidden messages and meanings. "Had she heard Pyotr Alexandrovich correctly?" the woman often asks the girl. "Was this what [her husband] meant?" (226).

As a codependent, Alexandra Mikhailovna kisses the hand that chokes her. She does not protest the abuse; rather, she asks for more. Without a doubt, the marriage between Alexandra Mikhailovna and Pyotr Alexandrovich is the apex of the addiction narrative in *Netochka Nezvanova*, if not in all of Dostoevsky's writing. Mochulsky's claim that wife loves husband "passionately" does not even begin to describe the tie between the couple.[16] As Netochka sees it, Alexandra Mikhailovna shows "too much fondness" (227) for Pyotr Alexandrovich. She cannot live without the man "for a single moment" (226). "From the depths of her heart," it is the wife's "wish to find a way to please [her husband] . . . [and to show] exceptional devotion . . . to his every need... word... and gesture" (226). Even with "no hope for success," Netochka notes, Alexandra Mikhailovna "begs for Pyotr Alexandrovich's approval" (207). She craves "the slightest smile on his face"; she hopes for the "least word of tenderness"; she receives his blessing with "reverence and gratitude" (207).

It is even more indicative of the addictive behavior between Alexandra Mikhailovna and Pyotr Alexandrovich that the slightest nod from the man triggers the "exact moment... [that begins] a completely timorous and hopeless love" (226) for him. When Pyotr Alexandrovich gives his mate a "disdainful squeeze"; when he notes "something in her... anything at all"; when he "takes it into his head to fondle one of their two small children" (one child or more?)—such moments "change [the woman] completely... [and make her] proud... instantly happier... and truly ecstatic" (226, 227). They even bring her to cross the boundaries imposed by the man. With trepidation and faltering voice, Alexandra Mikhailovna "makes bold" (227) to suggest that Pyotr Alexandrovich listen to a piece of music or give his opinion of a book. She even "goes so far" (227) as to ask the man to read a page or two of something that impressed her that day. When Pyotr Alexandrovich agrees to music lessons for the allegedly talented Netochka, Alexandra Mikhailovna even rushes to kiss the man's hand "as though something unbelievable had been done for her" (237).

Further telling of Alexandra Mikhailovna's addictive relationship with Pyotr Alexandrovich is that, in his absence, her heart grows panicky, not fonder. Whenever the man is away from home, she sends people to track his wanderings and deeds. She requires constant knowledge of where he is, what he has said, and whether he is "unwell, cheerful, or melancholy, and so on and so forth" (226). In fact, so extreme is Alexandra Mikhailovna's codependence on her husband that even (unidentified) orders to harness horses send her into a tizzy.

Given the extremely skewed tie between Alexandra Mikhailovna and Pyotr Alexandrovich, it is unsurprising that both crack under the strain. In her account of her life with the couple, Netochka takes care to note those times when Alexandra Mikhailovna does not suffer in silence. Even as the woman shows "invariable self-abasement and adoration of her husband," she also harbors a simmering "storm" (228) within. As with deific moments, Alexandra Mikhailovna cuts an impressive, if terrifying, figure. Angry hints and pauses become tears and sobs; then, as if in a "nervous crisis," she resorts to "outbursts of indignation, reproaches, complaints, and despair" (228). Although Netochka does not detail the cause of the distress, she is quick to render its effects. Reminiscent of the shoe-tying episode between herself and Katya, Alexandra Mikhailovna and Pyotr Alexandrovich suffer the tempest in mutual bending and bowing. An almost limbo-like how-low-can-they-go is the dynamic. When Alexandra Mikhailovna revolts against her life, Pyotr Alexandrovich does not respond with recrimination or rebuke. Rather, he drops to his knees, kisses his wife's hands, and weeps along with her. In the struggle for the bottom, the woman always does the man one better. Convulsing, she, too, falls to her spouse's feet to "beg for an [unspecified] forgiveness that would be immediately granted to her" (228).

Not surprisingly, the pardon brings no peace since neither is willing to resolve the addiction-related difficulties between them. For the moment, at least, the mutually groveling Alexandra Mikhailovna and Pyotr Alexandrovich achieve equality; but like all the downward-spiraling ties in *Netochka Nezvanova*, it is a parity of sorrow, split, and denial. The storm over, the two continue as before. Momentarily conquered, the forgiving Pyotr Alexandrovich is again the conqueror. He is as "severe, unapproachable, and self-absorbed as ever" (235). Alexandra Mikhailovna resumes subservience, but in an increasingly dualistic and destructive way. She persists in "tears, agonies of conscience, and new supplications for forgiveness" (228), even as she believes that her life has been and continues to be utopian. After all, the deluded woman tells Netochka, "everyone she has ever known . . . [has always been] so kind and fond of her," particularly Pyotr Alexandrovich, who is "always so worried . . . about her peace of mind, when really she was, on the contrary, so happy, so very happy" (229).

Alexandra Mikhailovna kids no one, least of all herself. Simply put, like Netochka's mother, she is dying a slow death by being "extinguished" (235) before Netochka's (and her readers') eyes. She is "weighed down . . . by something . . . mysterious . . . indefinable . . . and incomprehensible" (235). The woman's "ghastly torment [so] embitters her," her intelligence turns so "melancholy and dark" (235) that she becomes even more isolated and aloof than preciously. Even Netochka sees her "in a new way" (235).

SEEKING SPACE

Netochka understands as little of the skewed, addictive tie between Alexandra Mikhailovna and Pyotr Alexandrovich as she had of the codependent relationships between Efimov and her mother or the Prince and Princess. Gradually, she puts together the pieces of her latest domestic puzzle. As she had with previous husbands and wives, she now "watches, notices, and divines certain things" (228).

It is another sign of Netochka's growing maturity that she observes the relationship between Alexandra Mikhailovna and Pyotr Alexandrovich in a dispassionate way. Her role in the final part of her account is certainly not passive, as Terras asserts.[17] Rather, for the first time in her tale, she does not allow her heart to rule her head; instead, she seeks hypotheses and theses, causes and effects. Like the child hero in Belyi's *Kotik Letaev* considering a progressive cause-and-effect,[18] Netochka quests for a first "reason" for Pyotr Alexandrovich's sullenness; a second for his "double-edged compassion for his poor sick wife"; a third for Alexandra Mikhailovna's timidity before her husband; and a fourth "for the quiet, strange love which she dared not reveal to her husband" (228). Dostoevsky's heroine also seeks a "cause" (228) for Alexandra Mikhailovna's isolation (physical and spiritual), as well as for the facial blushes and deathly pallor whenever she is with her husband.

In her deliberations on the couple, Netochka gets nowhere. Codependent barriers again come to the fore. The girl "asks so many questions and looks at [Alexandra Mikhailovna] in such way . . . that [the woman] lowers her eyes . . . [and] withdraws from her more and more" (232). Unspecified "estrangements, secrets, mistrustfulness, perhaps even embitterment" (236) develop between them. In fact, Netochka believes that she has become such a "burden" to Alexandra Mikhailovna that it is "scarcely possible to be [her] friend" (232). The lessons that had so excited teacher and student fall by the wayside. Alexandra Mikhailovna now does not know what to read to Netochka. The two never get beyond the first page of a book; they avoid extended conversations; and when they do talk, Alexandra Mikhailovna again does with Netochka what she does with Pyotr Alexandrovich: she seeks "possible hidden meanings in every word, in every significant paragraph" (232). The benefactress even ignores her ward's sixteenth birthday.

It is little cause for wonder, therefore, that Alexandra Mikhailovna is now seen by Netochka as so "out of touch" (236) as to be oblivious to the girl's wants and needs. The codependence continues unabated, though. Like other break-ups in *Netochka Nezvanova*, benefactress and ward encounter even more pain when they go their separate ways. Netochka and Alexandra Mikhailovna "are never close again" (235); but they are still drawn to each other like moths about a flame. Netochka continues to love Alexandra Mikhailovna "more and more each day . . . with greater and greater devotion" (225, 235), but she does so only with "tears in [her] eyes . . . [and] a heart that bleeds with sympathy for [the woman]" (225, 228, 232, 235).

Clinging is again a fervent but fruitless option. "I would throw my arms around [Alexandra Mikhailovna]," Dostoevsky's heroine writes, "and hug her fervently" (232). The response is mutual. "In secret understanding," an equally lachrymose Alexandra Mikhailovna embraces Netochka "violently and desperately" (232).

A second reason for her failure to understand the dynamics between Alexandra Mikhailovna and Pyotr Alexandrovich is that Netochka, at long last, is going her own way. The external world no longer engages her exclusive attention; inner existence and growth also demand her focus. As in the first pages of her story, Dostoevsky's heroine boasts about her intellectual and emotional prowess, but now with increasing credibility. "I was developing and growing... out of childhood... very rapidly," she tells her readers, "and a wealth of new impressions, interests, and surmises was forming inside me" (228, 231, 232). Such ferment, she admits, so diverts her from observing her hosts that even her curiosity about them is "on the wane" (232). More and more, Netochka experiences a "curious and ever more frequent wish to be alone... to think, to do nothing but think" (232).

As Netochka soon realizes, this cerebral retreat has both strengths and weaknesses. Positively, it allows her to review and right past wrongs. Netochka now realizes that her earlier "brooding and fantasies" reduced her to a "wild beast lost in the fancies of her own creation" (232). Negatively, though, the mental retreat leads the girl to make the same mistakes as previously. That is, when Netochka engages in prolonged thinking, she finds not only that she is "less patient" with herself and life, but also that she is privy to such "new and unconscious impulses... [and to] such thirsts for activity and excitement... [that] she can no longer concentrate on one thing" (232). In the mental diffuseness, the desire is again to move from real to unreal realms. Netochka can no longer bear the "depressing monotony... [and] the spiritless and miserable circle" (235) that is her third home. "All [her] attention, heart, mind and soul," she writes, "were suddenly, with great intensity and fervor, directed to... another world" (232). Warning sirens sound, but to no avail. Like the zombie-like Raskolnikov in his perceived call to greatness in *Crime and Punishment*, Dostoevsky's heroine forges ahead blindly. "I had no time to turn back, look around, or change my mind," she confesses. "I might be on the way to my downfall," she adds, "but enticement proved stronger than fear... [so that] I closed my eyes and went ahead" (232).

If earlier Netochka indulged her fantasies outside her normal life, in a house with red curtains, she now fires her imagination inside her home, in the library there. The two places could not be more different. If the fantasy house stimulated Dostoevsky's heroine with lights, sounds, and action, the library is quiet, dark, and sinister. It is locked securely, and Netochka only gains entrance when she comes across the key.

With the same unrestrained enthusiasm and lack of discrimination that marked her readings with Efimov and Aleksandra Mikhailovna, Netochka lights on the first tome in the first bookcase. She does so with feelings that advance her to a self-styled but false epiphany. The "throbbing and flutters of [her] heart" give way to "a rush of terror and excitement . . . to a prescience of a great transformation in [her] life" (233). Quickly, Dostoevsky's heroine becomes addicted to reading. All the chaos of her mind and soul—"all [her] new cravings, recent ambitions, the still vague impulses of [her] adolescence, and the restlessness induced by [her] precocious development"— finds "newly discovered sustenance" (234) in books.

Ensconced in the library, Netochka achieves her long-desired goals. She bids joyous farewell to time and space. "Every book she reads . . . the passions, the enchanting pictures, and the life portrayed in such unfamiliar forms" cause her "mind and heart to become so enchanted" and her imagination "to develop so widely" that, once again, Netochka becomes "oblivious of the present . . . [and] alienated from reality" (234).[19]

Dostoevsky's heroine plays fast and loose with past and future. Her readings, she asserts audaciously, have not only "illumined [her] entire earlier life"; they have also convinced the girl that all she has lived through has been "noble and austere" (234). Nowhere, though, is there a trace of confessional remorse and restitution for past sins. Rather, recasting her life, the girl continues to seek new addictions. Like her ventures into history, the thrill of books moves Netochka as the heroine not only of her own story but also of "every novel [she] reads" (238). Fictional characters and events are for the girl so like the individuals and occurrences in her own life that somehow, someway, she believes that she "lived them all long ago" (234). Further, like any good utopian, Netochka uses books to seek a glorious, if ill-defined future. "Day and night" she directs her readings to step "onto an unknown path . . . [where] she alone is master" (234). Evoking the devil's temptation of Christ, Netochka even mounts "heights . . . [that show her] the future in a magic panorama, in a dazzling and alluring perspective" (234).

In her Eden, Netochka finds that it is not good for a girl to live alone. Just as earlier paradisial visions included singular ties with Efimov and Katya, so now does she invite her former playmate again to enter into everlasting codependent joy. To her disordered taste, Netochka finds that Katya has "never left [her]" (238). Rather, fired by her readings in the library, the girl asserts that she is "still immersed in [her] former love," so much so that Katya "still seems to live inside [her] . . . especially in all [her] dreams, in all the romances and adventures of [her] fantasies, where the two went hand in hand, inseparable" (238). Unsurprisingly, the resurrected image of Katya remains conveniently static. Dostoevsky's heroine finds it "quite inconceivable . . . [that the young Princess] could have changed in the slightest degree" (238). How easy, then, for Netochka, in the continuing story of her life—half "created" by her, half "borrowed shamefully from [her] favorite authors"—"always to find a place for Katya, [her] friend and Princess" (238). Like any fan of the future, Netochka finds that when, via the magic carpets that are her books, she fast forwards to other times and places, she is more than content to stay there. "I was destined to live in the future," she notes, a place only of "temptation and joy" (234). Foreshadowing the pseudo-philosophical meanderings of Raskolnikov in *Crime and Punishment* and Ivan Karamazov in *The Brothers Karamazov*, Netochka is not above exploiting her readings to dabble in personalized ideas of existence. She channels "all her strength and intuition" toward the "glimmering . . . [of what she sees as] a basic inner law of life" (234). Humankind, Dostoevsky's heroine asserts, seeks "salvation, preservation, and happiness" (234), but in so doing, it moves at will between a law of "fatality" on one hand, and on the other, a "spirit of adventure" (234). Like Dostoevsky's would-be thinkers, Netochka chooses the second over the first. The thinking-reading girl is no ordinary person. Rather, like the heroines of her novels, Netochka, too, feels destined for greatness. Her reservations about God and other celestial beings aside, she believes that a mysterious "someone . . . prompts [her] . . . to fulfill some prophecy . . . that grips [her heart] . . . with force and poetic fascination" (234). The precise nature of this prophesy is, of course, anyone's guess. Sufficient for Dostoevsky's heroine is that she is a superior being.

As is the case with all such self-elevated beings in *Netochka Nezvanova*, if not in all of Dostoevsky's writings, Netochka finds that extraordinary pretensions cause extraordinary doubts. As soon as she seeks the heavens, she fears the heights. Almost immediately, Dostoevsky's heroine becomes "instinctively nervous" (234) about her fantasy future. She is "content . . . [and] bold only in her dreams" (234). The girl realizes that whatever joys she has in the ethers are hers alone. "All that I had lived [with books]," Netochka recalls, "was so intimate, so close . . . [and] so distinctly reflected in those fantasies that . . . I might have been frightened and confused had anyone, no matter who, cast an indiscreet glance into my soul" (235). The result, she confesses, is that "all that is taking shape . . . in [her] dreams, hopes, thoughts, and passionate delights . . . [she] obstinately keeps to [herself]" (235).

For all the uncertainty, Netochka is unwilling to return the key and all that it holds to its rightful place and owner. At times, Netochka is uncomfortable with such an action. In fact, blithely ignoring her previous wrongdoings—her cruelty to her mother, her struggle with Efimov, her hijinks with Katya—Netochka sees the theft of the key as her "first evil act" (233) and enjoys her paradisial time in the library. "To think," she writes, "that this kind of life, a life of the imagination, a life absolutely divorced from my surroundings, could last for an entire three years!" (235). She even feels justified in such solitude. What other choice does she have, Dostoevsky's heroine postures, amidst the familial disengagement, where everyone "lived in such seclusion, in such isolation from the society, and in such cloistered stillness that we all had to develop an inner life of our own, a place of retreat" (235).

To her consternation, though, Netochka finds that, like all utopias in Dostoevsky (and in life), the paradise brought about by books is ephemeral, at best. Her experience with codependency teaches her that addictive highs charging the mind, body, and soul endure only for so long, and that, once they lose their strength and allure, they can plunge all three entities into the same distress that prompted the initial escape. Without warning, Netochka falls victim to a "depressing lethargy" (238). She realizes that "fantasies and enthusiasms subside"; daydreams "want from lack of energy" (238); and "youthful fervor... [moves to] cold indifference... heartache... foreboding... [and] a bitter and indefinite misery" (238, 239).

Such grief proves her salvation. Netochka is snagged from the existential void by a "strange occurrence," after which she moves from "dead calm to a genuine tempest," shaking her to the "depths of being... [with its] decisive effect" on her life (236, 239). Her intellectual and spiritual facilities are "strained so painfully... [that they] blaze forth in a bright flame of consciousness" (239). The effect she describes is a "foretaste of the future... something akin to a prophetic vision" (239). What Netochka sees (or thinks she sees) departs markedly from her alleged epiphany, as well as from the paradisial worlds she has envisioned for herself and others so many times previously. For once, something solid and salvific comes from codependent casting about. No longer is the future for Dostoevsky's heroine the deadening stuff of a red-curtained house or a secluded library or explicit contracts by which she and an exclusive other live by the rules of patriarchy and codependency in structured peace and joy. Rather, in this vision, Netochka's future is finally an intrinsic part of reality, of life with "all its mystery and incertitude, tempests and storms" (238). Like other individuals in Dostoevsky whose fevered deliberations on law and order lead them to physical and metaphysical dead ends, Netochka faces a choice: to live or die. Foreshadowing the decision that Raskolnikov in *Crime and Punishment* and Alyosha Karamazov in *The Brothers Karamazov* make at similar crossroads, Dostoevsky's heroine chooses life over death. "Alight with desperate hope," Netochka writes, her "entire being longs to live" (238).

A LETTER

Also like Raskolnikov and Alyosha, Netochka finds that even with such an insight, she still has a lot of living and learning to do. Life affords Dostoevsky's heroine a new lesson in codependence when, back in the library, she comes across a letter hidden in a book. The missive is addressed to Alexandra Mikhailovna by a certain "S.O."; it is tear-stained and worn; it has been "read . . . reread . . . and preserved as something precious"; and it contains words and lines that "leap to [Netochka's] eyes . . . [and] make [her] heart race" (239, 240). All of this allows the girl better to understand husband and wife. At last she has access to "an unlocked secret" about the couple whose existence she shares. She experiences a "revelation" that is like "a flash of lightning" (239, 240).[20]

The first thing that strikes Netochka about S.O.'s letter to Alexandra Mikhailovna is its pained and exacting tone. S.O.'s "thoughts and feelings were laid bare," she continues, "they were so intense and . . . implied so much" (240). In fact, so moved is Dostoevsky's heroine by S.O. that for the first time in her account, she reproduces the letter for her readers, standing aside to allow him to speak at length in his own right.

From the very beginning, the confession is pathetically, even laughably false. S.O. resembles Netochka in that he, too, draws his ideas on love from literature, not life. He also appears to have spent too many hours in a library, his first lines being the stuff of sentimental *romans d'amour*[21] and trite romantic fiction. "You said you would never forget me," S.O. writes to Alexandra Mikhailovna. "I believe it, and henceforth all my life rests in those words of yours" (240). On a melodramatic roll, he adds: "We must part, my sorrowful beauty . . . for our hour has struck" (240).

The confession has an important lesson. Close inspection of S.O.'s missive to Alexandra Mikhailovna reveals that just beneath the romantic twaddle is an almost textbook illustration of the workings of codependence, one that echoes and summarizes succinctly the nature of all the skewed relationships in the work. A first indication of emotional addiction is that the tie between S.O. and Alexandra Mikhailovna has meant only pain, so much so that S.O. is actually thankful that the relationship is over. Even as the man bemoans the "penalty of his lost happiness" (240), he relishes his freedom. "Throughout all the time you loved me," S.O. tells the object of his affection, "my heart so yearned and ached on account of our love that believe it or not, I feel relieved now" (240). A second indication of the addictive tie between S.O. and Alexandra Mikhailovna is that the writer of the letter takes no confessional responsibility for the affair but instead is mired in justification, pity, and excuses. Like all the other codependent figures in *Netochka Nezvanova*, S.O. is more than content to blame forces beyond his control. Fate and fortune conspire to destroy his life and love. "I knew long ago that it would be like this," the unhappy soul addresses his love, "that we were destined to this from the beginning! It is fate" (240).[22] Fortune, once his friend, is now his adversary. "I was given too much," S.O. tells Alexandra Mikhailovna, "but fortune erred and now she must correct her mistake and take everything back" (243).[23]

Even more telling of the skewed tie between S.O. and Alexandra Mikhailovna is the pronounced social distance between lover and loved. The two have never been "*equals*," he tells the woman, "I have felt that always" (240). Lest Alexandra Mikhailovna (or Netochka and her readers) miss the point, S.O. relishes his subservience in life. As was true of Efimov in relation to Netochka's mother, S.O.'s problems do not begin with Alexandra Mikhailovna; rather, in a sadomasochistic way, he has always loved life in the underground. "What was I compared to you?" the man asks. "How was I worthy of you? In what way did I excel . . . [or was I] remarkable?" (241).[24]

Like any mouse-louse in Dostoevsky, S.O. is only too happy to answer his own questions. Pre–Alexandra Mikhailovna, he was gloom and doom. As he tells it, "everything [in him] was somehow crushed . . . coarse and common . . . sullen and dejected . . . insignificant and low" (241, 242). He was a man of neither action nor thought. Prior to Netochka's benefactress, S.O. had no "desire for any sort of life"; he never "thought about existence"; he never "looked at it, or even wanted to look for it" (241). Even dreams and concerns for the future, passions that S.O. once had chased "like a fool" (241), lost their allure. Indeed, it was the unhappy man's "incontrovertible . . . resolution . . . [that] the sun would not shine again" (241). Simply put, the "withered" S.O. was a walking corpse; so much so that he could not even feel the "cold freezing his heart" (241). Most of all, like Efimov and Karl Fyodorovich, S.O. feared being ridiculous: "there is nothing worse than being absurd" (242).

Because he is ripe for codependence, it is not surprising that when S.O. first meets Alexandra Mikhailovna (the details of the encounter are unknown) he experiences not love at first sight but abject servility. Theirs is the most vertical codependent tie in *Netochka Nezvanova*. Initially, S.O. hardly dares raise his eyes to Alexandra Mikhailovna, as if he were nothing but a "slave" (241) to the woman. Unlike other addictive down-and-outers in *Netochka Nezvanova*, though, S.O. does not protest the skewed nature of their relationship. In contrast to his erotically driven colleagues, S.O. looks to Alexandra Mikhailovna in a way that is platonic, even ecological. He compares Alexandra Mikhailovna with a "beautiful sister" from whom the "light of God's day... [shines forth as] it warms... the lowest blade of grass... [alongside] a lovely flower" (241). He writes that she has "awakened... [and] filled with sweet hope" his "slumbering mind... [and] heart" (242).

The idyll does not last. An unidentified event—"that evening" of "finding out" something with "those words" (241)—changes everything radically. S.O. is "shaken to the depths of his soul"; he is "stunned, shattered... [and] overwhelmed" (241). More darkly, S.O. is moved to "understand" Alexandra Mikhailovna with a passion that "consumes [him] like fire... [that] flows like poison through his blood... [and that leaves him] intoxicated and possessed" (241).

For S.O., though, the sudden fervor for Alexandra Mikhailovna is short-lived, but it also leaves him with an emotional hangover and even more isolated and alone than previously. "Never, never" (242) could he be the equal of his love because with "so little faith in himself... [he is] unworthy of [her] affection" (241, 242). S.O. is the woman's "creation" (242), willing to become whatever she wants him to be.

Recalling Netochka's tie to Katya, S.O. expresses physical attraction to Alexandra Mikhailovna by first kissing her clothing, and then advancing to her hand. Both gestures are for him near-death experiences. "Oh! You never knew it," S.O. writes to his love, "but how many times did I kiss your dress secretly because I was not worthy of you" (242). Like the overcharged affection of Akaky Akakievich for his overcoat (in the eponymous 1842 story by Gogol), S.O.'s passion sparked by his love's apparel renders him "hardly [able to] breathe," with a heart that is "about to stop once and for all" (242). Similarly, the urge for Alexandra Mikhailovna's hand leaves the man "pale and trembling all over" (242). As their lips touch, S.O.'s eyes become shrouded in "mist"; his heart "stands still" (242). In fact, so shaken is S.O. by the alleged one-time physical closeness with Alexandra Mikhailovna that he wonders why he simply did not die at the place where, it will be recalled, he (and all characters in *Netochka Nezvanova*) are the most comfortable: "her feet" (242).

Given what he sees as the near-fatal experience of love, it comes as little surprise that S.O. keeps his boundaries intact. Alexandra Mikhailovna can go only so far into his mind, body, and heart, and her "purity of soul" (242) prevents him from accepting her beneficence. Just as Efimov, Netochka, and others in Dostoevsky's work bite the hand that feeds them, so does S.O. feel "burden[ed] and tortur[ed]" by Alexandra Mikhailovna's (unspecified) "constant and compassionate tenderness" (242). He also becomes mired in futile question-and-answer. "How can I tell you this?" S.O. asks the object of his affection. "How can I make myself understood?" (242). He fails miserably in the quest. "Ah," S.O. sighs in abject resignation, "I cannot tell you all that has been accumulating in my heart, longing to express" (242).

Like all characters in Dostoevsky (early and mature), S.O. fears genuine love. To his taste, how much less complicated, risky, and threatening is the platonic ideal over flawed flesh and blood. How much more comforting it is to address Alexandra Mikhailovna as "my sister! my sister!" (242) rather than to appeal to her in other ways. How much safer and more secure it is for him to say, "You loved me very much as a sister loves a brother" (242) rather than consider a fuller and more meaningful tie. The truth is that for all the erotic wallowing, S.O. is uncomfortable with his sexuality; not unlike Alyosha Karamazov, he would rather be an angel than a man. His "first excitement" subsiding quickly, S.O. can "contemplate" Alexandra Mikhailovna only "in boundless love, without ever approaching her ... in pure feeling, cleansed of all that is gross" (241).[25]

S.O. is also staunchly unwilling to pursue equality with the object of his affection. Genuine love, he discerns correctly, embraces "reciprocity and equality," entities he "fears" (242) greatly. Incessantly, this thought "hammers through [his] head and poisons [his] wounded heart" (243): he has failed at whatever Alexandra Mikhailovna has thought or desired him to be. To S.O., Alexandra Mikhailovna "loved the man [she] thought [she] had found in [him] but was deceived" (243). Such failed expectations, he continues, is more than he can bear. "This is what hurts, this is what tortures me," he tells Alexandra Mikhailovna, "this is what torments me to death if I do not lose my mind" (243). Small wonder that S.O. "dare not love" (242) in any genuine way, and that he experiences Alexandra Mikhailovna only with "surprise, confusion, and fright" (242).

Like Makar Devushkin in *Poor Folk* and Golyadkin Senior in *The Double* and the rumored women in their lives, S.O. is also deeply troubled by public knowledge of their time together. "Everything has come out," he writes to his love, "Oh, what a scandal there has been" (242). Although, characteristically, S.O. does not identify the whys and wherefores of the trouble, he makes clear not only the reason for the simmering tension between Alexandra Mikhailovna and Pyotr Alexandrovich but also his stance toward their codependent drama.

In the scandal over Alexandra Mikhailovna, S.O. wrings his hands that his sister-ideal is now a "tarnished woman ... [and] an outcast" (242). He exclaims: "My God, what a commotion they have raised! My God, what do they not say about you!" (243). His response is predictable. The cowardly S.O. does not step up to defend Alexandra Mikhailovna; rather, he leaves the woman to face her detractors alone. "I am terrified for you now!" (243), he writes. Perversely, such fear—more for himself than his love—is all S.O. needs to do what he does best: engage in new confessional rounds of self-recrimination.[26] "If you knew how humiliated I am in my own eyes" (242), he says. Indeed, S.O. reproaches himself that the public outrage over Alexandra's behavior has more to do with his own low station (because he stands "so low in [society's] eyes," 242) than with her morality. With the spotlight on himself, he laments, "If only I were somebody . . . if only I were of some worth in their eyes and could inspire them with respect . . . they might have forgiven" (242).

Like similar characters in *Netochka Nezvanova*, if not in all of Dostoevsky, S.O. believes that he has enemies everywhere. As is his stylistic wont, he often alludes to an unidentified "they" and "it" (whether real or imagined). "Who are they to make a fuss?" (242), S.O. asks. "They do not understand it, they cannot understand it, they are incapable of it" (243), he continues with a faux rhetorical flourish. "Blind . . . arrogant . . . [and] cold," he adds, "they do not see it, they will never see it" (243).

To the detractors, S.O. shows a typically bivalent response. They are right, S.O. tells Alexandra Mikhailovna, "because I am absurd and hateful even to myself" (242). Passing from self-styled crime to punishment, he elaborates: "I hate even my face, my figure, all my habits, all my ignoble ways. I have always hated them" (242). In fact, S.O. so applauds the public disparagement that he deems himself a buffoon. He has always been so weak, he says, that even he is "laughing at [himself]" (242).

At other times, S.O. cannot resist delusions of grandeur, and casts himself as a teacher-moralist-guide who, magnanimously, forgives and reconciles all who would harm him. Unwilling and/or unable to exonerate himself, he can exonerate others. His enemies, S.O. continues, do not understand what is splendid: "everything on this earth" that testifies to (his ideas of) goodness, beauty, and truth, as well as the "nobility . . . [and] innocence" (243) of Alexandra Mikhailovna—and by implication, himself. They will "cast the first stone," he continues, "boldly for they know how" (243). Still, S.O. affirms, they are not evil, only in dire need of (his) enlightenment. "If it were only possible to tell them everything quite openly and clearly," he writes to his love, "so that they might see, hear, understand, and believe!" (243). Somehow, sometime, he concludes, his detractors "will understand" (244). Even more condescendingly, S.O. bids Alexandra Mikhailovna to follow in his righteous path. "My poor darling," he tells the woman, "please forgive them as I am forgiving them" (244).

Either way, S.O. affirms that when the codependence gets rough, the codependent gets going. He seeks to escape, to break the tie. "Farewell, farewell!" S.O. writes to Alexandra Mikhailovna. "Now when everything has been discovered; when the hue and cry and the gossips begin (for I have heard them); when I have been humiliated, degraded in my own mind, made to feel ashamed of myself, ashamed for your choice; when I have cursed myself—now I must run away and disappear for your sake" (243).

Still, and as has been the case of every codependent relationship in *Netochka Nezvanova*, S.O. finds it difficult to let go. Again in the faux rhetorical style of his readings, S.O. intones: "We came together, we got to know each other, and now we must part until we meet again" (243). He does not let matters rest there. No addictive personality ever does. As was true of Netochka and company, visions of future bliss recapture S.O.'s fancy. No sooner does the man say a fervid good-bye to Alexandra Mikhailovna, than equally ardently, he requests a new (and a stylized) assignation with the woman. "Oh, tell me darling, where shall we meet again?" he pleads, "Where shall I find you? How shall I find you? How shall I know you, and will you know me then?" (243).

S.O. also wants even greater subservience to Alexandra Mikhailovna. "My whole soul is full of you," S.O. tells the woman, "teach me what I do not understand" (243). The yearned-for instruction, however, has little to do with genuine life and love. Rather, it points to Dostoevskian duality, to a painful split in self. It is more romantic than real, codependent than confessional when S.O. pleads with Alexandra Mikhailovna: "Teach me how to wrench my life in two, how to tear my heart from my breast, how to live without it" (243).

S.O. also bows submissively to Pyotr Alexandrovich. S.O. does not see the man as a rival for her affection. Unlike any disaffected lover, he does not damn the husband, expose his deficiencies, threaten his well-being, or compromise or cuckold him in any way. Rather, having only just met Pyotr Alexandrovich—the details and circumstances of the encounter remain obscure—S.O. actually places the man on an even higher pedestal than that of Alexandra Mikhailovna! Neither he nor the woman is "worthy" (243) of the man because the husband is everything the lover is not. Even "from the start," Pyotr Alexandrovich "knows ... [and] understands everything"— Netochka's readers should be so lucky to have such information!—he also "stands up [for his wife] heroically" (243). The codependent verticality thus assumes a third tier: Pyotr Alexandrovich over Alexandra Mikhailovna over S.O. The husband is "your savior," S.O. tells Alexandra Mikhailovna, "he will defend you ... against the uproar" (243). In fact, so awestruck is S.O. by Pyotr Alexandrovich that when the two meet, he follows the example of Alexandra Mikhailovna in rushing to kiss his hand. Moreover, when S.O. is ordered by Pyotr Alexandrovich to leave without delay, he does not protest the command. "It is settled" (243), he says in typical resignation.

Like other sham confessions and reconciliations in *Netochka Nezvanova*, S.O.'s attempts at rapprochement with Alexandra Mikhailovna, Pyotr Alexandrovich, and society only lead him to bitterness, isolation, and despair. In his view, he is the one who has suffered and lost the most. "They have taken more from me than from you!" (243), he laments. Once again, S.O. holds himself in contempt: "I am so weak and cowardly!" (243), he complains. Once again, he begs Alexandra Mikhailovna for pardon: "Forgive me for those tears!" (243), he continues. And once again, he resumes the verticality of their relationship, as he puts it, "to be at your feet once more" (243). Perversely, though, whatever S.O.'s feelings for Alexandra Mikhailovna, gratitude is not one of them. "I will not thank you" (244), he says in a final farewell. Like all codependent relationships in *Netochka Nezvanova*, what started as dream has transmuted to nightmare.

In S.O.'s letter to Alexandra Mikhailovna, there is a final issue: Has Netochka learned anything from the codependent affair between the two? The answer is yes. From the missive, Netochka receives a well needed jolt from her book-induced isolation. After three years of library-induced fantasies and dreams, "reality has caught [her] by surprise" (244). Even when measured against the partings with Efimov and Katya, nothing compares to the tumult Netochka experiences firsthand in the codependence engulfing S.O., Alexandra Mikhailovna, and Pyotr Alexandrovich. Having finished the letter, Dostoevsky's heroine sees that she has been an "involuntary participant" (244) in the family drama. Even as the "outsider" (244) in the threesome, what she experiences in their addictive realm is all too real. Netochka is so "shocked... frightened... [and] confused" by the unhappy couple that "it takes [her] awhile to realize what is happening [to her]" (244).

The changes are multiple. At long last, Netochka is stripped of her utopias and Edens: "Everything... even [her] hopes and dreams have been taken from [her] forever" (240). For the first time in her account, also, Dostoevsky's heroine experiences glimmers of a valid liberation. Feeling the "fetters" about her loosening, she again discerns "the beginnings of a new life... [and] a new role" (244), ones that contrast markedly with her previous existences and stances. For once in the narrative, readers of *Netochka Nezvanova* take heart that Dostoevsky's heroine is host to "impressions... [that are] strange and different from anything [she] has experienced before" (244). They rejoice over her claim that "something has been resolved... [and that] the old sadness has left her heart" (244).

Of course, Netochka soon finds that unlike her stay in safe and static Edens, genuine life, with its changes and risks, can be distressing for both herself and others. Aloud, the girl questions her resolve. "What ought I to do? ... What might come of it?" (244), she wonders. With no ready answers forthcoming, Dostoevsky's heroine resumes old addictive habits. Once again, she feels lost and unsure of "what she has discovered" (244). Once again, she does not know whether to "grieve or rejoice" (244) over her lot. Once again, she is beset by "thousands of still vague and confused questions [that] arise in [her] mind and weigh heavily on [her] heart" (244). Once again, she wants to cling, "to rush ... [and] hold someone tight" (244).

Further, like any wanderer, mythic or real, Netochka takes a longing look at a self-idealized past before she plunges into the unknown. "I felt like a person who is leaving for good a home and a hitherto peaceful and unruffled life" (244), Netochka writes. Whereas earlier she lived in the past and the future, she now finds herself where she truly belongs: the present. "I was setting out on a long and unknown journey," Dostoevsky's heroine continues, "looking around for the last time, bidding farewell thoughtfully to the past, feeling sick at heart, and full of misgivings about the harsh and hostile future that perhaps was waiting on this road" (244). For the first time in the narrative, readers of *Netochka Nezvanova* can accept and empathize with the girl's pain when she writes, "Eventually I broke into convulsions of sobbing and relieved my heart with hysterical tears" (244). Also for the first time in the account, they cheer and take heart that at long last, Netochka has had a valid epiphany. She also does not run away from the challenge she has set for herself. From the lessons of S.O.'s letter, together with her own accumulating life experiences, Dostoevsky's heroine does what no other codependent in *Netochka Nezvanova* has done to date: she faces up to the responsibility of living and promoting the examined life. "I could not remain silent," Netochka tells her readers, "I could not refuse to accept this role and seal up forever everything I now knew in my heart" (244).

POINT OF NO (CODEPENDENT) RETURN

If Netochka is ready to leave home, it is also because she now finds her domestic situation "impossibly difficult" (244). Caught between Alexandra Mikhailovna and Pyotr Alexandrovich, she wages a daily struggle for freedom and balance. Alexandra Mikhailovna continues to be a thorn in her side. The fact that the woman is now in "utter despondency" catches Netochka between old and new modes of being, "nervous strains ... [and] feverish states, verging on delirium," on one hand, and on the other, struggling to "regain self-possession ... [and] consider [her] position more clearly" (245). It is also because of her benefactress that Dostoevsky's heroine endlessly rereads

S.O.'s letter to the woman. Her mind wanders at will over the actors in the codependent drama as she thinks about the "long and hopeless suffering, martyrdom, and sacrifice [that Alexandra Mikhailovna] endures meekly, abjectly, and fruitlessly" and the "last and terrible cries of farewell [of S.O.] . . . in self-abnegation before his love . . . absurd . . . and ashamed" (245).

Netochka is even more confounded by Pyotr Alexandrovich. Even as Alexandra Mikhailovna continues to "fly [to her husband] with cries of joy," Dostoevsky's heroine finds that she is so "unable to control herself" (245) and that she rushes from the room whenever the man appears. It is a sign of Netochka's growth that whereas in the first part of her tale, she rationalized Efimov's abuse of her mother, she now, in the final section of her story, condemns Pyotr Alexandrovich for mistreating his spouse. "With her entire being," Netochka detests the "inequality . . . the supercilious condescension . . . [and] the intolerable looks" (227) that husband administers to wife. As she sees it, if anyone is the "criminal" (245) in the tormented trio, it is he.

Perversely, Netochka is intrigued by Pyotr Alexandrovich. His portrait gives her the opportunity not only to study her adversary but also to vent her feelings about the man and her own maturing sexuality.[27] On one hand, Netochka "shudders" (246) at Pyotr Alexandrovich's likeness. On the other hand, gazing at the picture, she experiences a "rousing . . . excitement [she] does not understand," so much so that she climbs on a chair to "scrutinize it [more] intently" (246). Dostoevsky's heroine encounters an immediate obstacle, though. She cannot conceptualize Pyotr Alexandrovich physically. If the eyes are the window to the soul, Netochka, in the portrait of Alexandra Mikhailovna's husband, has little sense of both. Without his glasses, his eyes are "duplicitous . . . [and] confused" (246). They also "avoid . . . [her] searching, questioning gaze" (246). No doubt about it, Netochka concludes, her "strange, unaccountable prejudice [about the man] . . . is justified" (246). The difficulty with Pyotr Alexandrovich's image is resolved when the man emerges, staring at her with the same intensity with which she has engaged his portrait. The encounter is brief, but charged. Pyotr Alexandrovich "reddens"; Netochka "blushes" (247).

Alexandra Mikhailovna, seeing that Netochka is flustered and flushed, and that Pyotr Alexandrovich is more talkative than usual, senses something amiss between the two. Just as, unfairly, Alexandra Mikhailovna has been judged guilty in an alleged affair between herself and S.O., so now, equally unjustly, does she assess a suspected liaison between Netochka and Pyotr Alexandrovich. Initially, Alexandra Mikhailovna confronts Netochka in gesture and mime. Silent, preoccupied, and disconcerted, she casts a "rapid, searching glance" (247) on the girl. Only the sudden entrance of

Pyotr Alexandrovich and the ubiquitous musician B. averts a showdown. Momentarily stymied, Alexandra Mikhailovna pursues another tactic. Calling Netochka "Annetta" (as if to emphasize that she is a woman in her own right) and requesting that the girl sing an unfamiliar aria, she strikes at Netochka's Achilles' heel, the question of whether she has true musical talent.

Uncertain and embarrassed, Netochka returns mime for mime. She answers Alexandra Mikhailovna's "lengthy and significant" stare with one of her own—"hotly . . . [and] in the eye" (247)—before she refuses the request. Matters go from bad to worse when Netochka rebels. To Alexandra Mikhailovna's coy observation that Netochka has turned pale, when only moments before she was so flushed, the girl bids the woman stop her taunting immediately.

Stunned by Netochka's response, Alexandra Mikhailovna reverts to a "poor thing . . . [who] with dropped eyes . . . pale cheeks . . . [and] suffused faint flush . . . seeing herself as guilty" (248) for the current fracas. But Alexandra Mikhailovna also shows "naive joy" (248) when a reconciling Netochka kisses her hand. She does not have long to wait for the status quo of their mutual addiction to be restored. To Netochka's request for forgiveness, the woman retreats even further from adulthood, reality, and moral avowal. It is her "meek . . . [and] naive . . . confession . . . [not only] that both [she and Netochka] are children . . . [but that she is also] terribly confused . . . frightened . . . much worse than [her ward] . . . and even worse than a child" (248).

Netochka does not bask in her triumph over Alexandra Mikhailovna; rather, she regrets her pique, particularly its effect on the woman. With the resumed codependence, Dostoevsky's heroine is at first "mortified," then at "the point of tears," and finally in a "state of deep depression" (248). She, too, resumes addictive patterns and realizes that like her benefactress, she also suffers from an "overwrought imagination . . . anxiety . . . inexperience . . . [and] the habit . . . of seeing . . . [and] exaggerating the importance . . . of only the external aspect of things" (248). Again, though, she makes little use of the knowledge. As do any such characters in Dostoevsky, the girl bypasses the difficult work of personal reconstruction. Telling her readers that "it is better not to think about anything," she claims, audaciously, to have "settled all her troubles with such exceptional facility . . . [and] to have carried out her resolve with equal ease" (248).

If other individuals in *Netochka Nezvanova* have cold water douse their dreams, Netochka's fantasies of reconciliation and peace are "scalded" (249) by the reentry of Pyotr Alexandrovich onto the scene. Neither is at ease with the other. A slight bow and a face that flushes crimson is all that is needed to reveal Netochka's confusion over the man and brings her close to tears. With her propensity for unmarked but pregnant pronouns, she also wishes to "make an end of it, to be rid of it all as quickly as possibly" (249).

In truth, an end to whatever Netochka thinks is going on between herself and Pyotr Alexandrovich is the last thing she wants. Just as Katya takes on Falstaff for dominance and control, so does Dostoevsky's heroine engage her adversary in a similar contest. Indeed, in her mind Netochka expands exponentially the erotically codependent pain and pleasure of such a tussle. "A thousand times I vowed to be more sensible," she tells her readers, "a thousand times I was overwhelmed with the fear of what I had to do" (249). On one level, Netochka hates Pyotr Alexandrovich with a passion. On another level, she is smitten by the man. Even as Dostoevsky's heroine despairs over her behavior, she admits that he causes her to lose control and even remain aloof from others, particularly Alexandra Mikhailovna, to hide her "agitation" (249).

Just as Pyotr Alexandrovich again comes crashing into her world, so does Alexandra Mikhailovna make a new, unexpected (and unwelcome) appearance. Any doubt about Netochka's attraction to the man gives way to the fact that when Alexandra Mikhailovna sees her ward, she almost cries out in horror. This time, though, the woman does not accuse the girl of shenanigans with her mate. Rather, Alexandra Mikhailovna treats Netochka "[with] kindness and concern" (249). Whether she does so from goodness, repression, or most likely a combination of the two, the effect is the same. The emotional outreach makes Netochka flaunt her misery in a display of "hysteria and tears" (249); it also triggers her desire to confess to the sins she believes she has committed against the woman.

As is the case with all confessions in *Netochka Nezvanova*, if not in all of Dostoevsky, though, the planned avowal fails on a number of counts. Resolving (again) to fall at Alexandra Mikhailovna's feet, Netochka seeks verticality, not equality. Unsure precisely what she wishes to disclose to Alexandra Mikhailovna, she remains silent on the subject of her attraction for Pyotr Alexandrovich, thereby bypassing a main source of doubt and suffering for both women. This conciliatory gesture is part of a pose, however, as Netochka's saccharine remarks about her rival suggest when she calls her benefactress a "martyr . . . [whom she wishes] to embrace . . . [with] a heart . . . [filled] with glowing infinite love . . . [and] unshakeable ardent feeling" (250).

Additionally, Netochka is careful to keep her boundaries intact by insisting that it is Alexandra Mikhailovna, not she, who has the problem with openness and sincerity. Even as Dostoevsky's heroine forgets the numerous tête-à-têtes she has had with Alexandra Mikhailovna, and even as she insists that if they met it would make "salvation more certain . . . [and] the effect of her words more powerful," Netochka also insists that she would be "the last person to whom [Alexandra Mikhailovna] could open up her heart" (250).

In all of this dissembling, Netochka raises this valid point: any confession to Alexandra Mikhailovna would only trigger new breast-beating and self-deprecation rather than genuine disclosure. Netochka decides to break the pattern of playing codependent limbo (the game of "how low can you go") with her benefactress. After all, the game would only let Alexandra Mikhailovna again win the race to the bottom. The mere thought that her benefactress could "possibly bow low before [her], below [her] judgment [of the woman]" (250) is more than Dostoevsky's heroine can bear. Such an idea leaves her "incensed . . . [and] aghast"; it "revolts [her] sense of justice"; it makes her heart "seethe with indignation" (250). It leaves the girl determined to win any vertical contest in self-abnegation and rebuke. "Poor darling, as if you were a sinner!" Netochka makes a mental note to Alexandra Mikhailovna. "This is what I would say to her as I wept at her feet" (250). Finally, Netochka's confession to her benefactress promises to bring about one of two equally undesirable ends. One is that it will result in reconciliation (i.e., when Alexandra Mikhailovna learns of Netochka's wrongdoing, her "tortured heart [will] rise to hope again," 250). The other, more likely end is that any avowal of S.O.'s letter will "kill the woman" (250).

The sudden reappearance of Pyotr Alexandrovich not only puts an end to Netochka's plans for ill-starred confession; it also affords her (and her readers) a unique opportunity to study the man in a way she has not done previously. Unnoticed, Dostoevsky's heroine sees Pyotr Alexandrovich standing in front of a mirror. "Stock-still . . . [her] curiosity . . . rooting her to the spot" (250), she sees no dour and burdened individual; instead, she witnesses a happy and contented man, smoothing his hair and humming happily. The man in the mirror seemingly "makes up his face . . . at a given signal . . . on command" (251). Indeed, without warning, the codependent theatricality becomes deadly earnest. A "look of bitterness" (251) seizes his content visage. The facial pain "appears to spring from his heart spontaneously, involuntarily" (251). It shows itself in a "spasm of pain . . . that distorts his mouth . . . creases his brow . . . [and] congeals his eyes deeply" (251).

Shocked by the masks she sees, Netochka experiences even more "intense astonishment" (250) after a flashback into times gone by. Just as, at the gathering at the Prince's home, the music of the violinist resurrects painful memories of Efimov, so now does Pyotr Alexandrovich's humming trigger a "spontaneous regression," both a "strange sensation . . . [and] an obscure, distant memory" (250): Netochka sees herself as a "little child . . . in the first year of life in that house" (250). The flashback is undefined but disturbing. The girl recalls not only that she "shuddered with the fear and dread of understanding what I had seen" but also that "from then on an uneasy disagreeable impression was locked in [her] heart forever" (251). She identifies this memory as the "genesis . . . [of her] inexplicable antipathy" (250) to Pyotr Alexandrovich.

Netochka's readers are left with only one option to fill the narrative void. The person who reenters the girl's consciousness must be none other than the Prince because he is the only individual who fits the recollection and because the similarities between the Prince and Pyotr Alexandrovich suggest a psychic tie between the two. Both men are handsome, successful, and wealthy but also solitary, shadowy, and serpentine. They both head households rife with secrets and skeletons. Indeed, it is plausible to infer that if Netochka is ill at ease with Pyotr Alexandrovich, the cause is not only the man himself but also the fact that he represents a type from her past. Past and present, the Prince and Pyotr Alexandrovich come together when Netochka recollects her adversary's "frowning, nervous air," his "frequently melancholy and despondent" face, and the "terrible misery . . . [of] the gloomy, oppressive scenes" (250) he effects in the home.

In the recollection, Netochka seems to be talking about Pyotr Alexandrovich, but—consciously or unconsciously—she also has the Prince in mind when she recalls her first moments in the second part of her tale. The girl reports being so ill at ease that she "hid in the corner as if [she] had done something wrong, praying that he would not notice [her]" (251).[28] Given the psychic coalescence of the two men, it is understandable that when Netochka returns to the preening Pyotr Alexandrovich, she shudders with a "vague, unchildlike feeling" (251). Just as the violinist's music provoked Dostoevsky's heroine to hysteria, so now does Pyotr Alexandrovich's tune cause in her a similar disequilibrium. With "bitter feelings . . . thumping in her heart," Netochka finds her "nerves beginning to quiver . . . [before] she bursts into peals of laughter" (251).

Such a response provokes an equally untoward reaction from Pyotr Alexandrovich. Just as Efimov was shocked to see the concert over his dead wife witnessed by his stepdaughter, so now is Alexandra Mikhailovna's husband similarly disconcerted to find that he, too, has been playing to an audience of one. "Shamefully caught in the act," Pyotr Alexandrovich "turns deathly pale . . . and [beside himself] with alarm, astonishment, and fury" (251). He does not send Netochka running, though. Rather, he finds the girl continuing to "laugh uncontrollably and nervously into his face" (251) as she strolls past him to Alexandra Mikhailovna's room. In the encounter, also, Pyotr Alexandrovich is compromised as head of the household. So stunned is the man by Netochka's reaction that like an exposed lover in a comedy or vaudeville, he hides behind the curtains, "paralyzed with cowardice and fear" (251). For once in the enduring standoff between the two, Netochka tastes victory and presses her advantage. With "nervous, [but] defiant impatience" (251) she watches to see what Pyotr Alexandrovich will do. With new confidence, Dostoevsky's heroine knows that her adversary will not follow her to Alexandra Mikhailovna right away. Indeed, the "poor man" (251) waits a full half hour before he faces both his wife and ward.

SHOWDOWN

Netochka cannot stand the strain of confrontation. She gasps for breath, cedes to hysterics, and loses consciousness. Regarded again by Alexandra Mikhailovna with "utmost perplexity," the girl responds to the woman as a codependent, kissing her hand as if "risen from the dead" (252).

The respite is short-lived: Pyotr Alexandrovich enters his wife's quarters, poised for battle.[29] Falstaff-like, he stands ready to reclaim his physical and psychic preeminence in the household. Appealing again to theatrics, Pyotr Alexandrovich resumes being gloomy and austere. Even as he greets Alexandra Mikhailovna coldly and sits without a word, he shows a face that is pale; a mouth that twitches; hands that tremble; and eyes that, bespectacled, fix pointedly on his ward. If Alexandra Mikhailovna senses trouble, Netochka is so seized by "incalculable terror" (252) that she almost cries out in dismay. Further, when Pyotr Alexandrovich takes the offensive by asking Netochka the reasons for her distress, she is angered but nonplussed. Inwardly, her "indignation" leaves her "barely able to breathe" (252), but outwardly, her fears bring beseeching glances to her benefactress.

Such an action has this unexpected result. Alexandra Mikhailovna, in a singular moment of dignity and strength, and despite lingering suspicions as to a liaison between her husband and ward, asks "Annetta" (252) to leave the room so that she can confront her husband alone. When Pyotr Alexandrovich again asks Netochka for the cause of her distress, the woman takes the man head-on. In an agitated voice, she responds: "Because you make her blush as you do me" (252). In choosing this manner of confrontation, Alexandra Mikhailovna signals to her husband that she has had enough of her husband abusing Netochka and herself and that the two are ready for battle.

The unhappy man does not retreat from the emerging coalition but, rather, goes on the offensive. With "callous, caustic sarcasm," the man more than alludes to her tie with S.O. and the marital difficulties therein when he says, "*I* make you blush, *I*? It is for me to blush, not for you, don't you think?" (252). The advance is successful. At the outburst, Netochka not only cries out in horror, but she also clasps her hands "with [such] entreaty" (253) that she stops the man in his tracks. The codependent struggle between husband and wife is no longer theirs alone. Pyotr Alexandrovich sees that Netochka now knows the "secret" between the couple and "understands fully" (253) the import of his words. The response of Alexandra Mikhailovna is even more searing. With S.O. out of the marital closet, she turns "deathly pale ... [in] surprise, pain, reproach and fear" (253). She shows "unbearable torture" in a face that is "stricken ... and deathly-looking"; and a head "held tightly between both hands" (253).

The triangular deadlock is broken only when Pyotr Alexandrovich hustles Netochka out of the room. Although he blames the girl for the crisis—"See what you have done, miss!" (253), he exclaims—the two do not continue hostilities. They do not, however, pursue the questions surrounding his knowledge of Alexandra Mikhailovna's relationship with S.O. Rather, in codependent fashion, they return the skeleton to the closet and Alexandra Mikhailovna to her codependent state. Netochka grasps Pyotr Alexandrovich's hand "warmly" (252) with a request that he spare his wife. She also sits idly by when, with a "strange look," he dismisses both her and his spouse with his claim that Alexandra Mikhailovna is undergoing "nothing but [an attack of] nerves" (253).

Believing herself to be "more to blame than anyone" in the three-way familial struggle, Netochka seeks to suffer the most. She spends three hours alone in her room, throwing herself on the sofa with her face hidden in her hands, and pacing the room, lost in thought in a "perfect," if unspecified hell (253). One moment Netochka sees herself as the odd man out, but the next she recognizes that she is a desired (and needed) member of the trio. Boundaries and borders rise and fall bewilderingly. On bad days, Dostoevsky's heroine senses from Alexandra Mikhailovna "inexplicable coldness ... awkward anxiety and annoyance ... [and] a cold, dry tone ... with peculiar pointedness" (254). On good days, she finds the woman seeking to "repent her harshness ... with affectionate and gentle words" (254).

Between the two, tension and hostility remain. Each seeks to flush out the other regarding S.O. and Pyotr Alexandrovich, the two men in their lives. Each wants to hear the other's confession, genuine or otherwise. When, at long last, Netochka queries Alexandra Mikhailovna "directly" as to the reasons for her distress and wants to know if her benefactress has anything to say to her, the smiling woman replies, "Nothing" (254). The same question to Netochka results in a similar "no" (254) and a resumption of the status quo. "Well, that is a good thing," Alexandra Mikhailovna says, "You do not know, my dear, how grateful I am for that good answer" (254). Eschewing confession, Alexandra Mikhailovna opts for a self-styled blameless life, wiping the slate clean of any perceived shortcomings in Netochka. Turning her back on everything she has thought about the girl and Pyotr Alexandrovich, she insists, "Not that I could suspect you of anything bad—no never" (254). Even worse, perhaps, the benefactress again indicts herself as the guilty one in the difficulties between herself and her ward: "I could not forgive myself such a thought—never" (254). In one fell swoop, everything is swept under the rug.

In this state of denial, Alexandra Mikhailovna regresses physically and mentally. "You have seen for yourself that I am ill," Alexandra Mikhailovna confesses to the girl, "and that I am like a child that needs to be looked after" (254). Nowhere does the unhappy woman find happiness and peace. Rather, in her unremitting demise, she continues to cite what she sees as her many failings, particularly the parenting of her ward. Although Alexandra Mikhailovna claims to have "more than enough love in her heart," she insists that she has not been a "proper mother" (254) to Netochka. "Forgive me," she begs the girl, "for having, perhaps failed, in spite of myself, to keep all the promises I made to you and my father when I took you into my house. I have been worried about that for some time now" (254).

Unsurprisingly, such a false confession evokes the appropriately codependent response. Netochka "bathes" (254) Alexandra Mikhailovna's hands with her tears. She joins the woman in regression, also resuming her stance as a "poor abandoned child" (254). Readily, too, Dostoevsky's heroine acquiesces to her benefactress's demand for renewed clutching and clinging, now made even more desperate by the woman's forebodings of impending death. "Hug me ... hold me tight!" Alexandra Mikhailovna tells Netochka, "This is the last time you will embrace me" (254).

Her words are prophetic. Externally, Alexandra Mikhailovna's face is thin and pale; her lips are parched with fever; her cheeks glow with "ominous patches of red" (255). Internally, the woman suffers "mute spiritual anguish" (255). Netochka sees that Alexandra Mikhailovna welcomes her end. "With the first snow, I shall die," the woman tells her ward, "but I do not regret it. Farewell" (255). In these self-styled last moments, Alexandra Mikhailovna conducts the same swan song on the piano that Efimov performs on the violin. Recalling Netochka's stepfather, she plays not music per se but something far more meaningful and profound. Striking a few chords, the unhappy woman snaps a string, causing it to quiver in a long, discordant note. Agitated, she reflects on her equally unstrung addictive life. "Do you hear, Netochka?" she asks the girl. "That string was strained to the breaking-point. It could bear it no more and has perished. Do you hear how plaintively the sound dies away?" (255).

Even on the verge of death, Alexandra Mikhailovna is not above seeking verticality and control. Masterfully, she plays with Netochka's mind; equally skillfully, she plucks the strings in the girl's heart. With a grave and mysterious air, Alexandra Mikhailovna drafts her last will and testament. The key demand is that Netochka go nowhere, but that she remain codependently in the household; she will be the new mother and wife. "You will not forsake [my children] when I die, will you Netochka?" she asks, "you will love them as if they were your own, won't you?" (255). With guilt-tinged finesse, she continues: "Remember, I have always considered you as if *you* were my own and made no distinction between you and my children" (255). Of her ward, Alexandra Mikhailovna asks an even more difficult task, to serve as go-between for Pyotr Alexandrovich and herself. In so doing, she insures not only that Netochka will remain in the family triangle but also that she will energize the codependence holding it together. "You both love me, don't you?" the woman asks, "Perhaps, you might perhaps tell him everything I said" (255, 256).

Alexandra Mikhailovna's farewell is narcissistic and insincere. In what is apparently her final encounter with her children, she sends them away as quickly as she asks for them, leaving readers with no information about the children's ages, genders, or even number. The meeting is also strikingly passive and aloof. Alexandra Mikhailovna "seems to relax as she watches [her offspring]" (255). More dramatically, in her self-styled demise, Alexandra Mikhailovna admits to playing games. Sensing Netochka's increasing distress, she backs away from her antics. With a flushed, sly glance, the woman confesses, "But I am only joking. Surely you did not believe me, did you?" (255). Indeed, her only honest confession is about her regression. "God knows why I say such things. I am like a child now. You must forgive me everything . . . I have been ill for a long time" (255, 256). Still, Alexandra Mikhailovna gets what she wants, but in an underhanded way. She is not Sonya Marmeladova in *Crime and Punishment*, Myshkin in *The Idiot*, or other genuine child-adults in Dostoevsky. Everything Alexandra Mikhailovna has asked for Netochka agrees to, but not with a free or right mind. "Yes, yes," the girl answers, but "not knowing what she is saying and choking with confusion and tears" (256). Such distressed acquiescence is of little concern to Alexandra Mikhailovna, though. Whatever she desires of Netochka in this life and the next, she seals with a "burning kiss" (256).

To Alexandra Mikhailovna's latest antics, Netochka responds in several ways. On one hand, she seeks to flee the woman. "I was glad to get away [from her]," Netochka writes, "I could not bear any more" (256). Indeed, her remark to her benefactress—"Stop, you are killing me!" (255)—can be understood on a deeper level (i.e., Netochka sees that, quite willingly, the dying Alexandra Mikhailovna is also causing her demise). On the other hand, the woman still looms large in her imagination because neither has resolved the issue of Pyotr Alexandrovich between them. Questions are conveniently dramatic and rhetorical. "Poor darling, poor darling! What kind of suspicions are you taking to the grave?" Netochka wonders. "What new trouble is poisoning and tormenting your heart, without your daring to talk about it?" (256). With a long overdue nod to her senior self, Dostoevsky's heroine comes to realize and articulate Alexandra Mikhailovna's plight. As a codependent, the woman is ensconced in a personal prison. She is "like a criminal, afraid of uttering the faintest murmur, the slightest complaint" (256). Her angst is intense, splitting, and enduring; it springs from mind and heart; it is rooted in fantasy and life. "Even now, *now*, almost on her deathbed," Netochka writes, "the pain is tearing her heart in two" (256). Alexandra Mikhailovna, she continues, also lets her imagination run away with her. She "imagines—invents—some new sorrow. In fact, she had already submitted to it, already resigned herself to it" (256). With the woman in her final days, Netochka also draws personal light from another's darkness. "I understand it so well now," she says, "this life without a ray of hope" (256).

With S.O.'s letter again in hand and in sync with the impending dusk, the girl yields to gloom and doom, even to premonitions of her own end. Codependence again drives her to the brink. Space and time resume being dark and threatening. Dostoevsky's heroine again sees the world as "cold and unknown, mysterious and hostile" as well as "closing in on her" (256). She is "lost" in the thoughts of the past; she is wracked with the pain of the present; she is horrified by the "threatening vacuum" (256) of the future. In fact, the suffering is so great that it forces her adult to step out from the shadows and intone, "I remember this moment as if I were reliving it now. . . . It cut into my memory so sharply" (256).

Netochka encounters still another threat to her being when suddenly, from nowhere, Pyotr Alexandrovich snatches S.O.'s letter from her. Opting to "face death" (256) in the ensuing tug-of-war, Netochka retakes the missive and, as a sign of her growing maturity, thrusts it into her bodice. The damage is done, but not in the way Netochka or her readers expect. Pyotr Alexandrovich, having made out the first lines, believes that it is a love letter addressed not to his wife, but to his ward!

Just as the unhappy man assumes the moral ascendancy with Alexandra Mikhailovna in her alleged affair with S.O., so now does he race to the ethical heights to judge Netochka for her supposed liaison. The anger he has for one, he extends readily to the other with a face that is pale, lips that are "blue and [quivering] with rage," and a voice that is "weak with emotion" (257). Netochka is no Alexandra Mikhailovna, though. Regarding what she sees as Pyotr Alexandrovich's "coarse brutality . . . outrage . . . resentment, shame and indignation," she cuts an equally impressive figure. Her eyes flash, her cheeks burn, and her body "trembles with excitement" (257). So aroused, Netochka not only halts further advances from Pyotr Alexandrovich, but together with the bodice-covered letter, she also addresses the underlying tension between them. "Your behavior is contemptible and dishonorable," the girl tells her adversary, "you are forgetting yourself! Let me go!" (257).

Although Netochka wrenches herself free from Pyotr Alexandrovich physically, she is dealt a near-knockout moral blow when the man, "still hardly able to restrain himself" (257), accuses her of a liaison. Presumed (if fictive) intrigues in *Netochka Nezvanova* now number three: S.O. and Alexandra Mikhailovna; Netochka and Pyotr Alexandrovich; and Netochka and a nameless partner. Even though Netochka is innocent of Pyotr Alexandrovich's claims of a lover, she so fears for Alexandra Mikhailovna's sanity that she appears guilty as charged. Her cries are frantic, her looks are horror-stricken, her eyes beg for mercy, and her face is despairing and pale. Demands that her adversary cease and desist—and even a threat ("Do not push me to the limit," 258)—have little effect. With a "strange smile" (256), Pyotr Alexandrovich presses the advantage. Believing that with the letter, he possesses "facts that speak for themselves," the man, unwittingly, comes very close to Netochka's shortcomings when he insists that she has a talent for falsehood, for pretending that things are other than what they are, and for "ideas" (258) that must be dismissed from her mind.

Taking flight, Netochka finds herself outside Alexandra Mikhailovna's study. The urge for confession, valid or otherwise, yields to an impulse that the woman be protected at all costs. "That letter!" she thinks, "No! Better anything in the world than that last blow to her!" (256). With Pyotr Alexandrovich quickly in tow, Dostoevsky's heroine seeks to derail his plans. Certain that the man will kill his wife if unopposed, she offers herself as a sacrifice. Her request to go "wherever [he] likes" (256), though, is met with an all too accurate countercharge: "It is you who is killing her" (256), Pyotr Alexandrovich responds.

The standoff ends with the appearance of Alexandra Mikhailovna. "Paler than ever . . . in terrible dismay . . . [and] barely able to stand on her feet"

(258), the woman is figuratively at death's door. Even here, though, she is host to Netochka's codependency, her bosom being the place where the girl buries her face in dread. Further, when Alexandra Mikhailovna tries to find out the reasons for "Annetta's" (259) distress, she finds that both she and the girl are drawn into court-like proceedings in which she is the arbiter, Netochka the defendant, and Pyotr Alexandrovich the prosecutor. "I want you to judge between us" (259), the man tells his wife.

Foreshadowing Dostoevsky's enmity toward lawyers, trials, and the faux evidence of prosecution and defense, the three roles break down immediately. Both women find themselves under fire by a self-styled magistrate who presumes them to be guilty. Legal formalities cede to no-holds-barred indictments. When Pyotr Alexandrovich hauls Netochka into the middle of the room, he does not inform the girl of the charges against her; nor does he ask her pertinent questions as to her thoughts and deeds. Rather, the man delivers the accused to her fate. On a matter that is for him "simple, plain, and vulgar in the extreme," he wishes to "judge [Netochka] in front of the woman who has been a mother to her" (259, 260). Similarly, Pyotr Alexandrovich confronts Alexandra Mikhailovna not only for her passionate defense of Netochka but also for her equally fervid suspicions that he has lusted after the girl. Between husband and wife, apparently, much has transpired behind the scenes concerning the third party in their midst. Insisting on this right to speak "plainly, simply, coarsely," Pyotr Alexandrovich is outraged that Alexandra Mikhailovna has "attacked [him] . . . for his *undue severity*" toward Netochka—a cruelty that, she adds, has been prompted by "*another* feeling" (259, 260). "Spitting out his words ruthlessly" (259), the serpent-like Pyotr Alexandrovich accuses his wife of jealousy. Unwittingly, also, he utters two truths that no one, himself included, has wanted to hear. The first is his allusion to the dissembling and charades that have passed for life in the emotionally addictive household. "Contemptuously . . . [with] a vindictive smile . . . [and] indescribable agitation," Pyotr Alexandrovich pronounces the tortured triangle of himself, Alexandra Mikhailovna, and Netochka as a "farce and nothing else" (260). The second is the purposeful repression of all three in matters of body and heart. In classic codependent denial and projection, what Pyotr Alexandrovich says about his wife can also be said about himself and his ward. Pointing to Netochka, he tells the woman, "I can assure you that *we* are not at all afraid of discussing such matters" (260). "We are not so innocent," the unhappy man continues, "[that we] blush and cover our ears when someone starts talking to us about such things" (260). Even as Pyotr Alexandrovich insists that only Alexandra Mikhailovna has been deceived by suspicion, he shows his own complicity and his own entanglement in the addictive web when his body says what his lips cannot. Moving nervously from head to toe, he tells his wife: "I cannot help my confusion or the color that flushes my face at that thought of your suggestion" (259).

Netochka and Alexandra Mikhailovna do not protest their innocence; rather, they stand guilty as charged. Blushing, her eyes lowered, Alexandra Mikhailovna "burns with shame . . . numbed and half-dead with horror" (259, 260) and blames herself for the familial discord. To both husband and ward, she says: "Forgive me, I am ill. . . . It is all my fault . . . my idea . . . a thoughtless joke" (259). Flustered and mute, Netochka likewise "wrings her hands . . . expecting no mercy" (259). Even as she "understands it all at last"—the suspicions and emotional addictions that send all three into a downward spiral; and even as she calls Pyotr Alexandrovich "beneath contempt . . . tyrannical, shameless, and horrible" (259), she does not stop him until he seeks to call attention to S.O.'s letter.

For the first time in her narrative, Netochka springs into action.[30] Knowing that such a move will kill Alexandra Mikhailovna, Dostoevsky's heroine moves to restrain the man by admitting to knowledge of the intimate problems between husband and wife. "To reproach me is the same as reproaching her," she tells the man. "I know everything . . . do you understand? *Everything!*" (260). The girl also seeks to deflect attention away from S.O.'s letter also by taking her turn at self-blame. "It is all my fault," she says, "I have been deceiving you all" (260). To a "wildly curious" Pyotr Alexandrovich and a "timid . . . anxious . . . [and] amazed" (260) Alexandra Mikhailovna, Dostoevsky's heroine tells a half-truth. She acknowledges her time in the library, but she sidesteps the infamous missive with this fabrication: Pyotr Alexandrovich has caught her with a tome that "should not have been in her hands" (260); this has caused the tension between them. "I am entirely guilty," Dostoevsky's heroine continues, "the temptation was too great, and having done wrong, I was ashamed to confess what I had done" (260). On the same uneasy footing as Pyotr Alexandrovich over their mutual attraction, Netochka concludes awkwardly, "That is all, almost all that has passed between us" (260).

Unsurprisingly, no one believes the story. Neither Netochka nor Pyotr Alexandrovich can identify the problematic book in question. To the girl's confession, also, Pyotr Alexandrovich bursts out laughing, responding, "How clever" (260). More darkly, Alexandra Mikhailovna "considers and weighs every word . . . with an unmistakable note of distrust . . . [before] she hides her face in her hands" (260). Although the woman insists that her "child [Netochka] . . . cannot tell a lie," her repeated questions—"Is that all, absolutely all that happened?" (261)—indicate otherwise. Again, though, the woman seeks peace at all costs. "I do not know what has passed between you" (261), she tells Pyotr Alexandrovich and Netochka, "but if that was all, then I do not know what cause we have for grief or despair" (261). Indeed, when the woman reiterates "if that *was* all" (261) she acts more like a mother with naughty children than as a woman and wife with a husband and ward bound in a tie that no one wants to confront. "Perhaps we have been keeping things hidden" (262), Alexandra Mikhailovna confesses in a startlingly frank acknowledgment of the codependence under her roof. "But again, what is there for us to be so upset for?" she continues, "the danger has passed" (261).

Evoking both the false reconciliation and moral posturing that S.O. seeks with the world, Alexandra Mikhailovna concludes: "Let us put aside our worries . . . let us dispel them with goodness and love" (262). How safe it is for the woman merely to close her eyes to the goings-on between Netochka and Pyotr Alexandrovich. How secure it is for her also to maintain sly glances and flushed cheeks as she resumes her cross of addiction. Absolving Netochka of all blame, citing her "noble and pure" heart, her "candid and clear" intelligence, and her soul that is "fearful of deceit" (261), Alexandra Mikhailovna calls to mind Netochka's specious absolution of Katya. Alexandra Mikhailovna's suspicions have been the stuff of "God knows what" (262). She is "more guilty than anyone . . . the first to conceal something . . . [and the one] to blame for everything . . . [and] to answer for it all" (261, 262). For her there is even no "great sin in which [she has suspected]" (262) the two people before her.

The response by Pyotr Alexandrovich is predictable and, if the truth be told, justified. Delighting in his wife's confusion, the man gives a derisory smile and a soft, jeering laugh. Suddenly, though, in a voice that is bitter and grave, the unhappy soul says what everyone, including Netochka's readers, already knows. "You poor woman, I do feel sorry for you," he notes, "you blind woman, you see nothing!" (262). Much in the way Netochka summed up the case against Efimov in the first part of her narrative, so does Pyotr Alexandrovich do likewise with Alexandra Mikhailovna in the last section of her story. With malice aforethought, the man rejects his wife's addictive bivalence as the best and least of creation. "You have adopted a stance you cannot maintain" (262), he tells the woman. He has no intention of assuming the bottom figure in the totem pole of codependency that Alexandra Mikhailovna has envisioned for her family. He refuses to be incited and aroused by new hints and old suspicions concerning his below-board interest in the girl. In a fighting mood, Pyotr Alexandrovich takes veiled issue with what his wife has seen as his stance toward herself and S.O. Publicly, the man is straightforward, intelligent, and strong; but privately, his "fits of magnanimity... [show a love] that is vehement, harsh, and grim" (262). For the "hundredth time" (262), Pyotr Alexandrovich rejects a liaison (real or imagined) with Netochka. Indeed, as he sees it, if anyone has been deceived by a suspected affair, it continues to be his wife.

Pyotr Alexandrovich acquits himself well in the role of prosecutor, judge, and jury. After his devastating self-defense (and prosecution of his spouse), Alexandra Mikhailovna retracts her suspicions. Although the woman challenges her husband because of his "insane behavior," she concedes that her suspicions of a liaison "may have been shameful" (263) and asks for punishment: "Let *me* suffer this!" she says, "let this be for *me!*" (263).

Although staggering from the struggle, Pyotr Alexandrovich and Alexandra Mikhailovna do not halt hostilities or retreat to their separate corners for a time-out. Rather, so determined is each to destroy the other that they find new energy for their contest by focusing on Netochka. Just as Efimov and his wife bounced Netochka back and forth in their game of codependency ping-pong, so Pyotr Alexandrovich and Alexandra Mikhailovna do the same. In truth, Dostoevsky's heroine is the last thing on either of their minds. Once again, in codependent style, it is all about them. Alexandra Mikhailovna appeals to Netochka only to underscore her own impotence in life. "My poor child," she says. "I am helpless to defend you!" (263). More bizarrely, perhaps, Pyotr Alexandrovich uses Netochka to reverse course on his spouse. Having just denigrated his wife *nec plus ultra*, he suddenly refashions the woman as an ideal, innocent and pure, but led astray by her ward. Just as the Princess blamed Netochka for Katya's ills, so does Pyotr Alexandrovich see the girl as the root of Alexandra Mikhailovna's ills. How disagreeable it has been for the man to see Netochka "beside [his wife], in [her arms], sitting at the same table as [she]" (264). In fact, the unhappy man concludes defensively, the "reason, and the only reason" (264) why he has watched the girl so obsessively is his fear of the harm she has caused the woman. Tearing Netochka's hand from his wife's, Pyotr Alexandrovich seeks to put further distance between the two when he tells the girl, "Away from her! I will not allow you to touch her; you pollute her, your presence is an insult to her" (263).

Pyotr Alexandrovich seeks the final siege of Netochka when, against her protestations, he holds up S.O.'s letter as a missive from her lover. "I have seen this letter, madam," Pyotr Alexandrovich tells Alexandra Mikhailovna, "It has been in my hands" (263). In grand rhetorical style, he concludes: "This is what is going on in our house! This is what is happening at your side! This is what you have failed to notice or even to see!" (263). What need of witnesses, Pyotr Alexandrovich concludes, as Netochka herself vents her guilt. "Only look at the girl," the man adds, "and see there is no question about it" (263).

The case seems so airtight that Netochka can barely stand from the assault.[31] Deathly pale, Alexandra Mikhailovna mounts only a half-hearted defense of her ward. After all, the love letters stir up her own shame and guilt over wrongdoing. When Alexandra Mikhailovna tells Netochka, "No, no, don't speak!"; when she cries out "Oh my God, oh my God!"; and when, one more time, she "sobs and hides her face in her hands" (263); readers of *Netochka Nezvanova* are correct to wonder if the woman is distressed for Netochka or herself. It is also not surprising that Alexandra Mikhailovna joins with Pyotr Alexandrovich in judging Netochka guilty. "Why did you not tell me about this before," she asks, "tell me everything and do not hide anything" (263).

Although inadvertently, Alexandra Mikhailovna makes a valid point—Pyotr Alexandrovich has "made a mistake . . . [he] has seen something else . . . he is blind" (263), she says—her reaction only spurs the man to new questioning of the girl. "Answer, answer immediately!" he demands of Netochka, "Did I not see the letter in your hands? . . . Is the letter from your lover? . . . With whom are you carrying on an intrigue?" (264). Netochka answers the first two questions affirmatively (but keeps mum on the third), but she does so only to protect Alexandra Mikhailovna and to end the collective codependent agony consuming all three. She fails miserably. Recalling other times of abuse in the narrative, the girl enters into disassociation when she hears the prosecuting/persecuting voice of Pyotr Alexandrovich "rising above her head" (264). By not resisting the man, though, Dostoevsky's heroine gives her adversary what he wants, Netochka—and by implication, his wife—have had illicit affairs. "How glad" (264), then, is Pyotr Alexandrovich to unmask Netochka before his wife. How equally delighted is he to say to his spouse, "You have seen and heard her. Well, what do you say now?" (264).

As before, the man is determined to destroy his wife more than his ward. With S.O. on his mind, and with as much carrot as stick, Pyotr Alexandrovich indicts the woman first for being too trusting and kind and then for her "sick imagination . . . [her] blindness . . . [her] God-knows-what suspicions . . . [and] something-or-other deductions" (264). Also, now that Netochka's tie to a lover is for him clear and beyond a doubt, Pyotr Alexandrovich seeks to restore codependent law and order in a single stroke. Netochka, he tells is wife, is to be banished from the home forever.

UNTIL (CODEPENDENT) DEATH DO US PART

Pyotr Alexandrovich is thwarted in his plans by Alexandra Mikhailovna. Like her husband, she, too, has had her fill of marital codependence. Her husband's bid for dominance and control, his overt and covert abuse, his attack on Netochka and herself, and her grief over S.O. all snap the piano chord to which, only recently, she has likened her life. For the first time in her marriage, Alexandra Mikhailovna makes herself heard. "Stop!" she "screeches" (264). Defending herself against the man—she now does not believe his charge against Netochka; she demands that he not "mock [her] . . . and look [at her] so fiercely"; she seeks to turn the tables by insisting that now she will be the one to "judge [*him*]" (264).

What Alexandra Mikhailovna has in mind contrasts markedly with the harsh verdicts of her husband. When, for a final time, the woman takes Netochka's hand, she does so not with the clinging and clutching that has marked so much of their time together. Rather, she attempts what is seen as a type of *sobornost'* or "spiritual union" that Dostoevsky, even in his early years, believed crucial to the understanding and salvation of humankind. When Alexandra Mikhailovna tells Netochka, "we are all sinners" (264), she accomplishes several things. She dismantles the codependence and verticality that have skewed her ties to Netochka and Pyotr Alexandrovich (not to mention all relationships in *Netochka Nezvanova*). In their place she vaunts an equality in which the genuine confession of human shortcomings is the first and crucial step to forgiveness and reconciliation, to love and peace among couples, families, and society. No longer is Alexandra Mikhailovna the self-styled least of God's creations who blames herself for the world's problems; rather, as Zosima in *The Brothers Karamazov* will do more than thirty years later, she takes the position that everyone bears the responsibility for evil—and good—in the world. Also, by openly and genuinely admitting her failings to her husband and ward, Alexandra Mikhailovna exhibits a strength and purpose she has not shown previously. To her husband's veiled threat to bring S.O. in the picture—"Madam! Restrain yourself! Do not forget . . ." he says—she does not fold like the flower to which S.O. compared her. She responds to Pyotr Alexandrovich's abuse ("You cannot harm me with your presence, for I too, *I too am a sinner*," 264) and refuses to be silenced: "I forget nothing"; "do not interrupt me . . . let me finish" (264).

Still another indication of Alexandra Mikhailovna's newfound fortitude is her willingness to clear Netochka (and by implication, herself) of any impropriety. If Pyotr Alexandrovich is the prosecuting attorney, she is the counsel for the defense. Does the letter prove that Netochka is a "criminal"?

(264) the woman asks her husband. "Does it justify treating her like this ... [and] in the eyes of your wife?" (264). Also, speaking about her alleged relationship with S.O. as much as about Netochka's supposed ties with a lover, Alexandra Mikhailovna brings both matters to bear when she queries Pyotr Alexandrovich: "Do you really know how it happened?" (264). She again ties the two unions together when she claims innocence and naïveté for Netochka. What if, Alexandra Mikhailovna wonders aloud, the girl fell victim to "her own inexperience with no one to guide her?" (265). Warming to the topic, the woman again hints at her own situation when she notes that Netochka does not compare to a "wife and mother [who] has forgotten her duties" (265). Still, for both herself and her ward, Alexandra Mikhailovna sees the case as closed. Netochka is for her as "innocent as a child" (269).

Heroically, Alexandra Mikhailovna resists attempts by Pyotr Alexandrovich to resume the codependent verticality of the past. To the mock offer that he beg Netochka's pardon; to the angry charge that he has lost patience; to his moral admonition that he rejects "trumpery . . . [and] gilded sin"; to his renewed menace that he will not remind his wife of her failings; to his condescending offer that he will help his wife; and finally, to his false braggadocio that he "sees through it all" (265) (of course the "it" remains unspecified)—Alexandra Mikhailovna does not yield. Rather, she charges her spouse with pride and blindness, for "failing to see the first thing" (265) about Netochka (and by implication, about herself). Indeed, the woman continues, if there is any wrongdoing among the three, it originates with Pyotr Alexandrovich. His "coarse suspicions . . . have insulted [Netochka's] maidenly feelings . . . and sullied [her] imagination" (265) more than any book, letter, or liaison could.

As a further finding against the man, Alexandra Mikhailovna contends that any admission of guilt from Netochka (and, by extension, from herself) occurred under duress. Again, the woman does not know how close she comes to the truth when she says that Netochka—"mortified ... tortured ... and torn with anguish" by Pyotr Alexandrovich—"did not know what to say" (265). Angry at her husband's addictive abuse not only of Netochka but also of herself, Alexandra Mikhailovna delivers her own judgment of him. He has been so cruel that he is beyond her pardon. "I shall never forgive you for this!" she continues, "never!" (265).

Free of the codependent bond, Alexandra Mikhailovna summons new strength against her husband. When Netochka, now under the threat of expulsion from the household, "clings" (265) to Alexandra Mikhailovna, falling to her feet and begging for mercy, the woman does not go to pieces as she has done previously. Rather, she rejects Pyotr Alexandrovich's bid to expel Netochka from the home.

Alexandra Mikhailovna is now the one who issues an ultimatum: If Netochka goes, she goes. "You know that if you turn [Netochka] out of the house," she intones, "you turn us out together, the two of us! Do you hear me, sir?" (265). Her image is as good as her word. For the first time in the novel, Alexandra Mikhailovna cuts an earthly figure. She is no longer an angel longing to leave this world; rather, she is a flesh and blood mortal determined to stay in it. Her eyes flash; her breasts heave; her "feverish excitement reaches a climax" (265).

At this point in the narrative, Alexandra Mikhailovna does not become an independent heroine in the style of George Sand. Repeatedly, Netochka has depicted the woman as incapable of such a transformation. Such an outcome is hardly surprising, given Dostoevsky's stronger love for problems than solutions in his early works. Indeed, it would take another twenty years or so before he could posit viable exits from the quagmire of addictive behavior, not to mention from a host of other human ills. So it is no surprise that in the final scene of *Netochka Nezvanova*, Alexandra Mikhailovna does not pursue her bid for freedom but returns to codependence. She "clutches at [Netochka] convulsively" (266) before fainting dead away. Netochka, in turn, cedes verticality and accepts defeat when she asks Pyotr Alexandrovich to have mercy on his wife. Pyotr Alexandrovich also fails miserably. Having won the battle, he has lost the war. Fearing that "it is all over . . . that he has killed [his wife] . . . he bites his nails until they bleed" (266).[32]

There is a moment of hope. Netochka recovers sufficiently to wage a second front against Pyotr Alexandrovich. Echoing Alexandra Mikhailovna, she berates the man for his "dark soul . . . merciless vanity . . . [and] jealous egoism" (266), and she indicts him for destroying his wife through his "wish for superiority . . . to prove to [her] that she has erred . . . [and that] he is the more sinless one." These actions have reduced his wife to a "ghost . . . [and] the last lament of a broken heart" (266). Netochka even goes so far to say that Alexandra Mikhailovna understands her husband's attraction for Netochka as "natural in the course of human affairs" (266).

She also knows that she cannot remain in the household any longer. "Farewell!" (266), she tells the man. Although she admits to being dazed by her decision—"I went to my room, hardly knowing what was happening to me" (267), she writes—and although, sadly, the manuscript of Dostoevsky's first novel ends precisely at this moment—readers of *Netochka Nezvanova* can be confident of one thing: from her time with Alexandra Mikhailovna and Pyotr Alexandrovich, Netochka has not only learned more about codependence, she has tied the addictive behavior of the third section of her story to the clinging and clutching of the first and second. In an intimate way, Dostoevsky's heroine has learned the difficulties (implicit and explicit) of addictive twosomes and threesomes fraught with bids for power and control, urges toward eroticism, evil masked as good, and violence and death. Indeed, her life with Alexandra Mikhailovna and Pyotr Alexandrovich has been as valuable as her time with Katya and her family, and with Efimov and her mother. The repeated emotionally addictive relationships with the people of her childhood, adolescence, and youth have taught Netochka about the content, form, and function of codependence.

CONCLUSION

On March 31, 1849, Dostoevsky wrote to Kraevsky, editor of *The Fatherland Notes*, that he would deliver the third part of *Netochka Nezvanova* in the first week of April, and that he planned to present the fourth and fifth parts of the work to him by mid-month. "Notwithstanding the fact that I have just finished the third section," Dostoevsky informed the editor, "I am now working on the fourth part [of *Netochka Nezvanova*] . . . not allowing myself a scrap of rest . . . since I definitely want . . . to publish the [next] two parts [of the work] in May" (vol. 28, bk. 1:152).

These hopes were soon dashed. The fourth installment of *Netochka Nezvanova* was proving so problematic that Dostoevsky was losing both momentum and interest in the work. "Even now," he lamented in the same letter to Kraevsky, "I am tearing out my hair over the fact that the [new] episode has not been presented in its entirety, but split up into three parts. Nothing has been finished, only [my] curiosity [in what I am writing] is still there. But curiosity at the beginning of the month is not the same thing as [curiosity] at the end of the month. It cools down and even the best works lose" (152–153).

Creditors, Kraevsky first among them, were also keeping Dostoevsky from his task. Despite the bluster—"Just consider the present winter!" he continued to the editor, "I have worked like a horse. The more I do, the more successful it becomes, [the more] the public likes my work" (153)— Dostoevsky had little time for writing other than projects to keep the wolf from the door. With the new sections of *Netochka Nezvanova*, he was already extending deadlines. "To my greatest regret, even if I worked until I had calluses on my hands," Dostoevsky confessed to Kraevsky, "I find it physically impossible to bring you the fourth part [of *Netochka Nezvanova*] by Saturday, but I will get to you by the 7th. But in the meanwhile it will be impossible for me to write. I have been tortured to the extreme because . . . creditors have made me [so] irritable [that] I will leap at outside things, that is, I will be forced to write some kind of fairy tale on the side. The saddest thing is that work on the side will sap the energy for my novel and the desire to continue again for half a month, and perhaps, for even a month" (154).

Little did Dostoevsky realize that it would be more than a decade before he would return to *Netochka Nezvanova*. On April 23, 1849, he was imprisoned in the Peter-Paul Fortress for his involvement in the Petrashevsky Affair, and on Christmas Day he was taken by sleigh from St. Petersburg to begin a decade-long exile in Siberia. Notwithstanding the trials and travails of his time in prison, Dostoevsky continued to worry about his novel. "Still one more request," he wrote to his brother Andrei on June 20, 1849. "I do not know if it is possible . . . but our brother Mikhail has a ticket to receive *The Fatherland Notes*. . . . The third part of [*Netochka Nezvanova*] was printed there, but without me, without my supervision, so that I did not even see the proofs. I am worried about what they printed and whether they mutilated my novel. So send the volume to me . . . or better still, come in person [with it]" (155–156).

Dostoevsky succeeded in his request. On July 9, 1849, Mikhail sent the issue to him, but with still another heartbreak. After Dostoevsky's arrest, Kraevsky had written to the Third Section asking permission to publish the third part of *Netochka Nezvanova*. On April 28, 1849, he received approval but only on the condition that the piece be published anonymously.

After exile, Dostoevsky chose not to continue his first novel. Rather, in a letter dated May 9, 1859, he wrote to his brother Mikhail that he planned to include the three parts of *Netochka Nezvanova*—"polished and which everyone liked" (326)—in an edition of his works that appeared a year later. Beyond minor alterations and stylistic tightening, he abandoned the work.

Given Dostoevsky's enduring fixation on suffering children, it is tempting to speculate on the fate of *Netochka Nezvanova* in the post-Siberian period. Indeed, it is not implausible to say that if Dostoevsky had continued his first novel, he would have moved his heroine along a path similar to that of Jane Eyre or other fictional heroines of the time. That is, Netochka would have been privy to multiple adventures in diverse homes as a governess or housekeeper amidst emotionally wounded children and adults. It would also be within the realm of possibility that, like the children in Dickens, Netochka would again come into contact with Katya, the Prince, and Pyotr Alexandrovich and begin with them anew.[1]

Two things would be certain. On one hand, given the stance of the adult Netochka toward codependence, as well as Dostoevsky's ongoing fascination with skewed relationships, it would be hard to imagine that his heroine would find the love of her life and settle down to domestic tranquility and bliss. The demons of addiction would continue to haunt and even possess her. On the other hand, whatever the obstacles to stability and peace, it would also be safe to assume that Netochka would live life on a more assured footing then previously. Judging from her growth in the third chapter of *Netochka Nezvanova*, she would not be savaged by her earlier relationship addictions. Rather, Netochka's time with Efimov, her mother, and the musician B.; with Katya and her household; and with Alexandra Mikhailovna and Pyotr Alexandrovich would have made Dostoevsky's heroine sadder but wiser about the causes and effects, stimuli and responses of codependence. Indeed, sensitive to the relationship addiction in herself and others to people, places, and things, and to images, ideas, and ideals, Netochka would seek out a denouement in which, not unlike the equally codependent Alyosha Karamazov (the subject of another study?) in the final pages of Dostoevsky's last novel, she would be seen as advancing the children in her care to the potential or possibility of agape and *sobornost'*, to a genuine understanding of love and community in life.[2] At the very least, Netochka would so understand relationship addiction as to be the first of Dostoevsky's heroines "to be granted the ultimate human status of choosing [her own] fate."[3] Unlike, say, Nastasya Filippovna in *The Idiot*, Netochka would be "ultimately willing to live."[4]

If after exile, *Netochka Nezvanova* was out of Dostoevsky's sight, it was certainly not out of his mind. As has been noted repeatedly in this study, many of the characters in *Netochka Nezvanova* appear in his other novels. If, as if in all his early and mature works, Dostoevsky left his first novel "open" and "unfinished,"[5] it was also with the knowledge that he would begin again, to reinvent the codependent men, women, and children of *Netochka Nezvanova* in new and different ways. Efimov and Netochka's mother reemerge as Marmeladov and Katerina Ivanovna in *Crime and Punishment*. Katya assumes new form in Polina in *The Gambler*, his 1867 novel about a young couple addicted to roulette. She also reappears as Aglaya Epanchina and Nastasya Filippovna in *The Idiot*, and Liza Khoklokova, Katerina Ivanovna, and Grushenka in *The Brothers Karamazov*. Alexandra Mikhailovna is a model for Maria Lebedyakina in *Devils*. Pyotr Alexandrovich retakes the stage as Prince Valkovsky in *The Insulted and the Injured*; Luzhin and Svidrigailov in *Crime and Punishment*; and Totsky in *The Idiot*. Netochka makes a second debut in Ippolit Terentiev in *The Idiot* and Ilyusha Snegiryov in *The Brothers Karamazov*.

The images and ideas related to codependency in *Netochka Nezvanova* also emerge not only as catalysts for all of Dostoevsky's mature writing but also as an impetus to the *proklyatye* or "damned" philosophical and religious questions that would inform *Notes from the Underground*, *Crime and Punishment*, *The Idiot*, *Devils*, and *The Brothers Karamazov*. Indeed, the tattered tangle of ties that bind Netochka with Efimov, her mother, Katya and the Prince, Alexandra Mikhailovna and Pyotr Alexandrovich would become the material for Dostoevsky's exploration of the more complex and convoluted relationships that bring addictive sorrow and suffering to Raskolnikov, Marmeladov, and Svidrigailov; to the Karamazovs; to Grushenka, Nastasya Filippovna, and the two Katerina Ivanovnas, and to Ippolit and Ilyusha Snegiryov.

Important here, though, is not what Dostoevsky would do in later fiction but what he did in *Netochka Nezvanova*. His lessons are many. Mired in codependence, in relationship addiction, Netochka and company seek war, not peace—hatred, not love. Not knowing who they are, what they are doing, and where they are going and distressed about their past, present, and future, they remake reality in their own image and likeness, or check out of it altogether. Fantasies and dreams, denial and delusion, masks and poses are the chosen *modi verandi*. Even more damaging is the fact that the love addicts of *Netochka Nezvanova* cling to their obsessions in such morbid fashion until physical or metaphysical death.

In their codependence, Netochka and her three families wreak havoc on themselves and others in self-canceling ways. They seek community in dominance and control; they desire equality as geniuses and gods. They live life in fairy tales, fiction, and utopias; they want love in narcissism, sadomasochism, and sexual perversity. They make false confessions and *apologiae pro sua vita*; they seek abusive bonds. Crying out for harmony and peace, they cleave themselves in two; unhappy with themselves, they seek out doubles that return them to the very distress from which they seek escape. They never learn from their mistakes; rather, they arouse themselves with addictions that allow them to live momentarily in heaven, but enduringly in hell. In a word, Netochka and her crew offer a textbook illustration of codependency: the ways—physical and social, intellectual and spiritual—in which individuals seek to possess anyone and anything to stem the restlessness, sadness, and emptiness within.

An equally important point is that Dostoevsky in *Netochka Nezvanova*, not Tolstoy in *Childhood*, was the first Russian author to create an indigenous model of family and the bildungsroman. If critics objected to *Netochka Nezvanova*, it was because of the unvarnished truth that Dostoevsky told about the family in his homeland, his exposé of the most sacred, private, and exclusive of human groupings to expose the flaws and failures of the national psyche. As Dostoevsky would make painfully clear in *The Diary of a Writer* and his mature novels, it was precisely the breakdown of the family—absentee fathers, unbalanced mothers, and neglected and abused children—that was sending Russia hurtling toward revolution and chaos. In no way, therefore, would or could *Netochka Nezvanova* be a model for fictional children in nineteenth-century Russia. The sweat that Druzhinin identified in the work was too unpalatable for readers who, like Netochka herself, preferred to read romantic idylls of Russian life. Indeed, the fact that Gorky's 1913 *Childhood* (which according to Wachtel was the first work to overthrow gentry myths of Russian childhood) appeared more than seventy years after *Netochka Nezvanova* shows how unwilling Russians were to accept the reality of families in their country.

If one agrees with Vyacheslav Ivanov that the child in Dostoevsky "is the central point of his doctrine concerning the world and humankind,"[6] one must also accept the crucial importance of *Netochka Nezvanova* in his corpus. One must also assent to the fact that in his first novel, Dostoevsky articulated a problem that he would explore more deeply in his later works: codependency. Throughout his career, Dostoevsky was fascinated by people who cannot live with—or without—each other. Dysfunctional bonds among lovers, spouses, and families, enduring struggles for power and control, physical and social aberrations, self-consuming revolts against reality, the overt and covert abuse of children, dreams of perfect worlds, and insatiable relationship addictions are all the stuff of codependency. True, Dostoevsky may not have understood addictive behavior from the vantage point of modern-day research, replete with research teams and statistical data. But he did not need to understand it this way. His insights into codependence were part observation, part intuition, and part consciousness into the workings of life. No doubt, Dostoevsky would have taken perverse delight in reading modern-day studies of codependency if only to see credentialed specialists reinvent the wheel. He would have agreed wholeheartedly that if such individuals had read *Netochka Nezvanova* and others of his works, they would have had a better handle on relationship addiction (content and form). Unfortunately, just as Dostoevsky's readers and reviewers refused to heed his warnings about men-gods, utopias, and distorted ideas of Christ and Christianity, so too did they close their minds and hearts to his admonitions about codependency. Indeed, one can even say that if they had read Dostoevsky's *Netochka Nezvanova*, they might have understood relationship addiction in others and, more importantly, in themselves. With Dostoevsky's first novel, they might also have seen that love may make the world go round, but codependency is the axis upon which it spins.

NOTES

Notes to Preface

1. See F. Dostoevskii, *Polnoe sobranie sochinenii v tridtsati tomakh* (Leningrad: Nauka, 1985), 28:148–149. All references to Dostoevsky's personal and aesthetic writings are to volume and page of this edition.
2. A. Druzhinin, "Smes," *Sovremennik* 2 (1849): 186.
3. L. Grossman, *Dostoevsky. A Biography*, trans. M. Mackler (New York: Bobbs-Merrill Company, 1975), 176.
4. G. Fridlender, *Realizm Dostoevskogo* (Moscow: Nauka, 1964), 88.
5. J. Frank, *Dostoevsky. The Seeds of Revolt, 1821–1849* (Princeton, NJ: Princeton University Press, 1976), 355 and 365.
6. V. Terras, *The Young Dostoevsky (1846–1849). A Critical Study* (The Hague/Paris: Mouton, 1969), 50; and E. Wasiolek, *Dostoevsky. The Major Fiction* (Cambridge, MA: MIT Press, 1964), 11.
7. L. Dostoevskaia, *Dostoevskii v izobrazhenii svoei docheri* (St. Petersburg: Andreev i sinov'ia, 1992), 45 and 50.
8. Frank, *Dostoevsky*, 366. Frank continues: "It is only with *Netochka Nezvanova* that we can see how Dostoevsky's explorations of personality have gradually led him not only to reverse the hierarchy between the psychological and the social assumed by the Natural School, but entirely to disengage his psychology from its earlier dependence on social conditioning." See Frank, *Dostoevsky*, 367.

Consider also Charles Passage's comment: "Least read, probably, of all of Dostoevsky's works, *Netochka Nezvanova* is nonetheless of great importance for the evolution of his art." See C. Passage, *Dostoevski the Adapter. A Study of Dostoevski's Use of* The Tales of Hoffmann (Chapel Hill: University of North Carolina Press, 1954), 82.

Additionally, note Lina Steiner's observations that Dostoevsky's "great achievement in [*Netochka Nezvanova*] is a very genuine portrayal of a growing human soul not as a rationalist abstraction, but rather as an unusually gripping, puzzling, and memorable story"; and that "situated halfway between a conventional analytical novel and what Lidia Ginzburg calls a 'human document,' this narrative experiment is interesting not only as one of Dostoevsky's first creative trials, but also as a precursor of a new psychological novel which incorporates both rational dialectic and the more immediate expression of the artist's sentiments and desires." See L. Steiner, "*Netochka Nezvanova* on the Path of *Bildung*," *Die Welt der Slaven* 51 (2006): 233–252.

9. Consider Grossman's claim that, despite its unfinished state, *Netochka Nezvanova* is the "most mature and successful of the early Dostoevsky's works." See Grossman, *Dostoevsky*, 124.

10. A. Kashina-Evreinova, *Podpol'e geniia. (Seksual'nye istochniki tvorchestva Dostoevsogo)* (Petrograd: Tret'ia strazha, 1923), 42.

11. "For the Russian imagination," Andrew Wachtel writes, "childhood was a gigantic *terra incognita*, waiting to be discovered. Until Tolstoy created Nikolai Irtenev [in *Childhood*], the Russian child lacked a voice of his own; he was a literary mute, sometimes seen but never heard.... Before 1852, there were practically no first-person accounts of childhood in Russia." See A. Wachtel, *The Battle for Childhood: Creation of a Russian Myth* (Stanford: Stanford University Press, 1990), 2–3.

12. W. Rowe, *Dostoevsky. Child and Man in His Works* (New York: New York University Press, 1968), 76.

13. F. Dostoevskii, *Polnoe sobranie sochinenii v tridtsati tomakh* (Moscow: Nauka, 1972–1990), 5:156. My translation.

14. "In Childhood," Wachtel continues, "Tolstoy presented Russian literature with a model for writing about childhood and proposed an interpretation of the meaning and purpose of this stage of life.... In his overall conception, in his descriptions and interpretations of Irtenev's surroundings, of his parents, and of Irtenev himself, Tolstoy invented a Russian gentry attitude toward childhood. In time, his personal myths of childhood became the foundation on which practically all future Russian works on the subject were constructed. In this sense he was not the historian of gentry childhood, but rather its creator, poet first and foremost." See Wachtel, *The Battle for Childhood*, 57.

Although Wachtel notes that "no full-fledged counter-myth of childhood arose in Russia until the twentieth century," it was Dostoevsky's *Netochka Nezvanova* that preceded, by more than sixty years, Maxim Gorky's 1913 *Childhood* deemed by Wachtel as the first successful attempt to overthrow literary myths of gentry formation. See Wachtel, *The Battle for Childhood*, 133 and 203.

15. Consider Terras's remark that Dostoevsky is "one of the first Russian writers to describe female homoeroticism in physical terms." See V. Terras, *A Karamazov Companion. Commentary on the Genesis, Language, and Style of Dostoevsky's Novel* (Madison: University of Wisconsin Press. 1981), 187.

16. Researchers estimate that "there are fifteen million Americans in nearly half a million recovery groups and that 100 million Americans are related to someone with some form of addictive behavior." See J. Rice, *A Disease of One's Own. Psychotherapy, Addiction, and the Emergence of Co-dependency* (New Brunswick: Transaction Publishers, 1996), 6 and 27.

17. Compare, for instance, the chapter "Enmeshment and Codependency: Just One Big Dysfunctional Family" in J. Davison, *Sweet Release. The Last Step to Black Freedom* (Amherst: Prometheus Books, 2008).

Also note L. McDowell, *Between the Sheets. The Literary Liaisons of Nine 20th-Century Women Writers* (New York: Overlook Press, 2010), in which the author examines what she sees as the codependence of such writers as Katherine Mansfield, Simone de Beauvoir, and Sylvia Plath on their partners, and how such ties liberated unspoken desires and encouraged innovation in art.

18. R. L. Jackson, *Dialogues with Dostoevsky* (Stanford: Stanford University Press, 1993); and W. Rowe, Dostoevsky. Child and Man in His Works (New York: New York University Press, 1968), 76.

19. L. Breger, *Dostoevsky. The Author as Psychoanalyst* (New York: New York Uni-

versity Press, 1989); and E. Dalton, *Unconscious Structure in "The Idiot." A Study in Literature and Psychoanalysis* (Princeton, NJ: Princeton University Press, 1979).

Particularly provocative is Dalton's objection to exclusively literary references for a text—i.e., "every fantasy or fear, every representation of aggression or sexuality can be accounted somewhere in the canons of comedy, tragedy, Gothicism, naturalism, courtly love, or whatever—with the result that literature appears to have no relation to human experience or feeling."

Dalton insists that literature is also "rooted in the gut and the genitals, as well as in the brain; in the infantile and regressive aspects of the psychic function, as well as in the maturely integrated ego; in delusion and dream, as well as in history, reality and rationality" (19).

20. L. Steiner, *For Humanity's Sake. The Bildungsroman in Russian Culture* (Toronto: University of Toronto Press, 2011); and "*Netochka Nezvanova*," 233-252.

21. O. Meerson, *Dostoevsky's Taboos* (Dresden-München: Dresden University Press, 1996). Specifically, in the idea of Robert Belknap, Meerson sees taboo secrets and sore spots as imposed by "the author's psychological identity, by governmental or ideological censorship, or by fear of displeasing some hegemonic economic or social force" (xiv).

Meerson adds: "After all, tabooing is the only thing definitely common to Dostoevsky's conscious narrative technique and his characters' involuntary embarrassed silence, conscience-sanctioned or God-imposed reticence, and dread at the prospect of eternal torment in hell. . . . Tabooing signals to the reader the values and sore spots of the characters, but while doing so, it also addresses the reader's own sore spots and values" (213).

To such a stance, Belknap responds: "This dangerous but exciting approach will have implications for many other books, primarily those whose authors were able to construct systems of taboos as instruments for the manipulation of their readers, exploiting the 'aha' that comes with the conscious and sometimes unconscious sense that one has participated in maintaining such a taboo" (xiv).

22. D. Martinsen, *Surprised by Shame* (Columbus: Ohio State University Press, 2003). Martinsen takes a similar approach to mine, i.e., she uses studies in shame by sociologists, anthropologists, philosophers, and psychoanalysts in analyses of *The Idiot, Devils,* and *The Brothers Karamazov.*

23. I. Erlich, "'The Peasant Marey.' A Screen Memory," *Psychoanalytic Study of the Child* 36 (1981): 384.

24. S. Fusso, *Discovering Sexuality in Dostoevsky* (Evanston: Northwestern University Press, 2006).

25. S. Grenier, *Representing the Marginal Woman in Nineteenth-Century Russian Literature. Personalism, Feminism, and Polyphony* (Westport: Greenwood Press, 2001).

26. G. Cox, *Tyrant and Victim in Dostoevsky* (Columbus: Slavica Publishers, 1983).

27. J. Andrew, "The Law of the Father and *Netochka Nezvanova*," in J. Andrew, *Narrative and Desire in Russian Literature, 1822-49. The Feminine and the Masculine* (New York: St. Martin's Press, 1993), 211-234; and "The Seduction of the Daughter: Sexuality in the Early Dostoevsky and the Case of *Poor Folk* (*Bednye Liudi*)," in *Polyfunktion und Metaparodie. Aufsätze zum 175. Geburtstag von Feodor Michajlovič Dostoevskij,* ed. R. Neuhäuser (Dresden/München: Dresden University Press, 1998), 172-188.

28. V. Golstein, "Accidental Families and Surrogate Fathers: Richard, Grigory, and Smerdyakov," in *A New Word on* The Brothers Karamazov, ed. Robert Louis Jackson (Evanston: Northwestern University Press, 2004), 90-106.

29. O. Rank, *The Double: A Psychoanalytic Study,* trans. Harry Tucker (Chapel Hill: University of North Carolina Press, 1971).

30. N. Ruttenburg, *Dostoevsky's Democracy* (Princeton, NJ: Princeton University Press, 2008).

31. R. Rosenthal, "Dostoevsky's Experiment with Projective Mechanisms and the Theft of Identity in *The Double*," in *Russian Literature and Psychoanalysis*, ed. D. Rancour-Laferriere (Philadephia/Amsterdam: John Benjamins Publishing Company, 1989), 59–88.

32. B. Paris, *Dostoevsky's Greatest Characters. A New Approach to "Notes from Underground," "Crime and Punishment," and "The Brothers Karamazov"* (New York: Palgrave MacMillan, 2008).

33. S. Rosen, "Homoerotic Body Language in Dostoevsky," *Psychoanalytic Review* 80, no. 3 (Fall 1993): 405–432.

34. S. Sunderwirth and J. Spector, "Codependency: When the Chemistry Isn't Right," *Family Dynamics of Addiction Quarterly* 2 (1992): 23–31.

35. L. Tepperman et al., *The Dostoevsky Effect. Problem Gambling and the Origins of Addiction* (Don Mills: Oxford University Press, 2013).

36. P. Brooks, "The Idea of a Psychoanalytic Literary Criticism," in *Discourse in Psychoanalysis and Literature*, ed. S. Rimmon-Kenan (New York: Methuen, 1987), 17.

37. James Rice notes: "In his own era the novels of Dostoevsky were psychologically enigmatic and intentionally mystifying; his genius consisted in designing problems of the psyche that began to ring true and find solutions only after the advent of modern psychological technique."

Consider also Terras's comment that "as a study of authentic 'child psychology,' the pathetic romance of little Netochka with her half-madman, half-scoundrel stepfather is far ahead of its time."

Finally, note Andrew's comment that "*Netochka Nezvanova* is a remarkable piece of writing, especially in its emotional intensity and its anticipation of Freudian (and post-Freudian) thinking." See J. Rice, *Dostoevsky and the Healing Art. An Essay in Literary and Medical History* (Ann Arbor: Ardis, 1985), 19; Terras, *The Young Dostoevsky*, 53; and Andrew, "The Law of the Father," 226.

38. William Mills Todd III, "*The Brothers Karamazov* Tomorrow," in R. L. Jackson, *A New Word*, 254.

39. C. Caruth, *Unclaimed Experience. Trauma, Narrative, and History* (Baltimore: Johns Hopkins University Press, 1996), 3.

40. Frank, *Dostoevsky*, 367.

41. For an example of successful reversals of this trend, see R. L. Jackson's study on "The Christmas Tree and the Wedding," in *Dialogues*, 94–103.

42. Consider also Terras's remark that "In spite of its still obvious incompleteness, *Netochka Nezvanova* is still a work of considerable merit, and we can only deplore the fact that we do not have the whole novel." See Terras, *The Young Dostoevsky*, 48.

Notes to Chapter One

1. Although the idea of codependency has a decades-long history in Western psychology—through early explorations of the phenomenon by Sigmund Freud, Carl Jung, Erik Erikson, Erick Fromm, Karen Horney, and others—it first gained momentum in extensions to both addiction and the public at large in the 1980s. See M. Babcock, "Critiques or Codependency: History and Background Issues," in M. Babcock and C. McKay, *Challenging Codependency. Feminist Critiques* (Toronto: University of Toronto Press, 1995), 4 and 11.

2. D. Finnegan and E. McNally, "The Lonely Journey: Lesbians and Gay Men Who Are Co-dependent," in *Co-dependency: Issues in Treatment and Recovery*, eds. B. Carruth and W. Mendanhall (New York: Haworth Press, 1989), 123.

Also see "Co-dependency," *Mental Health of America*, http://www.mentalhealthamerica.net/co-dependency, 1. Also see "Codependency Test and Definition," *E-Home Fellowship: Help with Life*, http://www.way2hope.org/codependency-test-definition.htm, 1; and "How to Understand Codependency," *Wikihow*, http://www.wikihow.com/Understand-Codependency, 2; and Babcock, "Critiques," 3.

One of the most interesting explanations of codependency is by James Morgan, who understands the phenomenon as (1) a didactic tool allowing individuals and families to understand dysfunctional behavior; (2) a psychological concept to describe and explain human behavior akin to defense mechanism, enmeshment, and the like; (3) a psychological disorder, even a "disease entity." James Morgan, "What Is Codependency?" *Journal of Clinical Psychology* 47, no. 5 (1991): 722.

Also, consider the remark by Charles Whitfield, who writes: "Codependence is a *contagious* or acquired illness. From the time we are born, it is modeled and taught to us by an endless string of important people in our life: parents, teachers, siblings, friends, heroes, and heroines. Co-dependence is reinforced by the media, government, organized religion, and the helping professions." See C. Whitfield, "Co-dependence: Our Most Common Addiction—Some Physical, Mental, Emotional, and Spiritual Perspectives," *Alcoholism Treatment Quarterly* 6 (1989): 22.

For more on the alleged disease of codependency, see R. Subby, *Lost in the Shuffle. The Co-dependent Reality* (Deerfield Beach: Health Communications, 1987), 83ff.; and C. Kasl, *Women, Sex, and Addiction: A Search for Love and Power* (New York: Ticknor and Fields, 1989), 31ff.

3. See Whitfield, "Co-dependence: Our Most Common Addiction," 19–36; Tab Ballis, "Codependency: The Most Basic Addiction," *Cape Fear Healthy Minds*, http://www.capefearhealthyminds.org/library.cgi?article'1118181493, 1; and D. Lancer, "Recovery from Codependency," *Psych Central*, http://www.psychcentral.com/lib/recovery-from-codependency/00014956, 1.

4. Investigators argue over the immediate and long-range effects of codependency, the prevalence of men or women with the addiction, the quantity and quality of skewed ties to people, places, and ideas. Other issues include whether codependency involves a partial or substantial alteration of self, whether it is an innate or learned characteristic, and whether it is a temporary or permanent condition.

See, for instance, R. Asher and D. Brissett, "Codependency: A View from Women Married to Alcoholics," *International Journal of Addictions* 23 (1988): 346–347.

5. C. Whitfield, *Co-dependence. Healing the Human Condition. The New Paradigm for Helping Professionals and People in Recovery* (Deerfield Beach: Health Communications), 1991), 3.

6. Rice, *A Disease of One's Own*, 82.

7. Whitfield, *Co-dependence. Healing the Human Condition*, 98.

8. Ibid., 28.

9. Kasl, *Women, Sex, and Addiction*, 36.

10. Babcock, "Critiques," 23.

11. M. E. O'Leary, "Codependency and Love Addiction," *InsideTherapy.com*, http://www.insidetherapy.com/codaloveaddict.html, 2.

12. C. Whitfield, *Healing the Child Within. Discovery and Recovery for Adult Children of Dysfunctional Families* (Deerfield Beach: Health Communications, 1987), 68.
13. Subby, *Lost in the Shuffle. The Co-dependent Reality*, 1.
14. Whitfield, *Healing the Child Within*, 117.
15. T. Gagnier and R. Robertiello, "The Clinical Usefulness of Distinguishing Between Two Types of Codependency," *Journal of Contemporary Psychology* 21, no. 4 (1991): 250.
16. A. Schaef, *Codependence: Misunderstood-Mistreated* (San Francisco: Harper, 1986), 76.
17. Finnegan and McNally, "The Lonely Journey," 127.
18. Ibid., 121.
19. M. Erekson and S. Perkins, "System Dynamics in Alcoholic Families," in Carruth and Mendanhall, *Co-dependency*, 60.
20. O'Leary, "Codependency and Love Addiction," 1.
21. Ibid.
22. Ibid., 2.
23. Ibid.
24. Schaef, *Codependence*, 51.
25. O'Leary, "Codependency and Love Addiction," 2.
26. Ann Carson and Richard Baker, "Psychological Correlates of Codependency in Women," *International Journal of Addictions* 29, no. 3 (1994): 404.
27. S. Cooley Ricketson, *The Dilemma of Love. Healing Co-dependent Relationships at Different Stages in Life* (Deerfield Beach: Health Communications, 1989), 49.
28. The conceptualization of codependency began in the 1940s when the wives of members of Alcoholics Anonymous formed a group (later called Al-Anon) to discuss their problems with their spouses. See P. O'Brien and M. Gaborit, "Codependency: A Disorder Separate from Chemical Dependency," *Clinical Psychology* 48, no. 1 (1992): 129.
29. See, for instance, C. Bepko, *The Responsibility Trap* (New York: The Free Press, 1985), 48–40; and Kasl, *Women, Sex, and Addiction*, 31ff.
30. M. Walters, "The Codependent Cinderella Who Loves Too Much... Fights Back," in Babcock and McKay, *Challenging Codependency*, 184.
31. R. Asher, *Women with Alcoholic Husbands. Ambivalence and the Trap of Codependency* (Chapel Hill: University of North Carolina Press, 1992), 19–20.
32. Ibid., 90.
33. T. Cermak, *Diagnosing and Treating Co-dependence. A Guide for Professionals Who Work with Chemical Dependents, Their Spouses, and Children* (Minneapolis: Johnson Institute Books, 1986), 5; S. Perkins, "Altering Rigid Family Role Behaviors in Families with Adolescents," in Carruth and Mendanhall, *Co-dependency*, 113 and 114; Rice, *A Disease of One's Own*, 59; and Schaef, *Codependence*, 41–42.
34. M. Erekson and S. Perkins, "Systems Dynamics in Alcoholic Families," in Carruth and Mendanhall, *Co-dependency*, 60.
35. All references to Dostoevsky are from F. Dostoevskii, *Polnoe sobranie sochinenii v tridtsati tomakh*, 30 vols. (Moscow: Nauka, 1972–1990). All translations are mine.
36. Ricketson, *The Dilemma of Love*, 29.
37. J. Davison, *Sweet Release*, 35.
38. "How to Understand Codependency," 3.
39. E. Larsen, *Stage II Recovery: Life beyond Addiction* (San Francisco: Harper and Row, 1985), 55.
40. See, for instance, P. Edwards et al., "Wives of Alcoholics: A Critical Review and Analysis," *Quarterly Journal of Studies on Alcohol* 34 (1973): 113, 114, and 119; and Subby, *Lost in the Shuffle. The Co-dependent Reality*, 86.

41. J. Jackson, "The Adjustment of the Family to the Crisis of Alcoholism," *Quarterly Journal of Studies of Alcohol* 15 (1954): 568; and Edwards et al., "Wives of Alcoholics," 113 and 114.

42. Larsen, *Stage II Recovery*, 21.

43. B. and J. Weinhold, *Breaking Free of the Co-dependency Trap* (Walpole: Stillpoint, 1989), 185.

44. Consider the claim by J. Deighton that "for many years, the ego deficiencies of the abuser have been blamed for child sexual abuse. Only with the past decade has incest been viewed as an expression of dysfunction, the result of undue tension with the family unit." See J. Deighton et al., "Group Treatment: Adult Victims of Childhood Sexual Abuse," *Journal of Contemporary Social Work* 66, no. 7 (1985): 406.

45. E. Shapiro and A. Carr, *Lost in Familiar Places. Creating New Connections between the Individual and Society* (New Haven: Yale University Press, 1991), 33; and Whitfield, "Co-dependence: Our Most Common Addiction," 22.

46. Tepperman et al., *The Dostoevsky Effect*, 104ff.

47. J. Cruse, *Painful Affairs. Looking for Love through Addiction and Co-dependency* (Deerfield Beach: Health Communications, 1989), 143.

Shapiro writes: "When the holding environment decays or is absent, as in borderline cases, the child feels unsafe in the world and is forced into premature maturation . . . an illusion of self-sufficiency. In some cases, this illusory self-sufficiency appears as detachment; in others, it is revealed through the denial of codependency combined with a chaotic and seemingly unrelated series of outbursts that demand a containing response." See Shapiro, *Lost in Familiar Places*, 36.

48. S. Karpman, "Fairy Tales and Script Drama Analysis," *Transactional Analysis Bulletin* 7 (1968): 40.

49. Ricketson, *The Dilemma of Love*, 28.

50. H. Garfinkel, "Conditions of Successful Degradation Ceremonies," *American Journal of Sociology* 61, no. 5 (1956): 421.

51. Subby, *Lost in the Shuffle. The Co-dependent Reality*, 86. Also see Whitfield, "Co-dependence: Our Most Common Addiction," 25ff.; and Cruse, *Painful Affairs*, 193.

52. See *Trauma. Contemporary Directions in Theory, Practice, and Research*, eds. S. Ringel and J. Brandell (Thousand Oaks, CA: Sage Publications, 2011), 6.

Many of the images and ideas of codependency bear a close affinity with the causes and concerns of "trauma theory," a relatively new discipline integrating psychology and the humanities. Embracing the work of Sigmund Freud, Paul de Man, Jacques Lacan, and others, trauma theory focuses (on one hand) on victim-survivors of incest, rape, domestic violence, early sexual abuse and (on the other hand) on victim-survivors of slavery, torture, famines, terrors, holocausts, and wars.

Like codependents, traumatized individuals manifest their wounds in states of anxiety, dysphoria, hyperarousal, and hypervigilance. Additionally, they often reexperience or reenact past events not only as repetitious, timeless, and unspeakable but also as literal, contagious, and frozen in time and space.

Traumatized individuals show shattered and dissolute selves in disassociation, dismemberment, learned helplessness, cognitive chaos, instinctive obedience, internal and external terror, and substance abuse and addiction. Further, as do codependents, traumatized individuals recall their early years via flashbacks; physical distress; divided consciousness; visual, auditory, and kinesthetic memory; sensations of "departure," "falling," and "burning"; and transference of pain and hurt from multiple pasts to multiple presents.

Finally, such souls engage in "trauma bonding"—i.e., they seek ties with kindred spirits in mutual torment and abuse.

However, healing, closure, and growth are possible for victim-survivors. Questioning and mourning the reasons for their trauma, they learn lessons, mythic and redemptive, sacred and sublime, and they can move to closure, to face life anew as reconstructed selves. See Caruth, *Unclaimed Experience*, 5.

Of interest here is Shoshana Felman's comment that the confession of the hero in Dostoevsky's *Notes from the Underground* can be understood as the writer's "belated testimony to [the] trauma" of his near-death experience at his mock execution in 1849 for his involvement in the Petrashevsky Affair. See S. Felman, "Education and Crisis, or the Vicissitudes of Teaching," in *Testimony. Crises of Witnessing in Literature, Psychoanalysis, and History*, eds. S. Felman and Dori Laub (Oxon: Routledge, 1992), 9–12.

53. Consider also the "inner-child state"—i.e., a conscious, consistent pattern of thoughts, feelings, attitudes, and behaviors that resemble or re-create the experience a person had as an actual child. See L. Weiss and J. Weiss, *Recovering from Co-dependency* (Deerfield Beach: Health Communications, 1989), 3. Also see Rice, *A Disease of One's Own*, 81; and Ricketson, *The Dilemma of Love*, 47.

54. Wienhold, *Breaking Free of the Co-dependency Trap*, 174. As Whitfield writes, "Co-dependence comes from our trying to protect . . . the child within from what may appear to be insurmountable forces outside ourselves." See Whitfield, "Co-dependence: Our Most Common Addiction," 22–23.

55. L. Weiss and J. Weiss, *Recovering from Co-dependency*, 9; and Rice, *A Disease of One's Own*, 81.

56. M. Fossum and M. Mason, *Facing Shame: Families in Recovery* (New York: Norton, 1986), 52 and 57; and Ricketson, *The Dilemma of Love*, 100.

57. M. Lambek, "The Past Imperfect: Remembering as Moral Practice," in P. Antz and M. Lambek, eds., *Tense Past. Cultural Essays in Trauma and Memory* (New York: Routledge, 1996), 235–254; and. L. Namka, *The Doormat Syndrome* (Deerfield Beach: Health Communications, 1989), 42 and 43. Also see Rice, *A Disease of One's Own*, 22; and Whitfield, "Co-dependence: Our Most Common Addiction," 34.

58. For Norman Denzin, individuals seeking to understand addiction experience a "doubling of self." That is, they "relive their past . . . from the vantages of new recovering selves. They exorcize themselves from their past as they retell stories about it. In the process they become different kinds of selves." See N. Denzin, "The Alcoholic Self: Communication, Ritual, and Identity Transformation," in *Communication and Social Structure*, eds. D. Maines and C. J. Couch (Springfield: Charles C. Thomas, 1988), 68.

59. D. Maines, "Narrative's Moment and Sociology's Phenomena: Toward a Narrative Sociology," *Sociological Quarterly* 34, no. 1 (1993): 26; and J. Bruner, "Life as Narrative," *Social Research* 54, no. 1 (1987): 12.

60. In studies of such narratives, several researchers posit a "universe of discourse" with several rhetorical indicators: (1) *biographical reconstruction* in which codependents seek healing to retrofit their life stories into new symbolic systems; (2) *the adoption of a master attribution scheme* by which they move their life troubles into a model that "authoritatively informs all casual attributions about self, others, and events in the world"; and (3) *a suspension of analogical reasoning* in which they interpret their adopted worldview literally, not metaphorically. See Rice, *A Disease of One's Own*, 144–145.

61. In Denzin's idea, codependents writing their histories "offer a privileged access to their inner thoughts and past experiences. . . . As dramatic narrators of life events, they

may be comic, serious, satiric, ironic, truthful, overly emotional, deadpan, deceptive, direct, or indirect. . . . [They may also be] objective, subjective, compassionate, neutral, personal, impersonal, humorous, pompous, ministerial, therapeutic, philosophical, fatherly or motherly. . . . They have become storytellers." See Denzin, "The Alcoholic Self," 68.

Maines also writes: "Time is seen as non-linear because the person can reconstruct pasts and project futures. Time is an activity that turns back on itself through the intersecting processes of cognition (memory) and sociality (keeping collective pasts alive through language and documents)." See Maines, "Narrative's Moment," 23.

62. As Deighton asserts, "Perhaps the major benefit [in reestablishing family ties post-abuse] . . . is the ability . . . of the victim to see that the adult perpetrator and the non-involved parent were victims, too." See Deighton et al., "Group Treatment," 408.

63. Cruse and Johnson "Codependency Treatment Strategies," *Professional Counselor* (1988): 51.

64. D. Maines, "Narrative's Moment," 23. Consider also Bruner's comment: "Eventually, the culturally shaped cognitive and linguistic processes that guide the self-telling of life narratives achieve a power to structure perceptual existence, to organize memory, to segment and purpose-build the very 'events' of a life. In the end, we *become* the autobiographical narrative by which we 'tell' about our lives." See J. Bruner, "Life as Narrative," *Social Research* 54, no. 1 (1987): 15.

65. In line with such writing is the idea of the "trauma novel," defined as a "work of fiction that conveys profound loss or intense fear on individual and collective levels . . . [embracing] the transformation of the self-ignited by an external, often terrifying experience which illuminates the process of coming to terms with the dynamics of memory that inform the new perceptions of the self and the world." See M. Belaev, "Trends in Literary Trauma Theory," *Mosaic* (Winnipeg) 41, no. 2 (2008): 150.

66. As Denzin notes, individuals seeking to understand addiction can locate themselves "within a structure of experience in which they are both objects and subjects. . . . In so doing, they provide the context for others who seek the same ends for themselves." See Denzin, "The Alcoholic Self," 71.

Consider also the experience of one codependent: "I have used a journal in my own recovery and noted that at the beginning there were many things I would not have said out loud to myself or to anyone else. Writing these things down was my first real experience with breaking the silence of the 'no talk' rules in my family history.

"I wrote about my relationships, my family, my feelings, my hopes, and my dreams. I wrote letters to myself and to the little boy in me. I wrote letters to my inner adult and parent. I wrote letters to my father, my mother, my sisters, and my brother.

"After a year or two of journal writing, I started to see certain patterns in my thinking, and I began to acknowledge some of the feelings I had inside. Eventually, I shared many of the things I wrote about with my recovering friends." See Subby, *Lost in the Shuffle. The Co-dependent Reality*, 134–135.

67. M. White and D. Epston, *Narrative Means to Therapeutic Means* (New York: W. W. Norton and Company, 1990), 126 and 127.

68. It is a key tenet of trauma theory that traumatized individuals need empathetic and powerful communities to hear their stories in order to help rebuild their lives and to prevent similar suffering and pain in the future. See K. Tal, *Worlds of Hurt, Reading the Literatures of Trauma* (Cambridge/Melbourne: Cambridge University Press, 1996), 126.

69. Rice, *A Disease of One's Own*, 173.

70. As R. Bauman writes: "Recent critical theory... has begun to mount a double attack on the autonomous narrative text, recontextualizing it from the various viewpoints of both author and reader. In reader-response criticism, in all its various guises, the focus is on the role of the reader, no longer as a passive receiver of the meaning inherent in the text, but as an active participant in the actualization—indeed, the production—of textual meaning as an interpretative accomplishment, much like the members of an oral storytelling audience....

"[There is] a concern with the formal devices employed by the author to engage the participatory involvement of the reader, again as an oral storyteller would do, such as metanarration, the textual creation of a communicative context for the narration, the leaving of gaps to be filled by the reader and so on.

"This effort to reset the literary narrative text in a web of communicative relationships and processes has, not surprisingly, induced some literary theorists to begin to consider—but only in a programmatic way as yet—that it might be productive to think of literary narration as akin to oral storytelling." See R. Bauman, *Story, Performance, and Event. Contextual Studies of Oral Narrative* (New York: Cambridge University Press, 1986), 112-113.

71. Cruse and Johnson, "Codependent Treatment Strategies," 51.

72. For Denzin, the codependent's self is a "group production, rooted in language, common sense meanings, and cultural understandings.... The self, its meanings and its changes are irrevocably grounded in the social group." See Denzin, "The Alcoholic Self," 71.

73. Deighton et al., "Group Treatment," 409; and L. Weiss and J. Weiss, *Recovering from Co-dependency*, 3.

In contrast to other kinds of recollections, "screen memories" feature an apparent discrepancy between intense affect and insignificant content. They also have a dramatic element; i.e., the individual resurrecting the past sees himself as a child performer amidst unusually bright, vivid, and sharp detail. See Erlich, "'The Peasant Marey,'" 384.

74. Carol Gilligan writes: "The middle years of women's lives readily appear as a time of return to the unfinished business of adolescence... [a time when] girls appear to confuse identity with intimacy by defining themselves through relationships with others. The legacy left from this mode of identity definition is considered to be a self that is vulnerable to the issues of separation that arise at mid-life." See C. Gilligan, *In a Different Voice. Psychological Theory and Women's Development* (Cambridge, MA: Harvard University Press, 1982), 170.

75. Maines, "Narrative's Moment," 23.

76. Asher, "Codependency," 28.

77. As Maines writes: "Inconsistency in self-narration is not isomorphic with lying and deception, but rather is an interpretative problematic." See Maines, "Narrative's Moment," 23.

78. E. Chiauzzi and S. Liljegren, "Taboo Topics in Addiction Treatment," *Journal of Substance Abuse Treatment* 10, no. 3 (1993): 308.

79. Ballis, "Codependency: The Most Basic Addiction," 1.

80. Regarding the title for Dostoevsky's work, Konstantin Trutovsky, a classmate at the Main Engineering Academy, where both he and Dostoevsky were students, and later a respected academician of art, recalled: "When I was eighteen, I fell in love....With youthful openness, I shared with Fyodor Mikhailovich all the ups and downs of the affair. With enthusiasm, I described to him my love's beauty, her movements, her words.... Her name

was Anna L'vovna, but at home she was called 'Netochka.' Dostoevsky liked that name so much that he titled his new story *Netochka Nezvanova*." See K. Trutovskii, "Vospominaniia o Fedore Mikhailoviche Dostoevskom," *Russkoe obozrenie* 1 (1893): 215.

81. V. Belinskii, *Polnoe sobranie sochinenii v trinadtsati tomakh* (Moscow: Izdatel'stvo Akademii Nauk SSSR, 1956), 12:335.

82. P. Semenov-Tian-Shanskii, *Detstvo i iunost' (1827–1855 gg.)* (Petrograd: M. Stasiulevich, 1917), 197.

83. O. Miller, "Biografiia, pis'ma i zametki iz zapisnoi knizhki," in F. Dostoevskii, *Polnoe sobranie sochinenii v chetyrnadtsati tomakh* 1 (St. Petersburg: Tipologiia A.S. Suvorina, 1883), 90–91.

84. Kraevsky had received permission from the Third Section to publish *Netochka Nezvanova* without Dostoevsky's name on April 28, 1849.

85. H. Murav, "Reading Women in Dostoevsky," in *A Plot of Her Own. The Female Protagonist in Russian Literature*, eds. S. Hoisington (Evanston: Northwestern University Press, 1995), 51.

86. As Wachtel notes: "In *Kotik Letaev*, Belyi can be said to have taken on two forms: adult narrator and child experiencer. The final lines of the introduction prepare the reader for their dialogue, which will be the formal basis of the entire novel: 'Below me is the first consciousness of childhood; and we—embrace: "Hello, strange one"!'" See Wachtel, *The Battle for Childhood*, 159.

87. The idea of "awakening" or "reawakening" is a key concept of trauma theory. See Caruth, *Unclaimed Experience*, 97ff.

88. Wachtel, *The Battle for Childhood*, 157.

89. M. Jones, "An Aspect of Romanticism in Dostoevsky's *Netochka Nezvanova*, and Eugene Sue's *Mathilde*," *Renaissance and Modern Studies* 17 (1973): 57.

90. Cf. Dostoevsky's claim in *The Diary of a Writer*: "Sometimes a five- or six-year-old child knows things about God or about good and evil that are so amazing and are of such surprising profundity that one cannot help but conclude that Nature has given this child some other means of acquiring knowledge, one that is not only unknown to us but which, on a pedagogical basis, we even ought to reject. . . .

"Try to get at *the essence of the child's understanding*, and you will at once see that the tyke . . . knows more than you do about good and evil and about what is shameful and what is laudable. . . . You will already see that the little one already knows a terrific amount, that he or she has already figured out a great deal with a most unnecessary precocity" (23:22).

91. Open to question is Barbara Heldt's contention that "Dostoevsky's conservatism does not allow an abused woman the right to remain angry and alive." See B. Heldt, *Terrible Perfection. Women and Russian Literature* (Bloomington: Indiana University Press, 1987), 36–37.

92. R. Nazirov, "Tragediinoe nachalo v romane F.M. Dostoevskogo 'Unizhennye i oskorblennye,'" in R. Nazirov, *Russkaia klassicheskaia literatura: sravnitel'no-istoricheskii podkhod. Issledovaniia raznykh let: Sbornik statei* (Ufa: RIO BashGU, 2005), 31.

93. Frank, *Dostoevsky. The Seeds of Revolt*, 353.

94. Kasl, *Women, Sex, and Addiction*, 172.

95. Passage, *Dostoevski the Adapter*, 82–83.

96. Wachtel, *The Battle for Childhood*, 198.

97. Ibid., 196.

98. Ibid., 180.

99. Martinsen, *Surprised by Shame*, 94.

100. Terras, *The Young Dostoevsky*, 103.

101. Consider Victor Pritchett's unflattering (and arguable) comment that *Netochka Nezvanova* is "Russified George Sand . . . [and] unreadable. It has the turgid air of conspiracy which certainly became a characteristic element of Dostoevsky's genius, but here the artist is cramming too much in." See V. Pritchett, *The Myth Makers. Essays on European, Russian and South American Novelists* (London: Chatto and Windus, 1979), 69.

102. Avdotya Panaeva's 1848 novel, *The Tal'nikov Family*, also features the first-person notes of a young cynic and survivor, Natasha, growing up amidst harsh surroundings, replete with a narcissistic, card-addicted mother; a murderously angry father; a hard-drinking grandmother; and her crazy, cowardly, breast-beating husband.

103. So well did Dostoevsky know *Mathilde*—a novel about a pure, innocent orphan girl who endures a tyrannical, sadistic aunt and a weak, immoral husband before marrying a handsome, honorable nobleman who remains her true (and platonic) friend—that he once planned to publish a translation of the work. The project never came to be, though. (*Mathilde* was eventually translated into Russian in 1846.)

104. The first installment of a Russian translation of *Jane Eyre*—Charlotte Brontë's classic account of the moral and spiritual sensibility of a girl in passage to adulthood, replete with explorations into sexuality, religion, proto-feminism, and class consciousness—was published in the May–June 1849 issue of *The Fatherland Notes*, the same issue that featured the third and last section of *Netochka Nezvanova*. See Grenier, *Representing the Marginal Woman*, 131.

105. The novels of Charles Dickens, including *The Old Curiosity Shop*, the story of the beautiful and virtuous Nell and her unnamed grandfather, and *Dombey and Son*, the account of a girl's anguished love for her neglectful father, were not only wildly popular in Russia but also a seminal influence on Dostoevsky and his writing. See Alexander Druzhinin's comparison of *Netochka Nezvanova* and *Dombey and Son* in Druzhinin, "Smes," 67–69. Also see M. Futrell, "Dostoevsky and Dickens," *English Miscellany* 7 (1956): 52–56.

106. Compare Apollon Grigoriev's 1848 statement that "all of contemporary literature is nothing more . . . than a protest in defense of women, on one hand, and on the other, of children, i.e., in defense of the very weakest [of society]." See A. Grigoriev, "N. V. Gogol' i ego 'Perepiska s druz'iami,'" *Sobranie sochinenii*, vol. 8 (Moscow, 1916): 28.

As will be seen, Dostoevsky's Netochka observes only several characteristics of what Wachtel identifies as Russian pseudo-autobiography. As the "sensitive central figure of the experiencing child," she experiences "an eccentric father" and "bittersweet nostalgia for lost time and space"; but she refuses "an idealized mother figure" and "idealization of life on a country estate." See Wachtel, *The Battle for Childhood*, 178.

107. Martinsen writes: "Faces mark the external boundaries between self and others. Also, as centers for verbal and visual reactions, faces become a locus for identity. Readers as witnesses judge interactions between characters by interpreting words, facial expressions, and body language, determining from these clues whether characters violate or demonstrate disrespect for self and others.

"Following unexpected exposure, shamed persons cannot control the autonomic responses that betray shame: pounding of heart, averting of eyes, contracting of posture, sweating, blushing." See Martinsen, *Surprised by Shame*, 15–16.

108. Terras, *The Young Dostoevsky*, 139.

109. A. Guerard, *The Triumph of the Novel: Dickens, Dostoevsky, Faulkner* (New York: Oxford University Press, 1976), 94.
110. Wachtel, *The Battle for Childhood*, 71–72.
111. Terras, *The Young Dostoevsky*, 102 and 266.
112. Heldt, *Terrible Perfection*, 35.
113. Ibid.
114. False, therefore, is Steiner's claim that "Netochka's quest is a harmonious and peaceful spiritual state akin to the lost state of innocence ... to rediscover an innocent, non-egotistical approach to the world." Even more objectionable is her allegation that *Netochka Nezvanova* "appears to be an optimistic precursor of some of Dostoevsky's major works centered on child-like heroes and education (Prince Myshkin and Alyosha Karamazov being the two most obvious examples)." See Steiner, "*Netochka Nezvanova*," 237, 238, and 239.
115. See ibid., 241. Also consider Lacan's idea that "[the] Name-of-the-Father is the Law. The legal assignation of a Father's name to a child is meant to call a halt to uncertainty about the identity of the father.... The Name-of-the-Father must be arbitrarily and absolutely imposed, thereby instituting the reign of patriarchal law." See J. Gallop, *The Daughter's Seduction. Feminism and Psychoanalysis* (Ithaca: Cornell University Press, 1982), 39.
116. Dostoevsky agreed. When asked by his second wife, Anna, that he call her Netochka because her relatives had tagged her as Netochka Nezvanova "to distinguish [her] from any other Netochka and at the same time to hint at [her] passion for Dostoevsky's novels," he replied, "No! My Netochka had to bear a lot of sorrow in life, and I want you to be happy." See A. Dostoevskaia, *Vospominaniia* (Moscow: Khudozhestvennaia literatura, 1971), 92–93.
117. Consider the claim by J. Framo that "despite the anxiety that most people have about raking up old coals, there is nonetheless a universal human need, pushed to some extent by nostalgic memories, to reconnect with one's estranged family." See J. Framo, "Family of Origin as a Therapeutic Resource for Adults in Marital and Family Therapy: You Can and Should Go Home Again," in R. Green and J. Framo, eds., *Family Therapy. Major Contributions* (New York: International Universities Press, 1981), 372.
118. As Wachtel notes, Gorky, in his fictional anti-childhoods, is able "to accept both the sweet and bitter throughout his life and to conceive of life as an organic process that can improve through the accretion of knowledge over time."

Wachtel continues: "For Gorky the positive aspects of childhood (that is, the malleability and optimism of the young) are potentially present at all times and need merely to be tapped rationally.... [With Gorky] it is only through the accumulation of knowledge and self-understanding (acquired through experience, not through self-analysis) that one can move forward, away from the ugly past and into the bright future."

If Dostoevsky's Netochka seeks to make peace with her past, Gorky's narrator seeks a more violent response—i.e., he sees his childhood, adolescence, and youth as a "truth that must be known to its roots so that it can be ripped out by those roots from the memory, from the soul." See Wachtel, *The Battle for Childhood*, 144, 145, and 147.
119. Terras, *The Young Dostoevsky*, 111.
120. Wachtel, *The Battle for Childhood*, 182.
121. Terras, *The Young Dostoevsky*, 289; and Fusso, *Discovering Sexuality*, 108.
122. As Dostoevsky wrote in *The Idiot*: "There is a limit to disgrace in the consciousness of one's own worthlessness and powerlessness beyond which a man cannot

go, and after which he begins to feel a tremendous satisfaction in his own disgrace." See Dostoevskii, *Polnoe sobranie sochinenii*, 8:343.

123. J. Coetzee, "Confession and Double Thoughts: Tolstoy, Rousseau, Dostoevsky," *Comparative Literature* 37, no. 3 (1985): 200; and Corrigan, "Amnesia and the Externalized Personality," 83.

124. Coetzee, "Confession and Double Thoughts," 216. One of the most interesting aspects of current studies of "false confessions" has been the investigations by lawyers and legal experts into Dostoevsky's works. See, for instance, Rinat Kitai-Sangero, "Can Dostoevsky's *Crime and Punishment* Help Us Distinguish between True and False Confessions?" *Ohio State Journal of Criminal Law* 9 (2011): 231–253; Robert Cochran, "Crime, Confession, and the Counselor-at-Law: Lessons from Dostoevsky," *Houston Law Review* 35 (1998): 327–397; and Peter Brooks, *Troubling Confessions. Speaking Guilt in Law and Literature* (Chicago: University of Chicago Press, 2000), and "Storytelling without Fear? Confessions in Law and Literature," *Yale Journal of Law and Humanities* 8, no. 1 (1996): 1–18.

125. Coetzee, "Confession and Double Thoughts," 194.

126. R. Miller, *Dostoevsky's Unfinished Journey* (New Haven: Yale University Press, 2007), 152.

127. Consider also R. Miller's comment that "the frame, the needy child, the trance-like state the precise description of the day on which the [alleged] conversion occurs, the subliminal memories that resurface 'at the needed time'—all these five elements function as mysterious talismans that, in one form or another, reappear in subsequent conversion scenes, almost as if Dostoevsky's individual stories and novels were themselves separate worlds, making mysterious contact with each other." See R. Miller, *Dostoevsky's Unfinished Journey*, 157.

128. As Rowe notes, Dostoevsky uses similar gradations in age with Ilyusha Snegiryov, Kolya Krasotkin, Nellie, and others of his fictional children. Nellie, for instance, is "described (at various stages of victimization) as potentially eleven, twelve, thirteen, fourteen, and fifteen." See Rowe, *Dostoevsky. Child and Man*, 206 and 210.

129. For instance, in *The Insulted and the Injured*, Ivan writes of Nellie: "Her pale and thin face had a sort of unnatural swarthy-yellow, bilious hue. But in general, despite all the hideousness of poverty and illness, she was actually quite pretty. Her brows were sharply outlined, delicate and beautiful; particularly pretty were her broad, somewhat low forehead and her lips, beautifully outlined, with a sort of proud, bold slant, but pale, with just a hint of color" (3:253–254).

130. N. E. Wright, *Psychoanalytic Criticism: Theory and Practice* (New York: Methuen, 1984), 109.

131. "Do you know what it means to abuse a child?" Dostoevsky wrote in *The Diary of a Writer*: "Their hearts are full of innocent, almost unconscious love, and blows such as these cause a grievous shock and tears that God sees and will count. For their reason is never capable of grasping their full guilt. Have you ever seen, or heard of little children who were tormented, or of orphans, say, who were raised among wicked strangers? Have you seen a child cowering in a corner, trying to hide and weeping there . . . not knowing himself what he is doing, not clearly understanding his own guilt, or why he is tormented, but sensing all too well that he is not loved?" (22:69).

132. P. Pol'zinskii, *Detskii mir v proizvedeniiakh Dostoevskogo* (Revel': Gimnaziia, 1891), 9.

133. Compare a similar situation with the child Matroysha in *Demons*. See Fusso, *Discovering Sexuality*, 101.

134. Wachtel, *The Battle for Childhood*, 44ff., and 202. Consider the author's rapture in *Childhood*: "Happy, happy irretrievable time of childhood! How can one not love, not cherish its memories?" See L. Tolstoy, *Polnoe sobranie sochinenii v deviatnosta tomakh* (Moscow: Khudozhestvennaia literatura, 1935), 1:43.

135. Compare the situation of Arkady in *A Raw Youth*, who, as Fusso writes, also "has acquired the habit of discovering the world on his own, making his own mistakes without guidance. He encounters the economic, spiritual, and sexual spheres of life in an experimental, blindly groping way; the last people he would turn to for advice are his mother and Versilov."

Similarly, about Alyosha in *The Brothers Karamazov*, Fusso adds: "Alyosha's mother is dead; and his father is incapable of offering moral guidance, especially in the sexual sphere, even if he were interested in doing so." See Fusso, *Discovering Sexuality*, 101–102.

136. Consider other accounts of childhood in nineteenth-century Russian fiction in which, as Wachtel notes, the child's voice "was generally quite simple, presenting the world as a conscious but not particularly sophisticated observer might have seen it ... one that was privileged only insofar as it was relatively happier than the adult's." See Wachtel, *The Battle for Childhood*, 159.

137. Rowe, *Dostoevsky. Child and Man*, viii.

138. Without foundation, therefore, is Steiner's comment that in *Netochka Nezvanova*, the "idea of early childhood or infancy ... [is] a redeeming spiritual state." See Steiner, "Netochka Nezvanova," 238.

139. Wachtel, *The Battle for Childhood*, 71.

140. Martinsen writes: "Pleasure in humiliation derives from multiple sources: exhibitionism, confirmation of negative self-image; aggressive sharing of blame, and engagement in a creative process. The process ... turns the passive victim of humiliation into an active humiliator. [The character] may be humiliated, but he [or she] is not humiliated. He [or she] finds pleasure in controlling the experience." See Martinsen, *Surprised by Shame*, 96.

141. Wachtel, *The Battle for Childhood*, 53 and 187.

142. Ibid., 53.

143. For more on exhibitionism in Dostoevsky, see G. S. Morson, "Prosaics, Criticism, Ethics," *Formations* 2 (1989): 77–95.

144. J. Kristeva, "On the Melancholic Imaginary," in S. Rimmon-Kenan, ed., *Discourse in Psychoanalysis and Literature* (New York: Methuen, 1987), 111.

145. Corrigan, "Amnesia and the Externalized Personality," 79.

146. In need of reevaluation, therefore, is Nazirov's contention that, in Netochka's story, "there are no secrets, but the prehistory of the heroes is given, their characters are described, and the realistic motivation of their actions is prepared in advance." See Nazirov, "Tragediinoe nachalo," 29.

It should be noted that "non-linear plots ... temporal fissures or narrative omissions ... [and] the withholding of graphic visceral detail to emphasize mental confusion, chaos, or contemplation" are all hallmarks of trauma novels. See Belaev, "Trends," 159.

147. Mochulsky, Terras, and Passage ascribe much of the chaotic nature of *Netochka Nezvanova* to Dostoevsky's off-hand, half-hearted attitude toward it. Given the notorious unreliability of Dostoevsky's speakers in his mature novels, a more tantalizing explanation for the marked randomness of the work is that Dostoevsky was experimenting with first-person narration and voice to show the inner distress of his characters. See K. Mochulsky, *Dostoevsky. His Life and Work*, trans. Michael Minihan (Princeton, NJ: Princeton University Press, 1967), 101; Terras, *The Young Dostoevsky*, 45; and Passage, *Dostoevski*, 83.

148. Wachtel, *The Battle for Childhood*, 3.

149. Consider Fusso's remark that "for Dostoevsky, the traditional relationship of parent and child must be preserved... and based upon the difficult, day-to-day labor of love." See Fusso, *Discovering Sexuality*, 116.

150. Consider again the case in Belyi's *Kotik Letaev* in which, as Wachtel notes, the child "can see and experience things that adults cannot... privileged by an inner vision to which the adult narrator is not privy." See Wachtel, *The Battle for Childhood*, 159.

151. Ibid., 167ff.

152. In *The Diary of a Writer*, Dostoevsky continued: "It is curious to observe how the most complex concepts develop almost unnoticed in a child—how the child, still unable to connect two thoughts, sometimes splendidly understands the deepest things in life. A certain German scholar said that any child, upon attaining the age of three, has already acquired an entire third of the ideas and concepts which he will take with him, as an old man, to the grave" (22:9).

Notes to Chapter Two

1. Wachtel, *The Battle for Childhood*, 96ff.

2. Ibid.

3. Frank's claim that the Italian is Efimov's "first instructor in the violin" has no basis in fact. See Frank, *Dostoevsky*, 353.

4. No evidence in the text exists for Passage's claim that the Italian conductor is "one of those figures, numerous in fiction, who are either devils temporarily incarnate on missions of soul-destruction, or, more commonly, who are quite human but have bartered their salvation for some earthly commodity, such as fame or wealth, and can escape the penalty of their misdeed only by engaging another human soul in a similar 'contract' with Hell." Passage's assumption that Efimov murdered the conductor, thereby "somehow impairing the magic of the instrument," also invites skepticism. See Passage, *Dostoevski*, 85 and 86.

5. See Terras, *The Young Dostoevsky*, 47; Frank, *Dostoevsky*, 353 and 355; and Grossman, *Dostoevsky*, 131. Also see A. Gozenpud, *Dostoevskii i muzykal'no-teatral'noe isskustvo. Issledovanie* (Leningrad: Sovetskii kompozitor, 1981), 55.

It should also be noted here that such benevolence has been extended to almost all of the highly flawed characters in *Netochka Nezvanova*. Nazirov, for instance, sees the landowner and the musician B., together with the Prince, Madame Leotard, Katya, and Alexandra Mikhailovna, as "humane people... [among whom] Netochka cannot perish." See R. Nazirov, "Tragediinoe nachalo," 5.

6. Frank, *Dostoevsky*, 353 and 365.

7. Consider Wasiolek's insightful remark: "We get in Efimov the first sketch of a character choosing circumstances to remake the world for a purpose.... We see in him what we will see often in the later heroes of Dostoevsky: a hero who paradoxically hurts not only those about him, but himself also; a hero who pursues, welcomes, and needs failure, hurt, and destruction." See Wasiolek, *Dostoevsky*, 15.

8. Without basis, Steiner accepts Efimov's bargain with the devil-Italian. "Dostoevsky's 'genius,' Efimov," she writes, "is not a beneficiary of a divine gift, but rather a victim of demonic possession; instead of yielding golden fruit, his artistic gift corrupts both his reason and his morals." See Steiner, "*Netochka Nezvanova*," 243.

9. Consider Wasiolek's apt remark: "There is much of the lackey about Efimov, albeit a rebellious lackey." See Wasiolek, *Dostoevsky*, 28.

10. Grossman, for instance, writes that Netochka's stepfather is an "outstanding musician ... crushed by poverty, dependence, and failure." Terras notes that Efimov shows "real promise" and "potential" as an artist. Fridlender adds: "Efimov is ... a talented and richly gifted Russian ... upon whom weighs the curse of Russian existence.... The tragic fate of Netochka's stepfather is for Dostoevsky not only a symbol of a certain timeless 'unavoidable' tragedy of the artist, but also an expression of the concrete physical and social conditions of the life of the people."

Finally, Steiner notes: "The portrait [of Efimov] that emerges is quite contradictory. He is both a genius and a wretch; his life—both a passionate drama and a failure. In short, Efimov's life presents an example of an unsuccessful *Bildung*—a failure to harmonize one's inner drive and the external conditions of one's life, to make a career out of one's vocation."

See Grossman, *Dostoevsky*, 127; Terras, *The Young Dostoevsky*, 121; Fridlender, *Realizm Dostoevskogo*, 89; Frank, *Dostoevsky*, 354 and 365; Wasiolek, *Dostoevsky*, 14; Passage, *Dostoevski*, 98; and Steiner, "Netochka Nezvanova," 241.

11. Terras, *The Young Dostoevsky*, 120. Steiner is even more accepting of Efimov's alleged giftedness. She notes that "Efimov inherits the Italian's occult power of unique musical perception ... to acquire his extraordinary ability to feel and understand music" and that "for six years immediately following the death of his first violin teacher, the demonic Italian, he has had enough patience to work on his art." She adds that Efimov's soul "has become seduced by the desire of absolute music: a perfect self-expression through a medium of pure sound, which requires neither the concern, nor the compassion of others; ... to realize his ideal of absolute music he must reach a non-human intelligence." See Steiner, "Netochka Nezvanova," 243–244.

12. Frank, *Dostoevsky*, 353.

13. In no way, therefore, is the musician B., as Steiner asserts, "the voice of reason and common sense." See Steiner, "Netochka Nezvanova," 241.

14. Wrongly, Steiner also indicts the world for Efimov's predicament. "How can the man's longing [for music]," she asks, "be satisfied in the world which imposes ordinary demands on one's profession, family and society?" See Steiner, "Netochka Nezvanova," 244.

15. Here Dostoevsky's Efimov bears a striking affinity to the Italian musician in Balzac's 1837 work "Gambara," about an insane enthusiast who creates new instruments and musical forms.

16. Necessarily open to question is Grossman's claim that Netochka grows up in an "environment saturated with an interest in art." Grossman, *Dostoevsky*, 127.

17. Terras, *The Young Dostoevsky*, 104.

18. Ibid., 105.

19. Compare the estate (and all that it implied) as the locus for the edenic garden in fictional accounts of gentry childhood. See Wachtel, *The Battle for Childhood*, 145.

20. Consider an early exploration into this aspect of Dostoevsky's life and writing in M. Kanzer, "Dostoevsky's Matricidal Impulses," *Psychoanalytic Review* 35 (1948): 115–125.

21. Contrary to the actual situation between Netochka and her mother is Steiner's idea that "early childhood is important to Dostoevsky first of all as an example of a non-egotistical approach to the world and a special non-subjective experience—the kind of experience that is akin to the bond of love uniting mother and child"; and that "Netochka's

entire story can be seen as an attempt to recover her original innocent experience, which Netochka remembers as sharing her bed with her mother and clinging to her." See Steiner, "Netochka Nezvanova," 238.

22. Wachtel, *The Battle for Childhood*, 125ff.

23. R. L. Jackson, *Dostoevsky's Quest for Form. A Study of His Philosophy of Art*, 2nd edition (Pittsburgh: Physsardt Publishers, 1978), 163.

24. Terras, *The Young Dostoevsky*, 70.

25. Wright, *Psychoanalytic Criticism*, 108.

26. Wasiolek is correct in his claims that "Netochka's attachment for her father [sic] is an erotic one" and that "striking ... is the boldness with which the erotic relationship [between her and Efimov] is pointed out and emphasized." However, another of his assertions is open to question, that the tie between them contains a "spiritual element" that is "more important [than the physical]." See Wasiolek, *Dostoevsky*, 42.

27. Terras, *The Young Dostoevsky*, 108. Consider also the explicitly erotic ties between Netochka and Katya in the second part of *Netochka Nezvanova* and between Netochka and Alexandra Mikhailovna in the third.

28. These characters include Nellie and Valkovsky in *The Insulted and the Injured*; the five-year-old girl and the moral monster Svidrigailov in *Crime and Punishment*; the child Liza and the landowner Velchaninov in Dostoevsky's 1870 novel *The Eternal Husband*; Nastasya Filippovna and her lover Totsky in *The Idiot*; and Matryosha and Stavrogin in *Devils*.

An example of aberrant sexuality in Dostoevsky's early works is the relationship between Yulian Mastokovich and the young girl in "The Christmas Tree and the Wedding" (1848).

Rowe, comparing the relationships between Liza and Velchaninov and between Nellie and Valkovsky, writes astutely: "The fathers seem to share a strange fascination for—that is, seem to be drawn uncannily towards—the girls and appear to experience a somewhat inordinate initial involvement in the girls' emotions.... A further factor uniting the circumstances of Liza and Nellie is that each girl lives in close quarters with a man who is not her father. Dostoevsky's apparent interest in such a situation can be construed to reflect the agitation typical of his more overt treatments of pedophilia." See Rowe, *Dostoevsky. Child and Man*, 15–16.

Terras hints precisely at this scene when he notes "the boldness with which the erotic aspect of the relationship [between Netochka and Efimov] is not only suggested and tolerated, but also pointed out and emphasized." See Terras, *The Young Dostoevsky*, 105.

For more on abused female children in Dostoevsky, see Fusso, *Discovering Sexuality*, 17–41; and Andrew, "The Seduction of the Daughter," 173–188.

29. Guerard, *The Triumph of the Novel*, 98. Consider also Andrew's claims that the scene is "structured in classically Oedipal terms ... [i.e.,] Netochka identifies with and privileges [Efimov's] phallus, at the expense of her mother's body"; as well as Rowe's assertion that "the Dostoevskian pedophilia victim ... has almost invariably the sexual desirability of an older girl, the helplessness of a younger girl, and a near woman's capacity for apprehending her victimization." See Andrews, "The Law of the Father," 220; and Rowe, *Dostoevsky. Child and Man*, 209.

30. Compare also Iza Erlich's analysis of Dostoevsky's 1876 story "The Peasant Marey," the quasi-autobiographical encounter between a gentry boy and a peasant. Specifically,

Erlich notes how Marey places his "thick finger" against the boy's "trembling" lips. Erlich also notes: "Child seducers need not be brutal; in fact, they are often quite gentle." See Erlich, "'The Peasant Marey,'" 387.

31. Consider here the "threshold dialogue" put forth by Mikhail Bakhtin. See M. Bakhtin, *Problems of Dostoevsky's Poetics*, 111, 116, and 128.

32. This statement undermines Andrew's claim that "we are left with [Netochka's] primal, unexplained and inexplicable rejection of the mother." See Andrew, "The Law of the Father," 220.

33. Implausible, therefore, is Steiner's remark that Netochka's love for Efimov is "an erotic attachment, which though not yet tied to the sexual instinct, is already selfish and possessive." See Steiner, "Netochka Nezvanova," 241.

Compare Vanya's paraphrase of Nellie's first story of her past in *The Insulted and the Injured*: "It was the strange story of the mysterious, even hardly understandable relationship between a half-crazy man and his tiny granddaughter, who was already able to understand him and who, although a child, was able to understand much that others do not grasp during the entire years of their smooth, secure lives" (3:299–300).

34. Consider a similar wake scene when Rogozhin and Myshkin attend the dead body of Nastasya Filippovna in *The Idiot*. Discussing this scene, Andrew wonders whether the demise of Netochka's mother is from murder or suicide, an additional explanation is that her codependence on Efimov is the genuine cause of her death. See Andrew, "The Law of the Father," 225.

35. Guerard, *The Triumph of the Novel*, 40.

36. There is every reason to question Terras's remark that when Efimov returns from S.'s concert, "there is still a faint glimmer of hope in his mind that he might duplicate the great fiddler's performance." See Terras, *The Young Dostoevsky*, 51.

37. Dostoevky's italics.

38. Dostoevsky notes a similar real-life incident in *The Diary of a Writer*. A seven- or eight-year-old girl begins to cry horribly at the sight of her dead mother. When she is reminded by a "stupid old woman" that her mother had once made her stand in the corner and hence did not love her, the girl stops crying immediately. The story does not end there. Dostoevsky continues: "The next day, at [her mother's] funeral, the girl was somehow affectedly cold and offended, i.e., '[her mother] did not love her.' She liked the idea that she was abused, unwanted, unloved. As God is my judge, this happened to a child of about seven or eight. But this child's 'fantasticalness' did not last long. In a few days, the child once more missed her mother, so deeply that she became ill, and never again in her entire life could this child remember her mother without a feeling of reverence." As quoted in Rowe, *Dostoevsky. Child and Man*, 9.

39. Revealingly, the hero in Gorky's *Childhood* experiences no grief at the death of his mother. See Wachtel, *The Battle for Childhood*, 136–137.

40. Catteau, Terras, R. L. Jackson, and others assert very plausibly that Efimov is most likely to "have been to a considerable extent a projection of [Dostoevsky's] own ego," specifically the writer's "fears, doubts, and miseries . . . [his] introspective analysis and self-criticism . . . [his] frequent and sudden jumps from exaggerated obsequiousness and self-depreciation to equally hyperbolic insolence and self-assurance . . . [his] tendency to exaggerate his every gesture, his every intonation . . . [and his] extreme impracticality in money matters." See J. Catteau, *Dostoyevsky and the Process of Literary Creation* (Cam-

bridge: Cambridge University Press, 1989), 120; Terras, *The Young Dostoevsky*, 121; and R. L. Jackson, *Dostoevsky's Quest for Form*, 181–182.

Terras and Frank both argue that Efimov's end is the result of not only his failure to develop his talent but also his surrender to romantic egoism. Terras writes: "I know of no *Künstlerroman* in which the author, for all his love and reverence for art, is so harsh to the artist who fails his calling." To this, Frank adds: "This first part of Dostoevsky's novel contains one of the most bitter indictments of Romantic egoism, in its 'artistic' variety, that can be found in literature of the time. Only Dickens's Harold Skimpole in *Bleak House* (published four years later) can compare with Efimov as a moral condemnation of the heartlessness of Romantic aestheticism." See Terras, *The Young Dostoevsky*, 51; also see Frank, 356.

Notes to Chapter Three

1. It is interesting to note that Grossman considers the second part of *Netochka Nezvanova* "one of the finest in Dostoevsky's early work." See Grossman, *Dostoevsky*, 28.

In the original manuscript for *Netochka Nezvanova*, Dostoevsky has the Prince also adopt a second child, Larya. Roughly the same age as Netochka, he was intended as the hero of the account.

Larya is a fascinating character. (He is often seen as a sketch for the already-noted Ippolit Terentiev in *The Idiot* and Ilyusha Snegiryov of *The Brothers Karamazov*.) Sickly, homely, and redheaded, he is the son of a poor spineless clerk and a doting, equally weak-willed mother. He tyrannizes over the two partly in response to his own mistreatment by schoolmates, partly as a consequence of his own disturbed personality.

"I would be so stupid and thoughtless," he tells Netochka, "that when I came home from school, I told [my mother] on purpose that the other boys had pinched me... because I knew that Mama would start crying when I told her everything" (444). Larya makes quite clear his joy over his maliciousness. "I liked it so much," he continues to Netochka, "that Mama was crying about *me*" (444).

Although Larya seeks to end such behavior—"I did feel sorry for Mama" (444), he tells his comrade—his wish is too little, too late. One night before Christmas, Larya's demands for expensive presents, coupled with his own willful behavior, causes his father to die of a heart attack and his grief-stricken mother soon to meet a similar fate.

Larya is then adopted by Fyodor Ferapontovich, a distant relative. In Fyodor, Larya has met his match. Like Efimov, Fyodor yearns morbidly (and theatrically) for recognition and respect. Adult and child clash, and Larya is only saved from ruin when Prince X. takes him in.

In his new home, Larya is even more problematic than Netochka. He cries a great deal, sulks in dark corners, refuses to study, and cedes to torturous dreams. He derives a morbid, sadomasochistic satisfaction not only from the fact that he caused the death of his parents but also that he will soon join them in death.

In a fashion typical of Dostoevsky's guilt-ridden characters, Larya seeks to force his own end. Similar to the way the ghost of Marfa Petrovna visits Svidrigailov in *Crime and Punishment*, Larya tells Netochka that every night his late mother visits him. Unlike Svidrigailov, though, Larya is so taken by what he sees as the joy and bliss of the woman's visits that he resolves to run away and die on her grave. Larya does not pursue his plan, though. Fortunately for both him and Netochka, the Prince places the boy with poor but honest relatives in Ukraine.

An interesting aspect of Larya is the way his guilt over his parents' demise spurs a desire to be humiliated and punished. When Netochka first meets Larya, she finds that the boy has not only missed supper on purpose but is also preparing to spend the night in a cold hall. Further, when Netochka seeks to return Larya to the nursery, the child begs on his knees for forgiveness for his crime against his parents.

Larya's most important apparent function is to prick Netochka's conscience over the death of her mother. Indeed, because of Larya the adult Netochka writes:

> In fact, all children carry within themselves facets that liken them [to Larya]. In the first place, they are all by nature sensitive and impressionable . . . miserly and greedy, egoists and sensualists to the highest degree. For that reason no one is as grateful for love as a child, but the attitude of the younger is often mercenary. This is his recompense for all the dotage and all the pleasures with which the youth is surrounded. (444)

The adult Netochka even takes this idea further, asserting that Larya informed his mother of his torments at school with the intention of inciting her to spoil him even more.

For an English translation of the episode with Larya in *Netochka Nezvanova*, see Terras, *The Young Dostoevsky*, 299–308.

2. Terras, *The Young Dostoevsky*, 146.

3. Frank's statement that Netochka, in the second part of her narrative, has moved to a world in which "a love of art is combined with the highest moral and human qualities" outlines the very opposite of what the girl actually finds there. See Frank, *Dostoevsky*, 356.

4. See Jones, "An Aspect of Romanticism," 49 and 51; Frank, *Dostoevsky*, 355 and 366–367; and Grossman, *Dostoevsky*, 131.

5. Wright, *Psychoanalytic Criticism*, 109.

6. See Wachtel, *The Battle for Childhood*, 148.

7. Steiner notes that the "drafts to *The Idiot*, *Devils*, and *The Adolescent* show . . . that the 'predatory' type occupied a prominent place in Dostoevsky's creative laboratory"; but, as with so many of the ideas and images of Dostoevsky's later fiction, the character of the predator appeared first in *Netochka Nezvanova*. See Steiner, *For Humanity's Sake*, 71.

8. Again, in the tyrannical old aunt, Dostoevsky copies a similar personage from Sue's *Mathilde*.

9. Such devastating flashbacks are a key factor in trauma theory, in the suffering and healing of traumatized individuals. See Caruth, *Unclaimed Experience*, 59 and 64.

10. See R. L. Jackson, *Dostoevsky's Quest for Form*, 64. Consider also Blank's claim that beauty in Dostoevsky has the "potential to act in both ways—to save and destroy, to inspire faith and to cause disbelief, to awaken love and to arouse carnal passion." See K. Blank, *Dostoevsky's Dialectics and the Problems of Sin* (Evanston: Northwestern University Press, 2010), 72.

11. Steiner, "*Netochka Nezvanova*," 245; and Grossman, *Dostoevsky*, 127 and 128.

12. This fact casts doubt upon Steiner's idea of Katya as the victim in her associations with Netochka. "That erotic desire for one person," Steiner writes, "can make one cruel and insensitive to others, as well as prone to selfishness and melancholia, is the main lesson that Katya, Netochka's 'beloved' and her pupil, is about to learn." See Steiner, "*Netochka Nezvanova*," 246.

13. In their view, the relationship is between an "extraordinarily strong and an extraordinarily weak individual," with Netochka as the "weaker, quasi-feminine partner," the bearer of "gentle amiability," the "head of an entire line of meek women in Dostoevsky," and the pièce de résistance, "the shy 'dreamer' . . . from the depths of the urban intelligentsia." See Grossman, *Dostoevsky*, 128; Terras, *The Young Dostoevsky*, 105–106; Wasiolek, *Dostoevsky*, 42; and Mochulsky, *Dostoevsky*, 109.

14. The academic rivalry between Netochka and Katya, not to mention the unhealthy relationship between the two girls, is inspired in some part by Mathilde and Ursula in Sue's *Mathilde*.

15. Compare Ivan's portrait of Nellie in *The Insulted and the Injured*: "Small of stature, with sparkling, dark, somehow non-Russian eyes, with luxuriant dark hair and an enigmatic, mute, and unyielding gaze, she would arrest the attention of any passerby on the street" (3:253).

16. Consider how the beauty of such "infernal" characters as Nastasya Filippovna in *The Idiot* and Grushenka in *The Brothers Karamazov* astound their hosts.

17. R. L. Jackson, *Dostoevsky's Quest for Form*, 238.

18. Compare the references to Falstaff in *Devils*, particularly the drunken officer Lebyadkin's identification with the character in the second part of the work.

19. Dostoevsky took the story of Falstaff, at least in part, from a French two-act melodrama, *Jocko, or the Brazilian Monkey* (*Jocko, ou le Singe du Brésil*), written by Edmond Rochefort in 1825. In it a rich Portuguese man traveling to Brazil captures a monkey, which, during a crossing of the Atlantic, saves the man's child from shipwreck but perishes in the process. (In later productions, the public demanded that the monkey survive.)

The play also gave rise to a ballet of the same name, one rendition of which was staged by Jean-Antonine Petipa (the father of the famous teacher, choreographer, and ballet dancer Maurius Petipa). Jocko is also seen as the precursor for the humanized monkeys in *King Kong* and *Planet of the Apes*.

The seven-year-old Dostoevsky saw *Jocko* in Moscow on February 1, 1828. About his reaction to the play, his brother Andrei writes: "One time we saw a play, entitled *Jocko, or the Monkey of Brazil*. I do not recall the content of the piece, but I do remember that the artist who played the monkey was also an expert tightrope-walker. For a long time my brother Fyodor was in raves over him and tried to imitate him." See O. Miller, *Biografiia*, 11.

20. Similarly, the narrator describes the dog in *The Insulted and the Injured*: "Why was it that the first time I saw [the dog] I immediately had this idea that it was not like all other dogs; that it was an unusual dog; that there had to be something fantastic and enchanted about it; that perhaps it was a kind of Mephistopheles in the guise of a dog and that its fate was connected by some mysterious, unknown means to the fate of its master?" (3:171).

21. In this, Dostoevsky is borrowing from Book Two of Rousseau's 1782 autobiographical *Confessions*, in which the hero, a young servant in the house of Comte de la Roque, steals a ribbon from Marion, a maid. When asked publicly by the Comte about the object, Rousseau insists that Marion has given it to him, implying that she has tried to seduce him.

In the public confrontation, Rousseau clings obstinately to his story, thereby ruining an innocent girl who does not flinch amidst his accusations. Unsurprisingly, both Rousseau and Marion are dismissed from their posts by the Comte, who notes that the conscience of the guilty party will avenge the innocent.

Rousseau proves the Comte correct: He suffers daily for his perfidy. He imagines that Marion, unable to find a new position, has become a prostitute. He himself suffers nighttime hallucinations in which he stands accused of the theft.

Notwithstanding the pain, Rousseau never confesses his crime, even to his closest friends. In fact, it is his conscience that spurs him not only to write his confessions but also to return to the incident after he has vowed never to speak of it again.

The theft of the ribbon also moves Rousseau to a classic "false" confession. As Paul de Man writes, "What Rousseau *really* wanted is neither the ribbon nor Marion, but the public scene of exposure which he actually gets. . . . The more there is to expose, the more satisfying the scene, and especially, the more satisfying and eloquent the belated revelation, in the later narrative, of the inability to reveal." See Paul de Man, "Excuses (Confessions)," *Allegories of Reading* (New Haven: Yale University Press, 1979), 285.

22. Terras, *The Young Dostoevsky*, 266.

23. Jones, "An Aspect of Romanticism," 53.

24. Frank, *Dostoevsky*, 360.

25. Conceivably, Dostoevsky is here polemicizing with a similar episode in Rousseau's 1762 novel *Emile, or On Education* (*Émile, ou De l'éducation*), in which a small boy is left in a dark room for several days to come to terms with his wrongdoing, the idea being that children, in and of themselves, can accept responsibility for their faults. Of course, with Dostoevsky's Netochka (not to mention the children in his mature fiction), just the opposite is the case. Indeed, the girl only justifies her codependency and other addictive behaviors.

26. See R. Miller, *Dostoevsky's Unfinished Journey*, 96. Rousseau deposited each of his five infant children from a liaison with his maid, Thérèse Le Vasseur, in a foundling hospital. Later, with great sentimentality, if breathtaking hypocrisy, he proclaimed himself a loving father and worthy teacher who continued to show concern for his brood.

Also relevant here is Julia Kristeva's claim of the "dismantling of the Christian-Rousseau myth of childhood. . . . Projected into the supposed place of childhood, and therefore universalized, one finds features that are particular to adult discourse; the child is endowed with what is dictated by adult memory, always distorted to begin with; the myth of human continuity persists (from child to parent, sameness prevails)." J. Kristeva, *Desire in Language. A Semiotic Approach to Literature and Art* (New York: Columbia University Press, 1980), 276.

27. Jones, "An Aspect of Romanticism," 53.

28. J. Meier-Graefe, *Dostoevsky. The Man and His Work* (New York: Harcourt, Brace, and Company, 1928), 75.

29. Frank, *Dostoevsky*, 365.

30. Recall the "feverish flush" and the "crimson, burning lips" of the five-year-old child in Svidrigailov's dream in *Crime and Punishment*.

31. Compare the kissing scene, replete with swollen lips, between Grushenka and Katerina Ivanovna in *The Brothers Karamazov*.

32. Steiner is therefore out of bounds when she observes that "the story of Netochka's friendship with Katya is a skillful narrative of suspense which titillates the reader by using the language of adult romance to describe the unfolding of an adolescent friendship, and yet which is more suggestive than revealing." See Steiner, "*Netochka Nezvanova*," 245.

Notes to Chapter Four

1. Terras, *The Young Dostoevsky*, 102.

2. Interestingly, Vissarion Belinsky, in his article "A View of Russian Literature in 1847" ("*Vzgliad na russkuiu literaturu v 1847 godu*"), saw Raphael's *Madonna* as the *idéal sublime du comme il faut*. Most certainly, Dostoevsky knew this piece. See V. Belinskii, *Polnoe sobranie sochinenii v tridtsati tomakh* (Moscow: Izdatel'stvo Akademii Nauk SSSR, 1956), 10:306.

3. R. L. Jackson, *Dostoevsky's Quest for Form*, 215.

4. Compare the pale face, hollow cheeks, and burning eyes that mark Nastasya Filippovna in *The Idiot*.

5. Charles Passage suggests, plausibly, that Alexandra Mikhailovna's birth may have been illegitimate. See Passage, *Dostoevski*, 102.

6. Alexandra Mikhailovna is for Terras "a virtuous and devoted wife," "the soul of generosity," and "the innocent victim of a cruel, unfeeling, and sordid world ... kindly, generous, and pure to the end." He describes her in this way: "Angelic simplicity, extraordinary nobility of emotions, loftiness of intellect—such are the basic traits of [Alexandra Mikhailovna's] character, which seem to lack negative traits altogether." See Terras, *The Young Dostoevsky*, 102; and Frank, *Dostoevsky*, 355 and 361.

7. Steiner unconvincingly portrays Netochka as an "orphan who gets adopted by two different 'accidental families,' is eventually able to transcend her coldness and alienation and develop friendships with Princess Katya and Alexandra Mikhailovna." See Steiner, "*Netochka Nezvanova*," 245.

8. Steiner clearly lacks evidence for the claim that in *Netochka Nezvanova*, Dostoevsky "suggests that any kind of productive learning and teaching happens only under the aegis of Eros." See Steiner, "*Netochka Nezvanova*," 246.

9. Here Dostoevsky again takes issue with Rousseau's *Émile*, in which the writer argues not only for the equality of teacher and student during instruction but also for the idea that emotion and experience offer the best lessons for life, and that children learn best when motivated by desire and pleasure, not coercion and force.

10. Andrew, "The Law of the Father," 218.

11. About his own youthful ambivalence over the works of Walter Scott, Dostoevsky wrote to Nikolai Ozmidov on August 18, 1880: "When I was about twelve years old, and on vacation in the village, I read all of Walter Scott and let develop in myself both fantasy and impressionability. But it was all to a good end ... since from my readings ... I seized upon ... many splendid and noble impressions ... which were seductive, passionate, and corrupting, and with which I struggled in my soul" (30, 1:212).

12. Contrary to the truth of the situation is Steiner's observation that "Netochka comes to love her new mother, Alexandra Mikhailovna, in the most selfless way; such a love resembles either a mother's life for her child or the poet's love for creation." See Steiner, "*Netochka Nezvanova*," 239.

13. Terras, for instance, writes that Netochka "appears to be a great voice, and promises to become a singer of considerable talent." Steiner adds that "*Netochka Nezvanova* was planned as a *Künstlerroman*—a type of bildungsroman describing the artist's apprenticeship." She also affirms that as an artist, Netochka is unlikely to repeat Efimov's mistakes: "Efimov's failure to transform his artistic gift into a redemptive resource serves an important lesson for the musically gifted Netochka. Like Efimov, she becomes an out-

cast taken in by strangers. But unlike her stepfather she will neither scorn their generosity nor betray their friendship. If we assume that Efimov has passed his demonic gift on to Netochka (such seemed to be the genealogy of her own talent), the rest of her story shows that Netochka does not blindly follow Efimov's path of alienation and madness, but manages to overcome his example."

Sounding a similar note, Frank pronounces it "very likely" that Netochka will become a great singer à la George Sand's heroines in her 1842–1843 novel *Consuelo*, or her 1846 work *Lucrezia Floriani*. Further, Frank believes it to have been Dostoevsky's goal to portray Netochka as a "character who unites a dedication to art with an equally firm commitment to the highest social-moral ideals." According to Frank,

> Netochka's life begins in the shadow of an artistic obsession that perverts her character and disorients her moral sensibility. But, triumphantly overcoming this initial handicap, her love of art would go hand in hand with a sensitive and fearless moral-social conscience. With [*Netochka Nezvanova*], then, Dostoevsky was endeavoring to steer a middle way between the discredited Romantic glorification of art on the one hand, and the temptation to discard the values of art entirely in favor of the utilitarian and the practical on the other.

In this vein, also, Frank believes that the hatred the child Netochka has for her mother "springs forth from a false belief that this parent blocks the way to the self-fulfillment of an artist, and to the life of ease and glory that artistic success would bring in its train." Also crucial to Frank's analysis is his idea that *Netochka Nezvanova* bears a "philanthropic" stamp. "Born of humble parents and living her earliest years in abject misery," he writes, "Netochka's success in becoming a great artist would reveal all the wealth of neglected talent hidden in the socially outcast as well as in her supposedly inferior sex."

See Terras, *The Young Dostoevsky*, 48; Frank, *Dostoevsky*, 350; and Steiner, "*Netochka Nezvanova*," 243 and 245. Also see Fridlender, *Realizm Dostoevskogo*, 88; Grossman, *Dostoevsky*, 128; Passage, *Dostoevski*, 98; and Andrew, "The Law of the Father," 217.

14. Mochulsky, *Dostoevsky*, 112.
15. Frank, *Dostoevsky*, 361.
16. Mochulsky, *Dostoevsky*, 111.
17. Terras, *The Young Dostoevsky*, 107.
18. See Wachtel, *The Battle for Childhood*, 174ff.
19. Consider also Andrew's claim that, in *Poor Folk*, the books Varvara receives from Pokrovsky, the poor tutor, afford her "unspeakable joy and coded sexual pleasure." See Andrew, "The Seduction of the Daughter," 181.
20. Fictional explorations of adultery (consummated or otherwise) were extremely popular in Russian fiction of the 1830s and 1840s. Elena Gan (writing under the pseudonym of "Zeneida R-va"), Maria Zhukova, and others portrayed "superior women" and "higher natures" who were prepared to violate marital conventions. Zhukova particularly objected to women who, for the sake of convenience, were married off by relatives and found little emotional or intellectual fulfillment with their mates.

It is also worth noting that in the 1840s, progressive writers and critics, Belinsky at their head, took up the issue of marital enslavement. They were particularly taken by the works of George Sand. In fact, the preface to Sand's 1834 novel *Jacques* entitled "Who Is to Blame?" is thought to have been the impetus for Alexander Herzen's 1847 novel of the same name (which also dealt with a love triangle involving a married couple). See Grenier, *Representing the Marginal Woman*, 66.

21. As Terras points out, these novels influence the style that Devushkin chooses in his letters to Varvara in *Poor Folk*. See Terras, *The Young Dostoevsky*, 182.

22. Given the earlier reference to Rousseau, it is remarkable how much of S.O.'s confession to Alexandra Mikhailovna is modeled on Rousseau's own avowal of personal failure—i.e., his complaint of circumstances beyond his control, his appeal to sickness and frailty, his misanthropy as a means of concealing social ineptitude, his feelings of persecution, his lofty words and base actions, and his flirtations and frantic correspondence with patroness-protectors for financial and emotional support.

Consider, for instance, the French writer's vaunted lack of responsibility for his moral behavior (i.e., when he calls the contradictions in his makeup "nature's doing, not mine"). See J. Rousseau, *Les confessions* (Paris: Tallandier, n.d.), 3:210.

Also consider Thomas Barran's comments that Dostoevsky attacks Rousseau-type confessions in three ways: (1) indiscriminate candor alone does not expiate sins or establish the moral worth of an individual, but rather dulls the ability to distinguish good from evil; (2) written confession, no matter how avowedly sincere, cannot avoid presenting the confessor as he wishes to see himself, and not as he actually is; (3) the very motives that impel men to confess on paper are all too often rooted in pride and contempt for others, rather than a desire to expiate guilt or express remorse.

For a fuller treatment of Dostoevsky, Rousseau, and confession, see R. Miller, "Dostoevsky and Rousseau: The Morality of Confession Reconsidered," in A. Mlikotin, ed., *Western Philosophical Systems in Russian Literature* (Los Angeles: University of Southern California Press, 1979), 89–101; and "Imitations of Rousseau in *The Possessed*," *Dostoevsky Studies* 5 (1984): 77–89. Also see T. Barran, "Dark Uses of Confession: Rousseau and Dostoevsky's Stavrogin," *Mid-Hudson Language Studies* 1 (1978): 97–112; and B. Howard, "The Rhetoric of Confession: Dostoevskij's *Notes from the Underground* and Rousseau's *Confessions*," *Slavic and East European Journal* 25, no. 4 (1981): 16–33.

23. Similarly, Rousseau writes in *Confessions*: "Fate, which for thirty years, promoted my inclinations, then interfered with them for thirty more; and this continual opposition between my circumstances and my inclinations gave birth to enormous faults, unprecedented misfortunes, and all the virtues, except for strength, which can do honor to adversity." See Rousseau, *Les Confessions*, 3:52.

24. Rousseau notes in *Confessions*: "[My] mediocrity was in large part the product of my ardent but feeble nature, less ready to undertake than easy to be discouraged, leaving a state of rest if jolted but returning it to weariness and from inclination, and which, always bringing me back, far from great virtues and ever further from great vices, to this idle and tranquil life for which I was born, never allowed me to achieve anything great, whether good or evil." See Rousseau, *Les Confessions*, 3:51–52.

25. In such comments, Dostoevsky again polemicizes with Rousseau who, in *The Confessions*, describes his reluctance to cross the boundary between desire and consummation, the result being that he remains in a world of pure feeling in which love can be idealized but for himself alone. See C. Apollonio, *Dostoevsky's Secrets. Reading against the Grain* (Evanston: Northwestern University Press, 2009), 38.

26. Consider Rousseau's similar self-baring in his *Confessions*. See Coetzee, "Confession and Double Thoughts," 207 and 208.

27. Steiner has argued that "the disenchanted tone of the later chapters [in *Netochka Nezvanova*] is due not only to Netochka's growing experience but also to her gradual loss of desire." This position warrants further consideration. See Steiner, "*Netochka Nezvanova*," 246.

28. Dostoevsky replays this angst with Nellie's distrust of her father, Prince Valkovsky, in *The Injured and the Insulted*. Nellie, too, hides in a corner from Valkovsky, who has an unhealthy fascination for the girl.

29. Terras sees the final scene of *Netochka Nezvanova* as the first example of a dramatic conclave in Dostoevsky's work. See Terras, *The Young Dostoevsky*, 54.

30. Steiner alleges that Netochka seeks to protect Alexandra Mikhailovna "to repay the debt of love and care she owes her dead mother." Given the problematic relationship between mother and daughter, not to mention the fact that Netochka fails to mention the woman in the second and third parts of the narrative, the claim hardly seems valid. See Steiner, "*Netochka Nezvanova*," 249.

31. So much for the invulnerability that Steiner claims for Netochka in the final chapters of the work. See ibid., 246.

32. The scene of scandal involving Netochka, Alexandra Mikhailovna, and Pyotr Alexandrovich invalidates Steiner's claim that "as Netochka's story progresses, she becomes less dependent upon conventional narrative styles, less graphic and more analytical." See ibid., 246.

Notes to Conclusion

1. Charles Passage suggests several Dickensian outcomes for the characters in *Netochka Nezvanova*: S.O. is murdered by Pyotr Alexandrovich. Alexandra Mikhailovna also dies at the hand of her husband, the victim of "music as a deft form of mental torture." Netochka is rescued by the musician B., who identifies S.O. as Netochka's biological father.

Passage also suggests that since S.O.'s letter is quite old, the addressee of the missive is not Alexandra Mikhailovna, but her mother, the old Princess (also named Alexandra), and that, courtesy of an early lover, she has given birth also to Netochka, who is the half-sister of both Katya and Alexandra Mikhailovna. "In this or some other way," Passage concludes, "it would seem inevitable that Netochka's rise in the world should culminate in her becoming the new Princess X." See Passage, *Dostoevski*, 103–104.

2. Consider Steiner's claims that Netochka emerges as "a figure of authority along the lines of Plato's Diotima," the philosopher-priestess in the *Symposium*, who originates the idea of Platonic love.

Steiner overstates things with the argument that Netochka "becomes more and more like the author himself: a wise seer into the human heart who can distance himself from immediate suffering in order to produce a work of art." After all, in 1849, Dostoevsky was at least fifteen years removed from becoming an artist-seer.

Steiner comes closer to the truth when she notes that "the most obvious explanation ... [for why] Dostoevsky lost interest in developing Netochka's story ... [is that] ... she became too much like himself." See Steiner, "*Netochka Nezvanova*," 236, 245, 246, and 249.

3. Heldt, *Terrible Perfection*, 35.
4. Ibid.
5. R. Miller, *Dostoevsky's Unfinished Journey*, 175.
6. V. Ivanov, *Freedom and the Tragic Life*, trans. N. Cameron (New York: Noonday Press, 1960), 95.

BIBLIOGRAPHY

Andrew, Joe. *Narrative and Desire in Russian Literature, 1822–49. The Feminine and the Masculine*. New York: St. Martin's Press, 1993.

———. "The Seduction of the Daughter: Sexuality in the Early Dostoevsky and the Case of *Poor Folk (Bednye liudi)*." In *Polyfunktion und Metaparodie: Aufsätze zum 175. Geburtstag von Fedor Michajlovič Dostojevskij*, edited by Rudolph Neuhäuser, 172–188. Dresden and München: Dresden University Press, 1998.

Apollonio, Carol. *Dostoevsky's Secrets. Reading against the Grain*. Evanston: Northwestern University Press, 2009.

Asher, Ramona, and Dennis Brissett. "Codependency: A View from Women Married to Alcoholics." *International Journal of Addictions* 23 (1988): 331–350.

———. *Women with Alcoholic Husbands. Ambivalence and the Trap of Codependency*. Chapel Hill: University of North Carolina Press, 1992.

Babcock, Marguerite, and M. Christine McKay. *Challenging Codependency: Feminist Critiques*. Toronto: University of Toronto Press, 1995.

Bakhtin, Mikhail. *Problems of Dostoevsky's Poetics*. Translated by Caryl Emerson. Minneapolis: University of Minneapolis Press, 1984.

Ballis, Tab. "Codependency: The Most Basic Addiction." *Cape Fear Healthy Minds*. http://www.capefearhealthyminds.org/library.cgi?article'1118181493, 1–2.

Barran, Thomas. "Dark Uses of Confession: Rousseau and Dostoevsky's Stavrogin." *Mid-Hudson Language Studies* 1 (1978): 97–112.

Bauman, Richard. *Story, Performance, and Event. Contextual Studies of Oral Narrative*. New York: Cambridge University Press, 1986.

Belaev, M. "Trends in Literary Trauma Theory." *Mosaic: A Journal for the Interdisciplinary Study of Literature* 41, no. 2, (2008): 149–166.

Belinskii, Vissarion. *Polnoe sobranie sochinenii v trinadtsati tomakh*. 13 vols. Moscow: Izdatel'stvo Akademii Nauk SSSR, 1956.

Bepko, Claudia. *The Responsibility Trap*. New York: The Free Press, 1985.

Berger, James. "Trauma and Literary Theory." *Contemporary Literature* 38, no. 3 (1997): 569–582.

Blank, Ksana. *Dostoevsky's Dialectics and the Problems of Sin*. Evanston: Northwestern University Press, 2010.

Breger, Louis. *Dostoevsky. The Author as Psychoanalyst*. New York: New York University Press, 1989 and 2009.

Brooks, Peter. "The Idea of a Psychoanalytic Literary Criticism." In *Discourse in Psychoanalysis and Literature*, edited by Shlomith Rimmon-Kenan, 1–18. New York: Methuen, 1987.

———. "Storytelling without Fear? Confessions in Law and Literature." *Yale Journal of Law and Humanities* 8, no. 1 (1996): 1–18.
———. *Troubling Confessions. Speaking Guilt in Law and Literature*. Chicago: University of Chicago Press, 2000.
Bruner, Jerome. "Life as Narrative." *Social Research* 54, no. 1 (1987): 11–32.
Carruth, Bruce, and Warner Mendanhall, eds. *Co-dependency: Issues in Treatment and Recovery*. New York: Haworth Press, 1989.
Carson, Ann T., and Richard C. Baker. "Psychological Correlates of Codependency in Women." *International Journal of Addictions* 29, no. 3 (1994): 395–407.
Caruth, Cathy. *Unclaimed Experience. Trauma, Narrative, and History*. Baltimore: Johns Hopkins University Press, 1996.
Cermak, Timmen. *Diagnosing and Treating Co-dependence. A Guide for Professionals Who Work with Chemical Dependents, Their Spouses, and Children*. Minneapolis: Johnson Institute Books, 1986.
Chiauzzi, Emil, and Steven Liljegren. "Taboo Topics in Addiction Treatment." *Journal of Substance Abuse Treatment* 10, no. 3 (1993): 303–316.
Cochran, Robert, "Crime, Confession, and the Counselor-at-Law: Lessons from Dostoevsky." *Houston Law Review* 35 (1998): 327–397.
Coetzee, Jacobus. "Confession and Double Thoughts: Tolstoy, Rousseau, Dostoevsky." *Comparative Literature* 37, no. 3 (1985): 193–232.
Corrigan, Yuri. "Amnesia and the Externalized Personality in Early Dostoevskii." *Slavic Review* 72, no. 1 (2013): 79–101.
Cox, Gary. *Tyrant and Victim in Dostoevsky*. Columbus: Slavica Publishers, 1983.
Cruse, Joseph, and K. A. Johnson. "Codependency Treatment Strategies." *Professional Counselor* (1988): 48–54.
———. *Painful Affairs. Looking for Love through Addiction and Co-dependency*. Deerfield Beach: Health Communications, 1989.
Dalton, Elizabeth. *Unconscious Structure in* The Idiot. *A Study in Literature and Psychoanalysis*. Princeton, NJ: Princeton University Press, 1979.
Davison, James. *Sweet Release. The Last Step to Black Freedom*. Amherst: Prometheus Books, 2008.
Deighton, Joan, et al. "Group Treatment: Adult Victims of Childhood Sexual Abuse." *Journal of Contemporary Social Work* 66, no. 7 (1985): 403–410.
de Man, Paul, "Excuses (Confessions)." In *Allegories of Reading: Figural Language in Rousseau, Nietzsche, Rilke, and Proust*, 278–291. New Haven: Yale University Press, 1979.
Denzin, Norman. "The Alcoholic Self: Communication, Ritual, and Identity Transformation." In *Communication and Social Structure*, edited by D. Maines and C. J. Couch, 59–74. Springfield: Charles C. Thomas, 1988.
Dostoevskaia, Anna. *Vospominaniia*. Moscow: Khudozhestvennaia literatura, 1971.
Dostoevskaia, Lyubov'. *Dostoevskii v izobrazhenii svoei docheri*. St. Petersburg: Andreev i sinov'ia, 1992.
Dostoevskii, Fyodor. *Polnoe sobranie sochinenii v tridtsati tomakh*. 30 vols. Leningrad: Nauka, 1972–1990.
Druzhinin, Aleksandr. "Smes'." *Sovremennik* 2 (1849): 183–187.
Edwards, Patricia, et al. "Wives of Alcoholics: A Critical Review and Analysis." *Quarterly Journal of Studies on Alcohol* 34 (1973): 112–132.

Erekson, Mary Talley, and Steven E. Perkins. "System Dynamics in Alcoholic Families." In *Co-dependency: Issues in Treatment and Recovery*, edited by Carruth and Mendanhall, 59–74. New York: Haworth Press, 1989.

Erlich, Iza. "'The Peasant Marey.' A Screen Memory." *Psychoanalytic Study of the Child* 36 (1981): 381–389.

Felman, Shoshana. "Education and Crisis, or the Vicissitudes of Teaching." In *Testimony. Crises of Witnessing in Literature, Psychoanalysis, and History*, edited by S. Felman and Dori Laub, 9–12. Oxon: Routledge, 1992.

Finnegan, Dana, and Emily B. McNally. "The Lonely Journey: Lesbians and Gay Men Who Are Co-dependent." In *Co-dependency: Issues in Treatment and Recovery*, edited by Carruth and Mendanhall, 121–134. New York: Haworth Press, 1989.

Fossum, Merle, and Marilyn Mason. *Facing Shame: Families in Recovery*. New York: Norton, 1986.

Foucault, Michel. *The History of Sexuality*. Translated by Robert Hurley. 3 vols. New York: Vintage, 1990.

Framo, James Laurence. "Family of Origin as a Therapeutic Resource for Adults in Marital and Family Therapy: You Can and Should Go Home Again." In *Family Therapy. Major Contributions*, edited by Robert Jay Green and James Lawrence Framo, 341–373. New York: International Universities Press, 1981.

Frank, Joseph. *Dostoevsky. The Seeds of Revolt, 1821–1849*. Princeton, NJ: Princeton University Press, 1976.

Fridlender, Georgy. *Realizm Dostoevskogo*. Moscow: Nauka, 1964.

Fusso, Suzanne. *Discovering Sexuality in Dostoevsky*. Evanston: Northwestern University Press, 2006.

Futrell, Michael. "Dostoevsky and Dickens." *English Miscellany* 7 (1956): 41–89.

Gagnier, Terri, and R. C. Robertiello. "The Clinical Usefulness of Distinguishing between Two Types of Codependency." *Journal of Contemporary Psychology* 21, no. 4 (1991): 247–255.

Gallop, Jane. *The Daughter's Seduction. Feminism and Psychoanalysis*. Ithaca: Cornell University Press, 1982.

Garfinkel, Harold. "Conditions of Successful Degradation Ceremonies." *American Journal of Sociology* 61, no. 5 (1956): 420–424.

Gilligan, Carol. *In a Different Voice. Psychological Theory and Women's Development*. Cambridge, MA: Harvard University Press, 1982.

Gozenpud, A. *Dostoevskii i muzykal'no-teatral'noe isskustvo*. Leningrad: Sovetskii kompozitor, 1981.

Grenier, Svetlana. *Representing the Marginal Woman in Nineteenth-Century Russian Literature. Personalism, Feminism, and Polyphony*. Westport: Greenwood Press, 2001.

Grigoriev, Apollon. *N. V. Gogol' i ego 'Perepiska s druz'iami.'* Vol. 8 of *Sobranie sochinenii*. Moscow, 1916.

Grossman, Leonid. *Dostoevsky. A Biography*. Translated by M. Mackler. New York: Bobbs-Merrill Company, 1975.

Guerard, Albert. *The Triumph of the Novel: Dickens, Dostoevsky, Faulkner*. New York: Oxford University Press, 1976.

Hartman, Geoffey. "On Traumatic Knowledge and Literary Studies." *New Literary History* 26, no. 3 (1995): 537–563.

Heldt, Barbara. *Terrible Perfection. Women and Russian Literature*. Bloomington: Indiana University Press, 1987.

Howard, Barbara. "The Rhetoric of Confession: Dostoevskij's *Notes from the Underground* and Rousseau's *Confessions*." *Slavic and East European Journal* 25, no. 4 (1981): 16-33.

Ivanov, Vyascheslav. *Freedom and the Tragic Life*. Translated by N. Cameron. New York: Noonday Press, 1960.

Jackson, Joan. "The Adjustment of the Family to the Crisis of Alcoholism." *Quarterly Journal of Studies of Alcohol* 15 (1954): 562-568.

Jackson, Robert Louis. *Dialogues with Dostoevsky*. Stanford: Stanford University Press, 1993.

———. *Dostoevsky's Quest for Form. A Study of His Philosophy of Art*. 2nd edition. Pittsburgh: Physsardt Publishers, 1978.

———. *A New Word on* The Brothers Karamazov. Evanston: Northwestern University Press, 2004.

Jones, Malcolm. "An Aspect of Romanticism in Dostoevsky's 'Netochka Nezvanova,' and Eugene Sue's 'Mathilde.'" *Renaissance and Modern Studies* 17 (1973): 38-61.

Kanzer, Mark. "Dostoevsky's Matricidal Impulses." *Psychoanalytic Review* 35 (1948): 115-125.

Karpman, Stephen. "Fairy Tales and Script Drama Analysis." *Transactional Analysis Bulletin* 7, no. 26 (1968): 39-43.

Kashina-Evreinova, Anna. *Podpol'e geniia. (Seksual'nye istochniki tvorchestva Dostoevskogo)*. Petrograd: "Tret'ia strazha," 1923.

Kasl, Charlotte Davis. *Women, Sex, and Addiction: A Search for Love and Power*. New York: Ticknor and Fields, 1989.

Kitai-Sangero, Rinat. "Can Dostoevsky's *Crime and Punishment* Help Us Distinguish between True and False Confessions?" *Ohio State Journal of Criminal Law* 9 (2011): 231-253

Kristeva. Julia. *Desire in Langauge. A Semiotic Approach to Literature and Art*. New York: Columbia University Press, 1980.

———. "On the Melancholic Imaginary." Translated by L. Burchill. In *Discourse in Psychoanalysis and Literature*, edited by Shlomith Rimmon-Kenan, 104-123. New York: Methuen, 1987.

Lambek, Michael. "The Past Imperfect: Remembering as Moral Practice." In *Tense Past. Cultural Essays in Trauma and Memory*, edited by Paul Antz and Michael Lambek, 235-254. New York: Routledge, 1996.

Lancer, Darlene. "Recovery from Codependency." *Psych Central*. http://www.psychcentral.com/lib/recovery-from-codependency/00014956.

Larsen, Earnest. *Stage II Recovery: Life beyond Addiction*. San Francisco: Harper and Row, 1985.

Maines, David. "Narrative's Moment and Sociology's Phenomena: Toward a Narrative Sociology." *Sociological Quarterly* 34, no. 1 (March 1993): 17-38.

Martinsen, Deborah. *Surprised by Shame*. Columbus: Ohio State University Press, 2003.

McDowell, Lesley. *Between the Sheets: The Literary Liaisons of Nine 20th-Century Women Writers*. New York: Overlook Press, 2010.

Meerson, Olga. *Dostoevsky's Taboos*. Dresden-München: Dresden University Press, 1996.

Meier-Grafe, Julius. *Dostoevsky: The Man and His Work*. New York: Harcourt, Brace, and Company, 1928.

Miller, Orest. *Biografiia, pis'ma i zametki iz zapisnoi knizhki*. St. Petersburg: Tipologiia A.S. Suvorina, 1883.

Miller, Robin. "Dostoevsky and Rousseau: The Morality of Confession Reconsidered." In *Western Philosophical Systems in Russian Literature*, edited by A. Mlikotin, 89–101. Los Angeles: University of Southern California Press, 1979.
———. *Dostoevsky's Unfinished Journey*. New Haven: Yale University Press, 2007.
———. "Imitations of Rousseau in *The Possessed*." *Dostoevsky Studies* 5 (1984): 77–89.
Mochulsky, Konstantin. *Dostoevsky. His Life and Work*. Translated by Michael Minihan. Princeton, NJ: Princeton University Press, 1967.
Morgan, James. "What Is Codependency?" *Journal of Clinical Psychology* 47, no. 5 (1991): 720–729.
Morson, Gary Saul. "Prosaics, Criticism, Ethics." *Formations* 5, no. 2 (1989): 77–95.
Murav, Harriet. "Reading Women in Dostoevsky." In *A Plot of Her Own. The Female Protagonist in Russian Literature*, edited by S. Hoisington, 44–57. Evanston: Northwestern University Press, 1995.
Namka, Lynne. *The Doormat Syndrome*. Deerfield Beach: Health Communications, 1989.
Nazirov, Roman. "Tragediinoe nachalo v romane F. M. Dostoevskogo 'Unizhennye i oskorblennye'." In *Russkaia klassicheskaia literatura: sravnitel'no-istoricheskii podkhod. Issledovaniia raznykh let: Sbornik statei*, edited by R. Nazirov, 21–35. Ufa: RIO BashGU, 2005.
O'Brien, Patrick, and M. Gaborit. "Codependency: A Disorder Separate from Chemical Dependency." *Clinical Psychology* 48, no. 1 (January 1992): 129–136.
O'Leary, Mary E. "Codependency and Love Addiction." *InsideTherapy.com*, http://insidetherapy.com/codaloveaddict.html, 1.
Paris, Bernard. *Dostoevsky's Greatest Characters: A New Approach to Notes from the Underground, Crime and Punishment, and The Brothers Karamazov*. New York: Palgrave MacMillan, 2008.
Passage, Charles. *Dostoevski the Adapter: A Study of Dostoevski's Use of The Tales of Hoffmann*. Chapel Hill: University of North Carolina Press, 1954.
Perkins, Steven. "Altering Rigid Family Role Behaviors in Families with Adolescents." In *Codependency: Issues in Treatment and Recovery*, edited by Carruth and Mendanhall, 111–120. New York: Haworth Press, 1989.
Pol'zinskii, Pyotr. *Detskii mir v proizvedeniiakh Dostoevskogo*. Revel': Gimnaziia, 1891.
Pritchett, Victor. *The Myth Makers. Essays on European, Russian and South American Novelists*. London: Chatto and Windus, 1979.
Rank, Otto. *The Double: A Psychoanalytic Study*. Translated by Harry Tucker. Chapel Hill: University of North Carolina Press, 1971.
Rice, James. *A Disease of One's Own: Psychotherapy, Addiction, and the Emergence of Co-dependency*. New Brunswick: Transaction Publishers, 1996.
———. *Dostoevsky and the Healing Art: An Essay in Literary and Medical History*. Ann Arbor: Ardis, 1985.
Ricketson, Susan Cooley. *The Dilemma of Love. Healing Co-dependent Relationships at Different Stages in Life*. Deerfield Beach: Health Communications, 1989.
Ringel, Shoshana, and Jerrold R. Brandell, eds. *Trauma: Contemporary Directions in Theory, Practice, and Research*. Thousand Oaks, CA: Sage Publications, 2011.
Rosen, Steven. "Homoerotic Body Language in Dostoevsky." *Psychoanalytic Review* 80, no. 3 (Fall 1993): 405–432.
Rosenthal, Richard. "Dostoevsky's Experiment with Projective Mechanisms and the Theft of Identity in *The Double*." In *Russian Literature and Psychoanalysis*, edited

by Daniel Rancour-Lafirriere, 59–88. Philadelphia/Amsterdam: John Benjamins Publishing Company, 1989.

Rousseau, Jean-Jacques. *Les confessions*. 3 vols. Paris: Tallandier, n.d.

Rowe, William. *Dostoevsky: Child and Man in His Works*. New York University Press, 1968.

Ruttenburg, Nancy. *Dostoevsky's Democracy*. Princeton, NJ: Princeton University Press, 2008.

Schaef, Anne. *Codependence: Misunderstood-Mistreated*. San Francisco: Harper, 1986.

Semenov-Tian-Shanskii, Pyotr. *Detstvo i iunost' 1827–1855 gg.* Petrograd: M. Stasiulevich, 1917.

Shapiro, Edward, and A. Wesley Carr. *Lost in Familiar Places: Creating New Connections between the Individual and Society*. New Haven: Yale University Press, 1991.

Steiner, Lina. *For Humanity's Sake. The Bildungsroman in Russian Culture*. Toronto: University of Toronto Press, 2011.

———. "Netochka Nezvanova on the Path of Bildung." *Die Welt der Slaven* 51 (2006): 233–252.

Subby, Robert. *Lost in the Shuffle. The Co-dependent Reality*. Deerfield Beach: Health Communications, 1987.

Sunderwirth, Stanley, and Judith Spector. "Codependency: When the Chemistry Isn't Right." *Family Dynamics of Addiction Quarterly* 2, no. 2 (1992): 23–31.

Tal, Kali. *Worlds of Hurt. Reading the Literatures of Trauma*. Cambridge/Melbourne: Cambridge University Press, 1996.

Tepperman, Lorne, et al. *The Dostoevsky Effect: Problem Gambling and the Origins of Addiction*. Don Mills: Oxford University Press, 2013.

Terras, Victor. *A Karamazov Companion: Commentary on the Genesis, Language, and Style of Dostoevsky's Novel*. Madison: University of Wisconsin Press. 1981.

———. *The Young Dostoevsky (1846–1849): A Critical Study*. The Hague/Paris: Mouton, 1969.

Todd, William Mills III. "*The Brothers Karamazov* Tomorrow." In *A New Word on* The Brothers Karamazov, edited by Robert Louis Jackson, 254–257. Evanston: Northwestern University Press, 2004.

Tolstoy, Leo. *Tolstoy. Polnoe sobranie sochienii v deviatnosta tomakh*. Vol 1. Moscow: Khudozhestvennaia literatura, 1935.

Torremans, Tom. "Trauma: Theory—Reading (and) Literary Theory in the Wake of Trauma." *European Journal of English Studies* 7, no. 3 (2003): 333–351.

Trutovskii, Konstantin. "Vospominaniia o Fedore Mikhailoviche Dostoevskom." *Russkoe obozrenie* 1 (1893): 210–217.

Wachtel, Andrew. *The Battle for Childhood: Creation of a Russian Myth*. Stanford: Stanford University Press, 1990.

Walters, Marianne. "The Codependent Cinderella Who Loves Too Much . . . Fights Back." In *Challenging Codependency: Feminist Critiques*, edited by Babcock and McKay, 181–191. Toronto: University of Toronto Press, 1995.

Wasiolek, Edward. *Dostoevsky. The Major Fiction*. Cambridge, MA: The MIT Press, 1964.

Weinhold, Barry K., and Janae B. *Breaking Free of the Co-dependency Trap*. Walpole: Stillpoint, 1989.

Weiss, Laurie, and Jonathan Weiss. *Recovering from Co-dependency*. Deerfield Beach: Health Communications, 1989.

White, Michael, and David Epston. *Narrative Means to Therapeutic Means*. New York: W. W. Norton and Company, 1990.

Whitfield, Charles. *Co-dependence: Healing the Human Condition: The New Paradigm for Helping Professionals and People in Recovery.* Deerfield Beach: Health Communications, 1991.

———. "Co-dependence: Our Most Common Addiction—Some Physical, Mental, Emotional, and Spiritual Perspectives." *Alcoholism Treatment Quarterly* 6 (1989): 19–36.

———. *Healing the Child Within: Discovery and Recovery for Adult Children of Dysfunctional Families.* Deerfield Beach: Health Communications, 1987.

Wright, Elizabeth. *Psychoanalytic Criticism: Theory and Practice.* New York: Methuen, 1984.

INDEX

A
abuse, covert, 9–11
abuse, overt, 8–9
abuse, sexual, 8–9, 167n44
adultery, 185n20
Al-Anon, 166n28
Alcoholics Anonymous, 166n28
alcoholism, 6–8
alcohol/vodka, 50, 52, 64
Alexandra Mikhailovna
    birth of, 184n5
    children of, 114, 143
    and codependency, 113
    death of, 142–43
    description of, 111, 112
    discussed, viii, 110
    last will and testament of, 143
    letter from S.O., 127
    marriage of, 112
    meets S.O., 128
    and scandal, 130–31
    Steiner on, 187n30
    Terras on, 184n6
Andrew, Joe, xi
Anna Karenina (Tolstoy), 118
Annetta (Netochka Nezvanova's formal name), 26, 29, 59, 136
aunt
    discussed, 80–81, 98–99, 181n8
    and Sir John Falstaff, 99–101
awakening/reawakening, 171n87

B
B. (musician)
    discussed, 25, 36–37, 54
    and Efimov, 46, 48–49, 52, 68
    and Efimov's family, 52
    Jackson on, 62
    and Karl Fyodorovich Meyer, 62
    on Netochka Nezvanova's singing, 117
    Steiner on, 177n13
    visits by, 112
Bakhtin, Mikhail, 179n31
Balzac, Honoré de
    "Gambara," 177n15
Barran, Thomas, 186n22
beauty, 181n10, 182n16
Beauvoir, Simone de, 162n16
Belinsky, Vissarion, 20, 185n20
Belknap, Robert, 163n20
Belyi, Andrei
    Kotik Letaev, 21, 122, 171n86, 176n150
Blank, Ksana, 181n10
Bleak House (Dickens), 180n40
borders/boundaries
    abuse/problems, 4, 5–6
    Alexandra Mikhailovna, 113
    Alexandra Mikhailovna and Netochka Nezvanova, 117
    and covert abuse, 10–12
    discussed, 4
    Netochka Nezvanova, 31, 80, 137
    S.O., 129
Breger, Louis, xi
Brontë, Charlotte
    Jane Eyre, 24, 172n104
Brooks, Peter, xi
Brothers Karamazov, The (Dostoevsky)
    and Alexandra Mikhailovna, 151
    and aunt, 80
    codependency in, xiii

discussed, xii, 175n135
and Efimov, 44
and Katya, 91, 157
and Katya and Netochka Nezvanova, 97
and Larya, 180n1
and Netochka Nezvanova, 56, 125, 126

C

cake, 65, 86–87
ceremonies of degradation, 12
characters, 157
childhood
    in Aksakov, 30
    Kristeva on, 183n26
    in Russian literature, ix, 36, 162n11, 162n13, 175n136
    Steiner on, 178n21
    in Tolstoy, 30
Childhood (Gorky), 27, 159, 162n13, 179n39
Childhood (Tolstoy), ix, 31, 34, 36, 162n13
"Christmas Tree and the Wedding, The" (Dostoevsky), 178n28
co-alcoholism, 6
codependency
    and alcoholism, 6–8, 166n28
    Alexandra Mikhailovna, 113
    Alexandra Mikhailovna and Netochka Nezvanova, 114, 116
    Alexandra Mikhailovna and Pyotr Alexandrovich, 119–21, 141
    Alexandra Mikhailovna and S.O., 127–28
    B and Efimov, 47, 51, 53
    B and Efimov's family, 52
    de Beauvoir, 162n16
    Denzin on, 170n72
    discussed, x–xi, xii–xiii, 1, 3–4, 162n15, 164n1
    in A Doll's House, xi
    in Dostoevsky's mature writing, 158, 159
    Efimov and landowner, 40, 44, 45, 46
    Efimov and Netochka Nezvanova, 56, 58, 60, 75
    Efimov and wife, 53
    Katya and Netochka Nezvanova, 83–84, 86
    Mansfield, 162n16
    Morgan on, 165n2
    Netochka Nezvanova, 32, 36, 55, 153–54
    in *Netochka Nezvanova*, 22–23, 35, 56, 133, 158
    Plath, 162n16
    symptoms of, 1–3
    and trauma theory, 167–68n51
    Whitfield on, 165n2
    of writers, 162n16
codependency, morbid, 4–5
codependent limbo, 138
cognition, 169n61
coins, 64, 65, 69, 70, 71
conductor, 38, 59, 176n3, 176n4
confessions, 137, 168n52, 186n22
Confessions, The (Rousseau), 182–83n21, 186n23, 186n24, 186n25, 186n26
Consuelo (Sand), 185n13
conversations, 119, 122
Count (conductor's employer), 38
court-like proceedings, 146
Cox, Gary, xi
Crime and Punishment (Dostoevsky)
    discussed, vii, 178n28, 183n30
    and Efimov, 42
    and Netochka Nezvanova, 27, 28, 64, 123, 125, 126
Crystal Palace, 58

D

D. (voice teacher), 118
Dalton, Elizabeth, 163n18
Debut, Ippolit, 21
defense mechanisms, 13–14, 62
Deighton, Joan, 167n44
delusions, 14
Demons (Dostoevsky), 174n133
denial, 14
Devils (Dostoevsky), 69, 79, 115, 178n28
Diary of a Writer, The (Dostoevsky)
    discussed, 159, 179n38
    excerpts from, 10, 12, 15–16, 17–18, 174n131, 176n152

Dickens, Charles
   Bleak House, 180n40
   Dombey and Son, 24, 172n105
   Old Curiosity Shop, The, 24, 172n105
disassociation, 14, 150
disengagement, 6–7, 55
Doll's House, A (Ibsen), xi
Dombey and Son (Dickens), 24, 172n105
Dostoevsky, Andrei, 156, 182n19
Dostoevsky, Anna, 173n116
Dostoevsky, Fyodor. *See also Netochka Nezvanova* (Dostoevsky)
   Barran on, 186n22
   beauty in, 181n10, 182n16
   Brothers Karamazov, The
      and Alexandra Mikhailovna, 151
      and aunt, 80
      codependency in, xiii
      discussed, xii, 175n135
      and Efimov, 44
      and Katya, 91, 157
      and Katya and Netochka Nezvanova, 97
      and Larya, 180n1
      and Netochka Nezvanova, 56, 125, 126
   "Christmas Tree and the Wedding, The," 178n28
   Crime and Punishment
      discussed, 178n28, 183n30, vii
      and Efimov, 42
      and Netochka Nezvanova, 27, 28, 64, 123, 125, 126
   Devils, 69, 79, 115, 178n28
   Diary of a Writer, The
      discussed, 159, 179n38
      excerpts from, 10, 12, 15–16, 17–18, 174n131, 176n152
   Double, The, vii, viii, 19, 20
   education of, 170n80
   Eternal Husband, The, 178n28
   fictional children of, 174n128, 174n129
   and gambling, xi
   House of the Dead, The, 28
   Idiot, The
      Andrew on, 179n34
      codependency in, xiii
      discussed, 79, 178n28
      excerpts from, 173–74n121
      and Larya, 180n1
   Insulted and Injured, The
      discussed, 79, 174n129, 178n28, 179n33, 187n28
      dog in, 182n20
   Kristeva on, 32
   "Landlady, The," vii
   Notes from the Underground, 28, 58, 168n52
   "Peasant Marey, The," 179n30
   Poor Folk, vii, viii, 19, 185n19, 186n21
   Raw Youth, A, 7, 175n135
   Rice on, 164n36
   on Walter Scott, 184n11
Dostoevsky, Lyubov, viii
Dostoevsky, Mikhail, 19, 156
Double, The (Dostoevsky), vii, viii, 19, 20
double-voicing, 21
doubling of self, 168n58
dramatic conclave, 187n29
Druzhinin, Alexander, vii

E

Efimov (Netochka Nezvanova's stepfather)
   and B., 46, 48–49, 52, 68
   Catteau on, 179–80n40
   and conductor, 38, 43
   and Count, 42
   death of, 77
   discussed, viii, 41, 44, 46–47, 50
   Frank on, viii, 177n10, 179–80n40
   Fridlender on, viii, 177n10
   Grossman on, 177n10
   Jackson on, 179–80n40
   and Karl Fyodorovich Meyer, 62
   and landowner, 41, 43
   as musician, 37, 41, 43, 44–45, 48
   and Netochka Nezvanova, 36
   Netochka Nezvanova on, 24–25, 37
   Steiner on, 176n8, 177n10, 177n11
   Terras on, viii, 48, 177n10, 179–80n40
   and violinist, 42
   Wasiolek on, viii, 176n7, 177n9
   and wife, 51–52

Emile, or On Education (Rousseau), 183n25, 184n9
enmeshment, 7
Erikson, Erik, 164n1
Erlich, Iza, xi, 179n30
Eternal Husband, The (Dostoevsky), 178n28
exhibitionism, 32, 175n143

F

faces, 172n107
facilitators/enablers, 7–8
false confessions, 27, 60, 99, 174n124
Fatherland Notes, The, vii, 20, 155, 156, 172n104
Fathers and Sons (Turgenev), 20
Felman, Shoshana, 168n52
Framo, James Laurence, 173n117
Freud, Sigmund, 164n1, 167n52
Friska (Sir John Falstaff's initial name), 94
Fromm, Erick, 164n1
Fusso, Susanne, xi, 175n135

G

"Gambara" (Balzac), 177n15
gambling, xi
Gan, Elena, 185n20
Gilligan, Carol, 170n74
Ginzburg, Lidia, 161n8
God
    and codependency, 3, 7, 12
    discussed, 27
    and Efimov and Netochka Nezvanova, 75
    and Netochka Nezvanova, 30–31, 81, 125
Gogol, Nikolai
    Overcoat, The, 129
Golstein, Vladimir, xi
Gorky, Maxim
    Childhood, 27, 159, 162n13, 179n39
    Wachtel on, 173n118
Great Exhibition, 58
Grenier, Svetlana, xi
Grigoriev, Apollon, 172n106
Grossman, Leonid, viii, 162n9, 177n10
Guerard, Albert, 25

H

Heldt, Barbara, 171n91
Herzen, Alexander
    Who Is to Blame?, 185n20
Homer
    Iliad, 54
Horney, Karen, 164n1
House of the Dead, The (Dostoevsky), 28
house with red curtains, 57–58, 59, 61, 78, 82

I

Ibsen, Henrik
    Doll's House, A, xi
Idiot, The (Dostoevsky)
    Andrew on, 179n34
    codependency in, xiii
    discussed, 79, 178n28
    excerpts from, 173–74n121
    and Larya, 180n1
Iliad (Homer), 54
impression management, 3
incest, 66, 167n44
inner child meditation, 13
inner-child state, 168n53
Insulted and Injured, The (Dostoevsky)
    discussed, 79, 174n129, 178n28, 179n33, 187n28
    dog in, 182n20
Ivanhoe (Scott), 116

J

Jackson, Robert Louis, xi, 62
Jacobo Sannazaro (Kukolnik), 63
Jacques (Sand), 185n20
Jane Eyre (Brontë), 24, 172n104
Jocko, or the Brazilian Monkey (Rochefort), 182n19
Jones, Malcolm, 22
Jung, Carl, 14, 164n1

K

Karl Fyodorovich Meyer, 62–63, 69
Katya (princess)
    discussed, viii, 83
    education of, 88, 182n14
    and mother, 85

key, 123, 125–26
king babies, 9
Kotik Letaev (Belyi), 21, 122, 171n86, 176n150
Kraevsky, Alexander, vii, 20, 155, 171n84
Kristeva, Julia, 32
Kukolnik, Nestor Jacobo Sannazaro, 63

L

Lacan, Jacques, 65, 79, 167n52, 173n115
"Landlady, The" (Dostoevsky), vii
landowner, 37–38, 39–40, 41, 43
Larya (child), 180–81n1
library, 123–24, 147
literature, 163n18
love addicts, 4, 5
Lucrezia Floriani (Sand), 185n13
L'vovna, Anna, 170n80

M

Madame Leotard
  discussed, 110
  and Katya and Netochka Nezvanova, 97, 107, 108
  and Netochka Nezvanova, 102
  as teacher, 88–89
Main Engineering Academy, 170n80
Maines, David, 169n61, 170n77
Man, Paul de, 167n52, 183n21
Mansfield, Katherine, 162n16
Martinsen, Deborah, xi, 163n21, 172n107, 175n140
Mathilde (Sue), 24, 172n103, 181n8, 182n14
Meerson, Olga, xi, 163n20
Meier-Graefe, Julius, 103
Miller, Robin, 174n127
minimalization, 14
Mochulsky, Konstantin, 118
moral inventory, 14
morbid codependency, 4–5, 32, 33, 95
Morgan, James, 165n2
Morson, Gary Saul, 175n143
mother, 51–52, 59, 65–66, 71, 74
Murav, Harriet, 21

N

Name-of-the-Father, 173n115
narrative voice, 34, 175n147
Nastya (servant girl), 104
Natural School, 24, 30
Nazirov, Roman, 175n146
Netochka Nezvanova. *See also* Annetta
  biological father of, 36
  education of, 88, 114–16, 118, 182n14
  and Efimov, 36
  on Efimov, 24–25, 37
  Frank on, 185n13
  Heldt on, 171n91
  Jones on, 22
  and Karl Fyodorovich Meyer, 63
  Kristeva on, 32
  and mother, 36, 56, 59, 65–66, 185n13
  names of, 26, 29, 59, 136
  and Pyotr Alexandrovich, 135, 137
  as reader, 124
  as singer, 117, 118, 136, 184–85n13
  Steiner on, 184–85n13, 184n7, 187n2, 187n30, 187n31
  Terras on, 23–24, 184n13
  Wasiolek on, 178n26
  as writer, 24–26
Netochka Nezvanova (Dostoevsky)
  abandonment/discontinuation of, viii, 156
  Andrew on, 164n36
  characters in, 157
  discussed, vii–viii
  Lyubov Dostoevsky on, viii
  Druzhinin on, vii
  ending of, 153
  excerpts from, 21
  Frank on, viii, xiii, 23, 161n8
  Ginzburg on, 161n8
  Grossman on, viii, 162n9, 180n1
  Guerard on, 25
  hypothetical endings of, 156–57, 187n1
  Nazirov on, 176n5
  original manuscript for, 180–81n1
  Passage on, 23, 161n8, 187n1
  plan for, 19–20, 21, 155
  Pritchett on, 172n101

publication of, vii, 21, 156, 171n84
Steiner on, 161n8, 187n32
Terras on, 164n36, 164n41, 187n29
title of, 20, 170–71n79
Notes from the Underground (Dostoevsky), 28, 58, 168n52

O

Old Curiosity Shop, The (Dickens), 24, 172n105
Overcoat, The (Gogol), 129
Ozmidov, Nikolai, 184n11

P

Panaeva, Avdotya
    Tal'nikov Family, The, 172n102
parentification, 9
Paris, Bernard, xi
Passage, Charles, 23, 161n8, 176n4
"Peasant Marey, The" (Dostoevsky), 179n30
pedophilia, x, 66, 178n29
Peter-Paul Fortress, 156
Petersburg period, ix
Petipa, Jean-Antoine, 182n19
Petipa, Marius, 182n19
Petrashevsky Affair, vii, 21, 156, 168n52
Petrashevsky circle, 20
Petrushka, 62, 63
piano, 117
Plath, Sylvia, 162n16
Plato
    Symposium, 187n2
polyphony, 24, 41
Poor Folk (Dostoevsky), vii, viii, 19, 185n19, 186n21
Prince X., 68, 72, 78, 79, 180–81n1
Princess (Prince X.'s wife), 80
Pritchett, Victor, 172n101
projection, 14
psychoanalysis, xi–xii
Pyotr Alexandrovich
    and Alexandra Mikhailovna, 118–19
    discussed, 118
    Frank on, 118
    humming of, 138, 139
    Mochulsky on, 118

portrait of, 135
and S.O.'s letter, 144

R

Rank, Otto, xi
Raw Youth, A (Dostoevsky), 7, 175n135
readers of a codependent's story, 16–17
reality testing, 16
regression/relapse, 18, 142
Rice, James, 164n36
Rochefort, Edmond
    Jocko, or the Brazilian Monkey, 182n19
Romantic Realists, viii, 24
Rosen, Steven, xi
Rosenthal, Richard, xi
Rousseau, Jean-Jacques
    Confessions, The, 182–83n21, 186n23, 186n24, 186n25, 186n26
    discussed, 30, 102–3, 183n26, 186n22
    Emile, or On Education, 183n25, 184n9
Rowe, William, ix, xi, 178n28, 178n29
Ruttenburg, Nancy, xi
R-va, Zeneida, 185n20

S

S. (violinist), 54, 68, 69, 72
Sand, George
    Consuelo, 185n13
    discussed, 172n101, 185n20
    Jacques, 185n20
    Lucrezia Floriani, 185n13
Sasha (Katya's brother), 93
scandal, 130–31, 187n32
Scott, Walter
    Dostoevsky on, 184n11
    Ivanhoe, 116
screen memories, 17, 81, 170n73
secrets
    and Alexandra Mikhailovna, 112–13
    and Alexandra Mikhailovna and Pyotr Alexandrovich, 119, 141
    Nazirov on, 175n146
    and S.O.'s letter, 127
Semyonov-Tyan-Shansky, Pyotr, 20
sex/sexuality

Alexandra Mikhailovna and
  Netochka Nezvanova, 178n27
"The Christmas Tree and the Wedding," 178n28
Efimov and Netochka Nezvanova, 66
Katya and Netochka Nezvanova, 98, 103–4, 178n27
Netochka Nezvanova, 135
in Netochka Nezvanova, x
S.O., 130
Shadow Self, 14
shame/shamelessness, 163n21
Shapiro, Edward, 167n47
Siberia, vii, 28, 156
Sir John Falstaff, 93–95, 99–101, 137. See also Friska
S.O.
  delusions of grandeur, 131
  discussed, 141
  enemies of, 131
  letter to Alexandra Mikhailovna
    discussed, 127–28
    and Netochka Nezvanova, 133, 135, 147
    Passage on, 187n1
    and Pyotr Alexandrovich, 144, 149
  meets Alexandra Mikhailovna, 128
  meets Pyotr Alexandrovich, 132
  physical attraction to Alexandra Mikhailovna, 129
  and scandal, 130–31
  sexuality of, 130
  subservience of, 128, 132
sociality, 169n61
societal imperatives, 79
Spector, Judith, xi
spirit of adventure, 125
spiritual union, 151
spontaneous regression, 17, 81, 138
Steiner, Lina, xi, 161n8, 173n114, 175n138, 178n21
stress, 12–13
Sue, Eugene
  Mathilde, 24, 172n103, 181n8, 182n14
Sunderworth, Stanley, xi
Symposium (Plato), 187n2

T

taboos, 163n20
Tal'nikov Family, The (Panaeva), 172n102
Tepperman, Lorne, xi, xiv
Terras, Victor
  on Efimov, viii
  on Netochka Nezvanova, 23–24, 26, 164n36
  Young Dostoevsky (1846–1849), The, xiv
Third Section, 156
threshold dialogue, 179n31
time, 169n61
Todd, William Mills, III, xii
Tolstoy, Leo
  Anna Karenina, 118
  Childhood, ix, 31, 34, 36, 162n13
trauma bonding, 168n52
trauma novels, 169n65, 175n146
trauma theory, 167n52, 169n68, 171n87, 181n9
Trutovsky, Konstantin, 170n80
Turgenev, Ivan
  Fathers and Sons, 20

V

Vasseur, Thérèse Le, 183n26
verticality
  Alexandra Mikhailovna, Pyotr Alexandrovich, and S.O., 132
  Alexandra Mikhailovna and Netochka Nezvanova, 137, 143, 151
  Alexandra Mikhailovna and Pyotr Alexandrovich, 151, 152
  Alexandra Mikhailovna and S.O., 133
  Katya and Netochka Nezvanova, 101, 106
  Netochka Nezvanova, 153
  Netochka Nezvanova and teachers, 115
violin
  discussed, 38, 39, 40
  and Efimov, 74, 176n3
  and Efimov and Netochka Nezvanova, 66–67
violinist, first, 40–41
violinist, French, 41

W

Wachtel, Andrew
    discussed, 172n106
    on Gorky, 173n118
    on Kotik Letaev, 171n86
    on Netochka Nezvanova, 23
    on Tolstoy, 162n11, 162n13
Wasiolek, Edward, viii, 177n9
Whitfield, Charles, 165n2, 168n54
Who Is to Blame? (Herzen), 185n20
writing, 15–16, 18–19, 168–69n60, 169n64, 169n66, 170n70

Y

Young Dostoevsky (1846–1849), The (Terras), xiv

Z

Zhukova, Maria, 185n20

www.ingramcontent.com/pod-product-compliance
Lightning Source LLC
Chambersburg PA
CBHW020118010526
44115CB00008B/882